INSIDE AND OUT
Universities and Education
for Sustainable Development

Edited by
Robert Forrant and Linda Silka
University of Massachusetts Lowell

Work, Health, and Environment Series
Series Editors: Charles Levenstein and John Wooding

Routledge
Taylor & Francis Group

LONDON AND NEW YORK

First published 2006 by Baywood Publishing Company, Inc.

2 Park Square, Milton Park, Abingdon, Oxon OX14 4RN
711 Third Avenue, New York, NY 10017, USA

Routledge is an imprint of the Taylor & Francis Group, an informa business

First isued in paperack 2017

Library of Congress Catalog Number: 2005054583
ISBN 13: 978-0-89503-361-1 (hbk)

Library of Congress Cataloging-in-Publication Data

Inside and out : universities and education for sustainable development / edited by Robert Forrant and Linda Silka.
    p. cm. -- (Work, health and environment series)
    Includes bibliographical references and index.
    ISBN 0-89503-361-5 (cloth)
    1. Community and college. 2. Sustainable development--Study and teaching. I. Forrant, Robert, 1947- II. Silka, Linda. III. Series.

    LC237.I57 2006
    378.1'03--dc22

                                        2005054583

ISBN 978-0-89503-361-1 (hbk)
ISBN 978-0-415-78434-4 (pbk)

Table of Contents

Introduction: Inside and Out—What's It All About? 1
Robert Forrant and Linda Silka

SECTION ONE:
University Space

1. Can Universities Contribute to Sustainable Development? 17
   Stephen Viederman

2. Education for a Transition to Sustainability 29
   Kenneth Geiser

3. Beyond Disciplines: Integrating Academia, Operations, and
   Community for Campuswide Education for Sustainability 41
   Robert Koester, James Eflin, and John Vann

4. The Role of the Humanities and Social Sciences in Education
   for Sustainable Development. 63
   *Daniel Egan, Vanessa Gray, Whitley Kaufman, and
   Chad Montrie*

5. Teaching Sustainability: The Case of the Incredible Shrinking
   Professor 79
   Elisabeth M. Hamin

6. Strategies Used to Embed Concepts of Sustainable Development
   in the Curriculum. 87
   Linda L. Lowry and Judy K. Flohr

SECTION TWO:
The Regional and Global Fabric

7. Building Sustainable Community/University Partnerships
in a Metropolitan Setting 105
  Alan Bloomgarden, Mary Bombardier, Myrna M. Breitbart,
  Kiara Nagel, and Preston H. Smith II

8. Education for Sustainability: Preserve Good Ideas—
Recycle Them 119
  Linda Silka, Priscilla Geigis, and Will Snyder

9. Merging Academics and Operations in a Statewide University
Consortium 135
  Patricia Jerman, Christy Friend, Corinna McLeod,
  Summer Smith Taylor, and Bruce Coull

10. Teaching Sustainability and Professional Ethics: Production and
Values In and Outside the Work Place 149
  William Mass

Contributors 169

Index 175

Introduction:
Inside and Out—What's It All About?

Robert Forrant and Linda Silka

In a collection of essays on the responsive university, Braskamp and Wergin state that "The academy does not often believe and act as though the campus is in the world and the world is the campus" (Braskamp & Wergin, 1998). In his examination of the University of Limerick, Dineen (1995) makes the point that in 1972 the idea that a university would have a direct interest in the economic and social development of its immediate region was "a radical departure from the existing concept and practice of university institutions both in Ireland and several other European countries" (p. 140). "Twenty years later," he notes, "there is still a degree of skepticism about university institutions which do not operate in 'splendid isolation' from their environment" (p. 140). In this book we intend to challenge such skepticism and make clear the case for the importance of an "engaged university" in the economic and social development process. We contend here that a university intent on playing a catalytic role in social and economic development beyond simply the theoretical can indeed have a sustained and positive impact when its on- and off-campus efforts are guided by a reflective institution-wide and region-wide discourse (Forrant & Silka, 1999).

In this introduction, we locate the University of Massachusetts Lowell (UML) within the history of its region. There follows a description of several projects underway in Lowell that reflect the University's efforts to broaden and deepen the discussion both between academic disciplines and in the area of what its role in the regional economy should be. The final sections sketch the content of the chapters. This book is the culmination of a series of conversations that led to a conference in the Fall of 2003 to discuss how, in and outside the classroom, universities could engage faculty, staff, students, and the wider community in the sustainable development process.

THE CITY, THE REGION, AND THE UNIVERSITY

UML is located in what at one time was a preeminent textile center. However, by the 1920s, Lowell's, and for that matter the majority of New England's textile mills, were closed. At the end of the Second World War, Lowell, a place that had offered economic hope to waves of new immigrants, was a decaying city with high unemployment and rising poverty. In 2004, with a population of 104,000, Lowell is the fourth-largest city in Massachusetts. It is located in the northeast part of the state, a region with 43 cities and towns and a population of roughly 750,000. It includes older mill cities as well as cities and towns that witnessed explosive growth tied to the expansion of high technology employment in the 1970s and again in the early 1990s. The economy is dominated by the Route 128/495 high technology and software industry corridor.

A city of immigrants in the 19th century, Lowell is still a city of immigrants today. Sizable Southeast Asian and Puerto Rican populations reside in Lowell— the second-highest concentration of Cambodian immigrants in the nation is found in Lowell. Several neighborhood census tracts contiguous to the university have minority concentrations greater than 50 percent. Economic prosperity in the early 1980s, especially in computer manufacturing, drew many of these newcomers to the city, but the sharp downturn in the late 1980s and early 1990s resulted in high unemployment. Thirty-seven percent of households in the city center are headed by females, and of these families, 62 percent live in poverty. Today the city's overall unemployment rate is approximately 4 percent; however joblessness in neighborhoods with high minority and immigrant concentrations is three times higher. Poverty, a shortage of affordable housing, and unemployment persist in immigrant neighborhoods.

UML's predecessor institutions—the Massachusetts State Normal School at Lowell and the Lowell Textile School—were established by the Massachusetts legislature in 1894 and 1895 respectively, to serve the region's industrial needs. The Lowell Textile School trained skilled workers, engineers, and supervisors for the region's mills. In 1932 the Normal School became the Lowell Teachers College, a four-year institution to prepare teachers for the Massachusetts public school system. In 1975 the institutions merged and became the University of Lowell. A sharp economic downturn in the late 1980s brought a rapid drop in state tax revenues and led to the rationalization of the state's public higher education system. As a result, in 1991 the University of Lowell became the University of Massachusetts Lowell, one part of the five-campus university system. UML was challenged to construct an explicit model of how a public university could organize its teaching, research, and outreach to help a region develop and maintain a thriving industrial economy. Realizing there was no quick technological fix, campus leaders set to work figuring out how UML could help the region avoid its historic patterns of economic boom and bust. At the same time, the University began to revamp curricula, reorganize academic departments and research institutes, and develop new ways to work with regional industries and communities. There are approximately 6,000 undergraduate, 3,000 graduate, and 4,000 continuing education students enrolled in the university.

BECOMING EMBEDDED IN THE REGION

The University soon articulated a mission predicated on the notion that a sustainable economy depends upon a skilled and ever-replenished workforce, innovative products, environmental protection, a strong public health infrastructure, and worker safety. In addition, as an integral part of the mission, the University fostered the enhancement and protection of the historical fabric of the community, supported K-12 and continuing education, and worked to strengthen the social and cultural life in Lowell and the region. Soon, several professors worked across their academic disciplines and colleges, an interdisciplinary graduate program in regional economic and social development began, students got involved as community researchers, and relationships strengthened between regional participants and the University. More recently, emphasis was placed on figuring out how to better involve the social sciences and humanities disciplines in the process for, as historian Chad Montrie points out, "First, studying the past can (depending on the quality and intent of a given investigation or interpretation) provide a better understanding of the present. In fact, I would argue that we cannot understand who, what, and where we are without knowledge of who and what came before us" (ch. 4). A growing body of academic and action-oriented research has been produced since 2000, including this volume (see Forrant, Pyle, Lazonick, & Levenstein, 2001; Pyle & Forrant, 2003).

To extend activities into the community, in the Summer of 1996 faculty—many of whom became members of the new Department of Regional Economic and Social Development—prepared a successful application to the U.S. Department of Housing and Urban Development (HUD) and established a three-year $400,000 Community Outreach Partnership program (COPC). Entitled The Lowell Community-University Partnership for Sustainable Development, the proposal articulated broad categories of work with numerous city partners. One objective was to promote research that provided information and analysis pertinent to the short-term resolution of significant urban problems as opposed to the more typical long-term research carried out by faculty and published in peer-reviewed journals. Under the grant, faculty engaged the community in defining research activities that centered on problem solving. The University administration agreed to institutionalize COPC-like activities by the end of the grant (Forrant & Silka, 1999).

The discussion about development and the University's role in the development process widened to consider among other things: how firms adopt cleaner production techniques and green chemistry; how production can be designed to be mindful of worker health; how communities can reduce their waste stream;

how to develop measures of sustainable production and community development; how the social sciences and the humanities can be brought into the discussion to more broadly define sustainable social and economic development; and how Lowell residents can participate in all of these discussions and make their ideas known to the University administration on a consistent basis. Faculty-led interdisciplinary research centers carried out many of these activities (www.uml.edu/research/centers.htm). One such group, the Committee on Industrial Theory and Assessment (CITA) was established in 1993 to shape new theoretical and pragmatic ways of thinking about development and explore the changing roles and functions of UML in the process (www.uml.edu/com/CITA/).

UNIVERSITIES AND SUSTAINABLE DEVELOPMENT

Members of the University community worked with local groups, Lowell National Historical Park and the Lowell Historic Board, neighborhood associations, the Lowell Public Schools, firms, and local development organizations to stimulate a collective learning process, influence commercial activity, preserve and reuse Lowell's industrial structures as a point of community pride and efficient renewal, and participate in the collaborative knowledge-generation needed to stimulate regional development. These efforts are instructive for their focus on how old industrial areas make transitions into more sustainable economic, educational, and cultural activity and for those who are keen on understanding how universities can shake what Storper calls "institutional sclerosis" and play a part in shaping learning regions (Storper, 1995).

Not richly endowed like the Massachusetts Institute of Technology or Stanford University, UML nevertheless strives to address issues that are useful to people interested in the role that "more ordinary" regional, and especially public, universities can play in development. Its experiences reflect the larger dialogue taking place as institutions of higher education consider whether and how to play a more catalytic role in their regional economies. In 2004 city and regional development centers are situated at numerous U.S. and European universities, and there is a growing body of literature and analysis of the university's role in development (see for example: Boucher, Conway, & Van Der Meer, 2003; Cox & Richlin, 2004; Dineen, 1995; Harris 1997; Jacoby, 2003; Labrianidis, 1995; Maurrasse, 2001; Mowery et al., 2004; Schmoch, 1999; Strand et al., 2003; Van Den Berg & Russo, 2004).

Two overarching questions seem to permeate the literature: 1) How does a university restructure its myriad activities, maintain its academic integrity, and have a transformative impact on the regional economy? 2) Who should participate in the discussions that frame and guide the internal restructuring process and off-campus interactions? For sustainable innovations to occur, whereby, for example, a new manufacturing process can be utilized by local industry, or a region is able to make a successful transition out of old industries and old ways of interacting into new ones that resolve difficult societal problems, regional participants must learn how to work together.

Our emerging perspective, based on research and projects in the field, is that long-term growth requires strategies geared to the scientific, technical, cultural, environmental, and social aspects of development. For this to occur, we must consider new ways to organize our teaching—an important theme of this volume. An iterative process is underway—one which involves professors from diverse disciplines, such as criminal justice, community psychology, sociology, work environment, public health, history, political science, philosophy, electrical and mechanical engineering, environmental sciences, nursing and health sciences, and education. Participating off-campus constituencies include neighborhood organizations, public schools, youth services, healthcare providers, and housing advocacy groups. Internal relationships among professors as well as between professors and administrators are being altered, while external relationships are being reconstituted to ensure that the campus listens better and engages the community in collaborative activities. To say the least, this is no small task! What follows is a brief description of some of the activities that demonstrate the range of efforts taking place.

WHAT WE ARE DOING

One strategic focus encompasses energy conservation, biodegradable materials, cleaner and safer production, and the environment. For example, the Toxics Use Reduction Institute (TURI), a multidisciplinary research, education, and policy center, works with firms, schools, and neighborhood groups to introduce the use of nontoxic materials into a variety of manufacturing processes (Geiser & Greiner, 2001). TURI researches, tests, and promotes pollution prevention and alternatives to the toxic chemicals used in Massachusetts industries and communities (www.turi.org). Through its participation in K-12 teacher institutes, TURI has helped disseminate information about nontoxic materials into the elementary and middle school science curriculum. The Lowell Center for Sustainable Production focuses on the development of specific links between community and regional economic activity that are conserving, nonpolluting, and efficient and promotes worker and neighborhood well-being (Kriebel et al., 2001). In order to promote sustainable production and consumption, recycling, and cleaner production research (www.sustainableproduction.org), the Center fosters collaboration between academic disciplines and among several constituents, including the environmental movement, trade unions, and state and federal governments.

The Institute for Plastics Innovation consortium offers research and product development services to leading firms, including 3M, Ford, and GE, as well as many others in electronics, computers, and automation technologies (www.ipi.org). Combined with the plastics engineering department, the Institute offers a comprehensive testing, research and development, and education and training program for plastics companies. The integration of scientific research across three disciplines—chemistry, plastics engineering, and biology—is an important attraction for the sponsoring companies because the development of novel materials has run well ahead of the development of processing procedures and environmental impact assessments. These exotic materials exist, but without widespread knowledge on how to utilize them; nor is there sufficient information on how they will interact in landfills and with various recycling techniques.

The Center for Family, Work, and Community (CFWC) is an outreach arm of the university that works to bring faculty, staff, and students together with community partners to solve long-standing problems in the region. A range of activities in local schools, neighborhood organizations and community nonprofits, are designed to create opportunities for the university to work with and learn from off-campus partners. The Center is currently taking the lead on the formation of a permanent community advisory board that will work with the chancellor and provost on issues of importance (www.uml.edu/centers/CFWC/).

Established in April 2004, the newly designed School of Health and Environment was created to promote human health and development thereby enabling people to live in safe and productive communities and environmentally sustainable economies. The new school brings together the University's long tradition of educating health professionals with an institutional focus on environmental and economic health. It includes the departments of Clinical Laboratory and Nutritional Sciences, Community Health and Sustainability, Nursing, Physical Therapy, and Work Environment. The School maintains working relationships with many organizations in the region, serving a fundamental educational role for students, while providing direct assistance to groups and individuals throughout the region. Additionally, the School offers community educational programs for citizens, community leaders, and healthcare providers regionally, nationally, and internationally. Faculty and student research to promote health and sustainability insure that the educational mission stays relevant and focused on real-world problems and solutions.

Novel approaches to research and science, new links between traditional professions and services, and the development of policies that can expand the ambitions and resources of current healthcare, public health, and environmental protection systems are part of the School's agenda. The School's establishment represents an important new phase in a continuing effort at the Lowell campus to become a model of innovation and interdisciplinary experimentation by pursuing a vision of regional sustainable development (www.uml.edu/College/she/).

The University has a unique multidimensional partnership with Lowell National Historical Park to help carry out the University's mission to build a vibrant and sustainable social, educational, and cultural life in the region, which in turn attracts the "creative class," makes the University more attractive to students, and strengthens regional tourism. In the 1970s University leaders worked with Senator Paul Tsongas and Lowell leaders to create Lowell National Historical Park (1978) and the Lowell Historical Preservation Commission. With this infrastructure in place, state and federal legislative delegations secured millions of dollars to fund preservation in Lowell's historic district and to sustain the downtown despite the exodus of major retail stores to suburban malls. These early efforts cut across institutional, ethnic, social, and political divisions to create a "culture of partnership" to initiate projects that would have long-term positive impact.

The Tsongas Industrial History Center, a partnership created in the late 1980s by UML and Lowell National Historical Park and located in the Park's restored Boott Cotton Mill, was a product of this culture of partnership and Lowell's activist legislative delegation. Park Service, University, and Lowell Public Schools leaders created a center for students to learn about the American Industrial Revolution through hands-on activities and engaging tours of the Park's restored structures and interpretive exhibits—discovering history where it happened. Today, 65,000 students "do history" each year by weaving, creating a canal system and testing water wheels, working on an assembly line, role-playing immigrants, or becoming inventors. By investigating industrial history, students also "do science, mathematics, and engineering," by testing river or canal water quality, tracing the flow of groundwater pollution, or discovering river cleanup techniques, and "read literature and do writing."

In serving as an interdisciplinary curriculum and professional development resource for K-12 teachers, the Center provides immediate dissemination of university research to K-12 teachers, models the university's "Community-as-Classroom-and-Laboratory" philosophy, and provides a unique setting for academic leaders, policy makers, and educators to come together to gain historical perspective on the modern global industrial economy and on issues of sustainability. The Tsongas Center is the largest fully functioning educational partnership in the National Park Service and serves as a model for other Parks (O'Connell & Hoermann, 2005). University and Park leadership are exploring other dimensions of this partnership, including the expansion of work with Lowell's diverse ethnic groups to both preserve and celebrate culture and to explore educational, economic, environmental, political, and social issues (www.uml.edu/tsongas/index2.htm).

A REFLECTIVE DISCOURSE

Much of the work discussed here and in the rest of this volume is at odds with traditional university practices for as Lerner and Simon point out, "too many of our faculty, in all of our disciplines, are far too insulated, too isolated, and in fact and perception are seen as indifferent to worlds other than their own" (1998, p. 3). The university tends to reproduce a culture that rejects direct interaction beyond the campus and across traditional academic departmental boundaries. Yet, interdisciplinary work is important because it more aptly mirrors what is taking place in the regional economy as firms collaborate across manufacturing boundaries and community organizations and neighborhood groups work to solve common urban problems. At the same time, tensions exist between research and its application. Too often "the actions of faculty suggest that they view the real intellectual work as having been completed by the time attention turns to application and community collaboration" (Silka, 2001, p. 490). Much of this tension is bound up with the internal academic evaluation processes associated with the granting of tenure.

At least three institutional/organizational obstacles inhibit success. At Lowell: 1) there has not been a consistent campuswide discussion of what a sustainable economy is, and whether and how the various academic and technical programs on campus can support it; 2) there is no consensus when it comes to understanding the importance of community collaborations and applied community research; 3) structural barriers such as tenure and promotion make it difficult for this type of work to be evaluated. There remains a need for a synthesis to identify which particular university/community institutional arrangements are effective in fostering economically and socially vibrant regions.

For Lowell, the starting point has been the consideration of the emerging collective understanding of how and why, in general terms, regional economies grow and decline. We believe the capacity of an industry or a regional economy to provide well-paying jobs and a broadly shared sustainable prosperity is contingent upon the ability to learn new things and resolve problems as they manifest themselves (for a discussion, see for example: Knudsend, 1997; Lazonick, Fiddy, & Quinby, 2003; Morgan, 1997; Storper, 1995). In "Toward the Learning Region," Richard Florida (1995) outlines the shift to knowledge-intensive capitalism and makes the case for a firm's need for a broader knowledge infrastructure than that which evolves solely in-house if they are to keep up with the shortened product and technology cycles that exist today. Florida explains that learning regions require an infrastructure of knowledge workers who can apply their intelligence to production. The education and training structure must facilitate lifelong learning and provide the high levels of group orientation and teaming required for knowledge-intensive economic organization (Florida, pp. 533-534).

To define a sustainable regional economy necessitates the integration of the social sciences and humanities into the discussion and requires that campus efforts be linked in substantial ways to off-campus constituencies. Many critical questions cannot be investigated without this approach. For example, does sustainable development imply an expanded economic pie—a larger tax base, more jobs, new firms—with little regard for wages paid or who gets the additional slices of the larger pie; does it foster economic stability and an end to the boom-and-bust cycles that Lowell, for example, witnessed for much of the 20th century. Does it mean a general increase in the levels of income of the entire population, an increase in the political and economic empowerment of citizens, a nurturing of start-up enterprises, improved health and healthcare delivery, neighborhood empowerment, or more jobs for youth? Our sensibility is that an encompassing definition of development requires programs and policies that promote a far more equitable distribution of new jobs and income while also boosting the region's capacity to innovate. Too narrow a focus on firms will fail to link residents to employment, while too narrow a focus on neighborhood development will not foster sustainable economic growth. Links between these developmental paths need to be explored.

WHAT'S INSIDE?

What is distinctive within the range of scholarship and practice in this volume is the inclination on the part of increasing numbers of professors on more and more campuses to collaborate across disciplinary lines. The deliberate convergence of several hitherto distinct fields of study, including planning and regional development, economic geography, ergonomics, work design, green chemistry, community and neighborhood studies, health-related and environmental studies, and gender, race, and ethnic studies is taking place. Universities need to persist in the advancement of cross-community, cross-firm, and cross-institutional learning. Centers and institutes appear to offer what Lerner and Simon (1998) call "ideal vehicles for this purpose" (on centers and institutes, see Brabeck, 1998; Harkavy, 1998). Because they "transcend disciplinary boundaries and disciplinary ways of framing problems, centers can be effective mechanisms for advancing outreach scholarship, particularly as issues and concerns undergo shifts and changes" (Silka, 2001, p. 502).

The learning dynamics and knowledge diffusion generated by collaborative activities and new approaches to teaching can invigorate all phases of learning at the university. In this way, the university advances its activities beyond an indiscriminate approach to development, maximizes the use of its resources, and performs an integrative and innovative role in the cultivation of equitable and sustainable regions. The chapters in this book move beyond the traditional focus in education for sustainability by taking on all three "legs": economics, equity, and the environment. The authors illustrate the strikingly different ways in which universities pursue integrated education for sustainability by focusing on all three themes.

The chapter by Robert Koester, James Eflin, and John Vann highlights a full-campus approach and asks us to consider how integration across an entire campus can best be achieved so that goals for the curriculum, the physical plant, and the administration are all aligned with sustainability. The authors examine a decade of successes at Ball State University, but also point to continuing challenges and unresolved issues in achieving all of the goals for sustainability they have set for themselves. This chapter calls our attention to questions about whether university change is most easily initiated and maintained through "top-down" or "bottom-up" approaches and whether strategies for change that are successful at one university can be adapted for others. Ball State could be said to have all of its ducks in a row. The discussion in this chapter raises the question of whether universities for which this is not the case can still draw from the Ball State model.

A multi-university focus is taken in the South Carolina and Western Massachusetts chapters. Each group of authors examines the question of how universities by working together, can advance education for sustainability. The chapters provide us with differing views in their descriptions of two very different regions, two very different partnerships with different goals, and two different points in time within those same partnerships. These chapters highlight the promise when systems work together, but also shed light on the differences in institutional practices that continue to thwart efforts aimed at bringing universities together when there are deep differences in campus cultures, skill bases, and tenure practices.

The question of disciplines and what they might offer is taken up in the Dan Egan et al. as well as Linda Lowry and Judy Flohr chapters. Here, the authors examine the question of how disciplines often considered to be out of the sustainability mainstream in fact can go to the very heart of unresolved questions of sustainability. Lowry and Flohr take us through the process by which courses in a leading department of tourism and hospitality are infused with sustainability, while the Egan et al. chapter looks at four different disciplines in social sciences and humanities—sociology, history, political science, and philosophy—whose potential to make significant contributions to the theoretical base of sustainability and to the problems and perils of sustainability has yet to be fully recognized. Education for sustainable development, Egan et al. note, "must first acknowledge the value-laden nature of the concept and then make explicit the particular values that are to be taught. Only after an ongoing social dialogue can we arrive at a consensus on a working definition of sustainable development. This is a task for which the humanities and social sciences can make a major contribution" (ch. 4).

The Elisabeth Hamin and William Mass chapters look at the level of individual courses and guide us through the transformations that are needed if courses in particular disciplines are to become better vehicles for conveying the complexities of sustainability. Both chapters make the compelling case that little will be achieved in education for sustainability if transformation does not reach down to the level of individual courses because these, after all, are the heart of the university. For Hamin, "Unlike biology, say, which creates biologists, or planning which creates planners, there is not a profession of 'sustainer'." The pedagogic goal, she notes "is to encourage a world view, one in which students will become citizen activists for sustainability after they graduate, whether in the civic sphere or by bringing sustainability criteria to bear on their work" (ch. 5).

The chapters noted above assist us in looking at education for sustainability where much of the focus is on the university itself: the students, the curriculum, and the physical plant. The Geiser chapter and the Silka, Geigis, and Snyder chapter take on the challenges posed when universities direct their educational efforts toward other audiences. Geiser describes a university's work with international environmental justice leaders where clean production principles become the means of overcoming attempts to pit the goals of equity, economy, and the environment against each other. For Geiser, "the education and training required to be an effective advocate for a sustainable future is often learned on the job and through direct personal experience. Universities can play an important role in such education by providing students with a broader awareness, values clarification, technical and historical information, personal and professional skills, and an opportunity to share experiences" (ch. 2). Silka et al. consider the ways in which universities can work more closely with policy makers to reach local leaders and precollege youth with sustainability themes. Both chapters explore new ideas—cleaner production and community preservation—and both note the value of addressing past problems by generating new conceptual approaches. Are universities equipped to take on these tasks that move them out of their traditional roles?

The Western Massachusetts chapter suggests some of the difficulties that can arise when an entire city becomes the focal point for efforts on the part of a five-campus consortium. The difficulties are illustrative of how college and university governance systems and definitions of "scholarship" make such multicampus collaborations difficult. This chapter illustrates how difficult it is for community organizations to find their way into the labyrinth that is the university.

While many of the chapters written from within universities argue that these institutions are well-situated to be leaders in furthering education for sustainability, the Viederman chapter raises core questions about the extent to which this notion is indeed the case. He wonders whether universities are in fact equipped to offer solutions. This chapter suggests that within universities, people are usually good at learning from those within their own disciplines, but most sustainability issues call for work that crosses interdisciplinary lines and here, he argues, universities have yet to come to terms with the fundamental problem of disciplinary fragmentation. Viederman notes:

> The world has problems; universities have disciplines. Inter-, trans-, non-, multidisciplinary approaches are rooted in the disciplines. Sustainability is about the whole, about the sum of and the relationships among the parts of systems. Universities excel at parts, not the whole. The search for knowledge is defined as that which is researchable. Expertise is valued. But as the eminent microbiologist Erwin Chargoff suggested, where expertise prevails, wisdom vanishes. Can higher education cultivate wisdom as well as it does knowledge (ch. 1)?

Viederman sees this fragmentation as permeating all parts of the university: whom faculties direct their research to, how courses are organized, how the curricula are designed, and how the very structure of the university as a knowledge-generating and disseminating entity is organized and maintains itself. Thus, an interesting argument goes on among these chapters about the extent of present and future leadership roles for universities.

The implied or explicit goal or end result of the various chapters also varies. Geiser calls for creating movements that bring academics together with those who have traditionally been excluded from sustainability discussions. Other chapters look to enlarge the ideas that serve as the foundation for education for sustainability. As more disciplines are brought into the discussion, better ideas are expected to result. Others focus on how students, upon leaving the university and becoming practitioners, can make a difference in their professions in tourism, engineering, and the like. But very different positions are taken here: Hamin calls for students to understand policy; she sees a focus on individual, personal change as not particularly useful and as somewhat beside the point. Other chapters highlight the importance of personal change. A comparable theme of personal change versus policy change also shows up at the university level. Should universities be focused on changing themselves (such as greening campuses), their structures, and their practices? Or is it universities in their idea-generating, policy-promulgation role that should be the focus of attention and efforts? Again, the chapters read together, convey an intriguing give and take on these important issues.

In addition, the problems the authors are trying to solve are quite different and very instructive. Some are trying to better understand what particular disciplines can offer. Others are attempting to identify those strategies best suited for moving ahead whole institutions. Some are seeking to understand which courses should be changed and what those changes might look like if they are truly to affect views on sustainability. Others are trying to look at how groups of institutions can work better together. Some are trying to understand how community outreach can become a core feature of a university's approach to education for sustainability. There are many differences among these perspectives, but also some important commonalities. All, in some sense, point to the fact that universities' resources remain to be effectively used. Here the chapters unearth and examine different resources: the variety of disciplines, the focus on research, the access to funding, and the opportunities to involve students and enrich their educational experiences. Ultimately, most university faculty do best when they are confronted with challenging problems in need of solutions: the question remains whether and how we can harness this motivation effectively. The chapters in this book point to innovative ways in which universities have begun this task in the area of education for sustainability.

REFERENCES

Blewett, M. (1995). *To enrich and to serve: The centennial history of the University of Massachusetts Lowell.* Virginia Beach, VA: The Donning Company.

Boucher, G., Conway, C., & Van Der Meer, E. (2003). Tiers of engagement by universities in their region's development. *Regional Studies, 37,* 887-897.

Braebeck, M. (1998). Changing the culture of the university engaged in outreach scholarship. In R. M. Lerner & L. A. K. Simon (Eds.), *University-community collaborations for the twenty-first century: Outreach scholarship for youth and families.* New York: Garland.

Braskamp, L., & Wergin, J. (1998). Forming new social partnerships. In W. G. Tierney (Ed.), *The responsive university: Restructuring for high performance* (pp. 62-91). Baltimore: The Johns Hopkins University Press.

Cox, M., & Richlin, L. (Eds.). (2004). Building faculty learning communities. A special issue of *New Directions for Teaching and Learning,* Spring, p. 97.

Dineen, D. (1995). The role of a university in regional economic development: A case study of the University of Limerick. *Industry & Higher Education,* June, 140-148.

Florida, R. (1995). Toward the Learning Region. *Futures, 27,* 527-536.

Forrant, R., & Silka, L. (1999). Thinking and doing, doing and thinking: The University of Massachusetts Lowell and the community development process. *American Behavioral Scientist, 42,* 808-820.

Geiser, K., & Greiner, T. (2001). Innovation and adoption of cleaner production technologies. In R. Forrant, J. Pyle, W. Lazonick, & C. Levenstein (Eds.), *Approaches to sustainable development: The public university in the regional economy* (pp. 219-241). Amherst: University of Massachusetts Press.

Harris, R. (1996). The impact of the University of Portsmouth on the local economy. *Urban Studies, 34,* 605-626.

Harkavay, I. (1998). Organizational innovation and the creation of the new American university: The University of Pennsylvania's Center for Community Partnerships as a case study in progress. In R. Lerner & L. Simon (Eds.), *University-community collaborations for the twenty-first century: Outreach scholarship for youth and families.* New York: Garland.

Jacoby, B. (2003). *Building partnerships for service-learning.* San Francisco: John Wiley & Sons.

Knudsend, D. (1997). What works best? Reflections on the role of theory in planning. *Economic Development Quarterly, 11,* 208-211.

Kriebel, D., Geiser, K., & Crumbley, C. (2001). The Lowell Center for Sustainable Production: Integrating environment and health into regional economic development. In R. Forrant, J. Pyle, W. Lazonick, & C. Levenstein (Eds.), *Approaches to sustainable development: The public university in the regional economy* (pp. 295-308). Amherst: University of Massachusetts Press.

Labrianidis, L. (1995). Establishing universities as a policy for local economic development: An assessment of the direct impact of three provincial Greek universities. *Higher Education Policy, 8,* 55-62.

Lazonick, W., Fiddy, M., & Quinby, S. (2003). Grow your own in the new economy: Skill formation challenges in the New England optical networking industry. In J. Pyle

& R. Forrant (Eds.), *Globalization, universities and issues of sustainable human development*. Northampton: Edward Elgar Publishing.

Lerner, R. M., & Simon, L. A. K. (1998). The new American university. In R. M. Lerner & L. A. K. Simon (Eds.), *University-community collaborations for the twenty-first century: Outreach scholarship for youth and families*. New York: Garland.

Maurrasse, D. (2001). *Beyond the campus: How colleges and universities form partnerships with their communities*. New York: Routledge.

Morgan, K. (1997). The learning region: Institutions, innovation and regional renewal. *Regional Studies, 31*, 491-503.

Mowery, D., Nelson, R., Sampat, B., & Ziedonia, A. (2004). *Ivory tower and industrial innovation*. Stanford: Stanford University Press.

O'Connell, P., & Hoermann, E. (2005 in press). *Educational partnerships in the National Park Service: Six case studies*. National Park Service.

Pyle, J., & Forrant, R. (Eds.). (2003). *Globalization, universities and issues of sustainable human development*. Northampton: Edward Elgar Publishing.

Schmoch, U. (1999). Interactions of universities and industrial enterprises in Germany and the United States—A comparison. *Industry and Innovation, 6*, 51-68.

Silka, L. (2001). Addressing the challenge of community collaborations: Centers as opportunities for interdisciplinary innovation. In R. Forrant, J. Pyle, W. Lazonick, & C. Levenstein (Eds.), *Approaches to sustainable development: The public university in the regional economy* (pp. 358-382). Amherst: University of Massachusetts Press.

Storper, M. (1995). The resurgence of regional economies, ten years later: The region as a nexus of untraded interdependencies. *European Urban and Regional Studies, 2*, 191-221.

Strand, K., Marullo, S., Cutforth, N., Stoecker, R., & Donohue, P. (2003). *Community-based research and higher education: Principles and practices*. San Francisco: John Wiley & Sons.

Van Den Berg, L., & Russo, A. (Eds.). (2004). *The student city: Strategic planning for student communities in EU cities*. Burlington, VT: Ashgate Publishing.

SECTION ONE:
University Space

CHAPTER 1

Can Universities Contribute to Sustainable Development?*

Stephen Viederman

> The obscure takes a while to see, the obvious, longer.
> —*Anonymous*

Going to a conference away from home is an exercise in unsustainability. The trip to and from the airport usually requires a car or taxi ride, single occupancy. The flight contributes to global warming and is a microcosm of class structure: first, business, and economy. The crowded highways traversed are multilane, having devoured green space and fertile farmland. Often they are lined with factories or the headquarters of corporations responsible for the manufacturing of the "excessities" that symbolize our modern age and the billboards that urge us to buy more. And these excessities are unequally distributed. The highways to and from the airport are often bordered with urban blight. The occupants of these neighborhoods suffer noise, air pollution, and other social ills not found in the suburbs. This view of the landscape often goes unnoticed because of its familiarity and because the traveler's thoughts are elsewhere. This view of the world is not what we want for our children, our grandchildren, and ourselves.

This chapter addresses a necessary process for envisioning a sustainable future and presents a brief overview of the meaning of the terms sustainability and sustainable development going well beyond the conventional focus on the environment. It looks at the structure of the institutional setting and particularly the control of disciplines, and departments, and related matters. In addition, constraints affecting knowledge generation for policy needs are addressed, focusing

---

*Any essay that refers to "universities" generically is painting with a broad brush. Thus, there may be some number of institutions of higher education that are to a greater degree exceptions to the characterizations offered here. Of one thing I am certain, however; they are too few and the "great and the good" are not among them.

particularly on the different questions and time frames that both the policymakers and the general public place on research. The chapter notes the failure of most institutions to look systematically at their own footprint on sustainability, whether it be in the form of the impacts of their investments, their labor practices, their procurement, their relationship to the communities in which they are located, and the like, and ends with some suggestions about what might come next.

VISION

A vision of a sustainable society is necessary to challenge all institutions in society to create the circumstances that will lead to changes in the institutions themselves and in the society as a whole. Envisioning clarifies goals and the processes of change that are needed. The emphasis on a vision of a desired future is essential because it forces a comparison of an ideal state with the situation that currently prevails or would likely occur if present trends continued with little or no societal intervention. Envisioning a sustainable society is a process with a beginning and no end because new circumstances will continually arise that require attention. The challenge of the process is to create better conditions for ourselves while ensuring that we leave options open for future generations to make the changes they envision as necessary.

Envisioning a sustainable society requires new approaches to understanding and creating change that is systemic and structural, rather than ameliorative. It requires the involvement of a range of people: individuals, groups, and communities that are usually not invited to sit at the decision-making table. It requires a broader democratic and participatory "we" than is often the case. Envisioning is a process for clarifying values, helping to create a deeper understanding of who we are, and at the same time, what we want to be, and what we want to facilitate for the benefit of future generations. Envisioning challenges the acceptance of attainable goals as ends in themselves, forcing formulation of goals that are just and needed, even though at any given point in the process they seem unattainable. The concept of acceptable risk as a part of the process, for example, raises a number of questions: Acceptable to whom?" "Decided upon by whom?" and "With what consequences for whom?" Acceptability is usually predicated on the opinion of external "expertise," often with conflict among those "experts," and decision making without consultation with those who are most affected by the risk. Citizens are therefore at the mercy of experts, diminishing their own power to control their communities.

Envisioning is proactive, not a passive acceptance of the present situation. Focusing on root causes of unsustainability rather than just symptoms creates opportunities to plan new courses of action more effectively, thereby avoiding being victims of fate. It requires attention to first principles: what is it we want for ourselves? For our children and their children? For all children? It demands an assessment of the present system of capitalism as a barrier to a just, equitable, and environmentally sound society. It calls for and empowers the search for a new "ism" that would facilitate the goals envisioned.

Envisioning a sustainable society is a social construct that goes against a notion that is central to our ways of thinking, the notion that gives primacy to science and technology as the basis of the solutions for all of human problems. Attention to the technical means of achieving sustainability is important, but cannot become a preoccupation until we know where we are going. There are no formulae to define sustainability, nor are there equations to measure it. Einstein's observation concerning mathematics applies equally, especially to sustainability: "[T]he laws . . . as far as they refer to reality, are not certain, and as far as they are certain, do not refer to reality."

Offered here is an unexceptional personal vision of sustainability that informs the thoughts that follow, underlining the breadth of the changes that are needed well beyond environmental issues. The world envisioned would be a peaceful world in which communities control their own economies and where peoples of different races, classes, ethnicities, ages, and sexual orientation live together learning and benefiting from social diversity. It would be a world in which the air is clean, the water pure, and where neither the poor nor the rich need to be concerned about environmental assaults on their health. It also would be a world where work is satisfying, provides a living wage and pay equity, with good benefits and the right to organize; a world where education would be freely available and that focuses attention on the obligations of citizenship as well as the needs of lifelong learning for pleasure and advancement. Finally, it would be a world where justice, equity, and fairness exist within and among nations and where power is used to enrich, not to diminish people.

SUSTAINABILITY

The terms "sustainable development" and "sustainability" gained prominence in the last decades of the twentieth century as a critique of development models that resulted in the destruction of nature. Governments and inter-governmental organizations established national and international commissions whose reports have long since been buried. Nongovernmental organizations at local, national, and international levels proliferated, countless conferences were held, books and papers published, and Web sites created. Today even the corporate world has accommodated the language of sustainability. The discussion has been sustained, but the world looks much the same as it did before.

The discussion then and now is still largely organized around discrete, though clearly interrelated issues—the environment, women, development, and population. And within these broad areas, the foci are narrow and unconnected. The emphasis on the environment is still foremost and even today the word "sustainability" is usually shorthand for environmental sustainability, for "greening." Trying to deal with all of the parts of the problem of unsustainability together remains elusive, in part because of the absence of an envisioning process. You cannot get anywhere without knowing where you are going. The problem is also complex and chaotic and thus difficult to confront directly. Our institutions are not structured appropriately. They tend to be organized horizontally with little vertical integration. Raising issues of the whole requires dealing with the systems in which the parts are embedded. This prospect, in turn, challenges too many beliefs and behaviors, raising questions about the use and abuse of power within institutions in the modern world. The political will necessary to reduce the dissonance between creed and deed, as Gandhi described in the mid-twentieth century, does not exist.

Moving toward a vision of sustainability is an extremely complex problem, and there has been little resolution of the key underlying issues. Einstein observed "perfection of means and confusion of ends seems to characterize our age." Mechanisms to address these questions as a whole, or at a minimum to put the parts together, and ways of creating opportunities for change are lacking. The focus is on details with no assurance that they are the most important details. Without a sense of the whole, there can be no understanding of the inter-relationship of the parts. By focusing on the parts rather than the whole, it becomes convenient to avoid explicit attention to what are arguably the two most impor-tant and difficult interrelated issues for sustainability and development: the global economy and the distribution of power among the peoples of the world. Sustainability is not a technical problem to be solved. It is ultimately about what a society values, not in the technical sense of economic valuation, but in the sense of human concerns and aspirations.

HIGHER EDUCATION AND SUSTAINABILITY

In his 1974 Nobel acceptance speech, economist Fredrich von Hayek began by observing the irony that economists at that time were being called upon to correct the problems for which they themselves were responsible. Little has changed, and economists are not the only ones at fault.

Higher education will play a role in shaping the vision and practice of a sustainable society for better or worse. It has a responsibility and an obligation for the better. Its graduates will be leaders of countries, corporations, religious institutions, art, thought, science, engineering—people of power. They will also be citizens, great and small, asked to participate in decision making for the commonweal. Its faculty will have access to the halls of power and will be called upon by society for assistance.

Higher educational institutions' efforts to respond to the challenges of sustainability must begin with an honest institutional assessment of the obstacles they face. Focusing on obstacles is not a counsel of despair, but a necessary first step toward the changes that are necessary. It is also a way of assessing the limits of institutions to respond to the challenge of sustainability. The focus then will be on what can be done in the short term, and the changes that are possible over time.

At a conference to a group of parliamentarians and religious leaders on global education held in Moscow in 1990, Nobel laureate Elie Wiesel offered this critique of the education of those Germans who allowed the atrocities against Jews and Russians during World War II.

> They [the Germans] did not come from the underworld; some came from some of the best and most prestigious Universities in Germany: they had degrees and even doctorates in medicine, philosophy, jurisprudence and theology. In other words: they were not shielded by their education. What was wrong with it? It emphasized theories instead of values, concepts rather than human beings, abstraction rather than consciousness, answers instead of questions, ideology and efficiency rather than conscience. Thus in the name of a theory based on conquest and domination, multitudes of men and women, and—woe unto us—children too, were reduced and diminished only to be seen as tools; their lives used as instruments. The sacredness of the human being, the uniqueness of the person, the right of every individual to immortality were negated and discarded at the whim of those who possessed power—either political or intellectual.

What is the relevance of Wiesel's criticisms of pre–World War II German education as a guide for the discussion of higher education and sustainability today? The world has changed in many ways in the last sixty years. But "conquest and domination" are still all too common, over nature and humans.

Domination and mastery of the environment is a recurrent theme in modern life. Yale's president, economist Richard Levin, began his inaugural address in October 1993 by quoting Sophocles: "Numberless are the world's wonders, but none more wonderful than man," adding that "the chorus sings of humanity's power over nature." Continuing, Levin observed, "We celebrate today our University—a monument to the achievement Sophocles extols. We preserve humanity's achievement [in controlling nature]. We impart an appreciation of that achievement by our teaching and augment it by our research." But what is the extent and what are the unintended consequences of our efforts to control and manage nature for present and future generations?

In a 1996 conference on philanthropy, James Gibson of the Urban Institute noted that many social problems, like poverty, might now best be thought of as organic to capitalism and not subject to "cure." Further discussion suggested that over the long haul efforts to deal with social ills should seek equilibrium rather than a cure. If social problems are rooted in the very nature of capitalism, then that is the problem to be solved. This issue was not raised. This at best amoral discussion reflects all too well the concerns expressed by Wiesel that are too common in academia.

WHY CAN'T UNIVERSITIES FOSTER LEARNING
AND BEHAVIORAL CHANGE TOWARD SUSTAINABILITY?

The world has problems; universities have disciplines. Inter-, trans-, non-, multidisciplinary approaches are rooted in the disciplines. Sustainability is about the whole, about the sum of and the relationships among the parts of systems. Universities excel at parts, not the whole. The search for knowledge is defined as that which is researchable. Expertise is valued. But as the eminent microbiologist Erwin Chargoff suggested, where expertise prevails, wisdom vanishes. Can higher education cultivate wisdom as well as it does knowledge?

While president of Columbia University in the 1990s, Michael Sovern observed that the most exciting issues confronting society seemed to fall "at the interstices between the departments," an admittedly unexceptional observation. But then more than two hundred years after the founding of that university (now 250 years old) and after decades of discussion and debate over "interdisciplinarity," he and his colleagues could do no better than to suggest that they needed to figure out how to deal with this reality! Derek Bok, who retired from the presidency of Harvard in 1992, observed:

> Our universities excel in pursuing the easier opportunities where established academic and social priorities coincide. On the other hand, when social needs are not clearly recognized and backed by adequate financial support, higher education has often failed to respond as effectively as it might, even to some of the most important challenges facing America. Armed with the security of tenure and time to study the world with care, professors would appear to have a unique opportunity to act as society's scouts to signal impending problems long before they are visible to others. Yet rarely have members of the academy succeeded in discovering emerging issues and bringing them vividly to the public's attention. What Rachel Carson did for risks to the environment, Ralph Nader for consumer protection, Michael Harrington for problems of poverty, Betty Friedan for women's rights, they did as independent critics, not as members of a faculty. Universities will usually continue to respond weakly unless outside support is available and the subjects involved command prestige in academic circles. (1990, p. 105)

In March 1994 James E. Welch Jr., GE chair, offered an alternative view of what is possible outside the bonds of academia. He argued that "boundaryless" is an essential operating principle in business. By that comment he meant "piercing the walls of hundred-year-old fiefdoms and empires called finance, engineering, manufacturing, marketing, and gathering teams from all those functions in one room with one shared coffee pot, one shared vision and one consuming passion— to design the world's best jet engine, or ultrasound machines, or refrigerator." The principle should apply equally to colleges and universities where education for sustainable development is a more important priority than the goal of producing a more refined product.

A question that educators concerned with learning about sustainable development must ask: Can a student receive an A in ecology and an A in economics? If he or she really understands the key concepts of the disciplines and is willing to point out the contradictions between these disciplines to the professor, is there the risk of receiving a lower grade? In economics, for example, equity is not about justice, but ownership; the focus is on the short term rather than the long term—witness the discounting of the dollar—and externalities to the society as a whole are not accounted for. The words ecology and economics both have the same root: *ecos,* home. But their architecture is very different. And neither focuses on issues of equity and justice. It is symptomatic of the systemic problem with which higher education must grapple.

The search for a technological fix is reflected in the management of a problem. For example, weather modification research to manage climate issues is pursued. New engines are designed that might reduce the guilt of single occupancy driving. But the new congestion occurring as a result creates a new problem for us to manage. Management efforts tend to be ameliorative and important in the short term. But not dealing with the consequences and effects of our actions in the long term is symbolic of the problems of universities. These institutions teach management that, as the Canadian philosopher John Ralston Saul writes, "is a tertiary skill—a method not a value. And yet we apply it to every domain as if it were the ideal of our civilization." It's like the cartoon of two cavemen talking about the future: "Let's concentrate on technology for a couple of thousand years, and then we can develop a value system." Management is not about people and their needs.

The culture of colleges and universities makes it difficult for fundamentally different views to prevail or even be fully addressed. As Duke University law professor James Coleman observes, "[I]n reality, the young scholars as they seek to win tenure, are forced to approach certain problems in a certain way that leads them to the same conclusions. You don't get as much independence of thought as the tenure system seems to promote." And you don't get to ask fundamental questions, such as ones about the failures of capitalism.

In economics, ethics and the real world seem to be intrusions. On receiving the Nobel Prize for economics, Amartya Sen was praised for his strong ethical sensibilities despite his technical capabilities. Another Nobel laureate, Robert Mundell, was notable, according to his teacher Charles Kindelberger, because "he brought into international economics some theoretical background, but a great deal of worldly wisdom along with it. He had a very well-developed, quick and imaginative sense of the real problems of the real world." Adds journalist Will Greider, "[I]t would make an interesting experiment if economics professors agreed to forfeit their protected status and submit to the invigorating competition of free labor markets (as they regularly recommend to workers). Would market forces generate freer thinking in the academy than the professors' protected guild status? You can be sure we will not find out." To repeat, Einstein's observation about mathematics applies equally to economics and to science in general as we try to deal with the policy process for sustainability: "[T]he laws of mathematics, as far as they refer to reality, are not certain, and as far as they are certain, do not refer to reality."

Politics is omitted from the sustainability disciplines and, more importantly, from the real world of sustainability. Lord Kenet, a British negotiator at the Montreal intragovernmental conference on climate change, suggests "[P]olitics is the art of taking good decisions on insufficient evidence." Paul Hawken, a businessman-turned-ecologist, goes further in his critique: "We know how to transform this world to reduce our impact on nature by severalfold, how to provide meaningful, dignified living-wage jobs for all who seek them, and how to feed, clothe, and house every person on earth. What we don't know is how to remove those in power, those whose ignorance of biology is matched only by their indifference to human suffering. This is a political issue. It is not an ecological problem."

Science does not reduce uncertainty. Rather it creates greater uncertainty. As science writer Andrew Revkin notes, "Like a flickering compass needle, science offers a trajectory toward truth, but not a recipe for dealing with it." In the real world, philosophers of science Silvio Funtowicz and Jerry Ravetz observe that "facts are uncertain, values in dispute, stakes high and decisions urgent." We must learn to live with and deal with uncertainty, which creates considerable discomfort in us all, in and out of academia.

The "precautionary principle" is more the product of renegade scientists than of those in the mainstream.

There is little acceptance of the validity of indigenous knowledge. The view of the forest is lost because of the focus on the trees. And some of the disciplines have disappeared, spawning new narrower focused disciplines. Biology has begot zoology and botany, and they have begot microbiology, molecular biology, genetics, physiology, and more, all separated from the whole. Rutgers University ecologist David Ehrenfeld points out that "loss of knowledge and skills is now a big problem in our universities, and no subject is of greater danger of disappearing than our long accumulated knowledge of the natural world. . . . We are on the verge of losing our ability to tell one plant or animal from another and of forgetting how the known species interact among themselves and with their environment."

Scientific research in colleges and universities is usually investigator generated and increasingly responsive to the needs of industry; this has co-opted the research process. But the need for knowledge generated by a vision of sustainability must be driven not only by the researchers but also by the participants in the envisioning process. The perception of what is most needed, particularly in the short-term, is likely to be in conflict. Researchers may believe that global climate change is a preeminent issue. Members of communities fighting for their survival may see job creation and toxics as high priorities.

How can colleges and universities respond, especially when the guild-like tenure system rewards the former rather than the latter? And in what time frames? Research is often a leisurely process, but policy makers and communities need answers or at least a sense of direction sooner than suits many academics. Muddling through often trumps the peer-reviewed article. And expert knowledge is rarely sufficient for action.

WHAT CAN BE DONE?

When he was president of the University of Chicago, Robert Hutchins observed, "[I]t is not a very good university, but it is the best we have." The constraints and issues described here are systemic and cannot be dealt with piecemeal. Nothing less than system change can effectively strengthen colleges and universities in their pursuit of learning and acting for sustainability. It is perhaps too flippant to assert that nothing less than a totally new institution, one that we cannot yet even begin to describe, is needed for education and learning that is related to sustainable development. This change is not likely to occur in the foreseeable future, which places a great burden on existing institutions to muddle through, doing the best they can.

Systems have specific purposes within the larger context in which they operate. The ways that parts of systems are arranged determine their performance. Educational institutions teach, train, and produce research and are historically organized around disciplines. This structure is dysfunctional with regard to sustainability and, as in the case of economics and ecology (as presently taught and researched), the disciplines are often in conflict. Disciplines are the problem and not part of the solution.

Ultimately, the issue confronting higher educational institutions is one of fundamental culture change. System change of the magnitude needed engenders fear of losing power and authority. This fact, in turn, makes the very possibility of change seem impossible. Systems need feedback; but it is not clear where that comes from in a university. Students are always in transition. Alumni are distant. Faculty are distracted by their own needs. Administrators raise money, and money from governments and corporations talks. Communities are subjects not objects of concern.

Relationships to outside constituents such as community organizations must be developed in a meaningful way. It is not simply a matter of what the institution believes it may contribute to the community, but the need for the institution to develop a way of listening and responding to the community. The institutions also need to develop appropriate governance structures to receive and respond to feedback from all of their constituencies. With universities' increasing obligations to the corporate world for research support, real conflicts arise.

The process of change in research, training, relationship to the community, governance, and so forth must become a singular focus of the institution to see how it might be restructured with a vision and goal of sustainability. This is not a task for a department or a new institute for the study of change, but for the institution as a whole. Ideally, this process would be carried out in conjunction with the community in which the institution is located and from which it can learn. This approach is for mutual benefit, not *noblesse oblige*.

Most efforts at social change are, in effect, ameliorative: they seek to remedy immediate problems, but do not deal with root causes. Efforts at reformation can create some change, but they remain within the limits of existing systemic constraints. The most significant and lasting forms of social change are revolutionary. They pose fundamental challenges to existing systems, seeking to envision and create new systems. This transformation should be the long-term goal of colleges and universities.

Nothing less than a redefinition of what an economy can and should be is in order, reflecting the vision "we" create because the university does not exist in a vacuum. Scale is an important matter to consider. Have we gone beyond what we can deal with? And if scale were smaller, as Grieder observes, "The principles of economics would look utterly different, since the meanings of profit, loss, and productive output would be revalued to conform better with society's understandings [and vision] of what is gain and what is loss." Can capitalism be redefined in theory and in practice to encompass justice, equity, and the environment? If not, what would the new "ism" look like? And who will initiate the discussion and with whom?

But initiating such a process of transformation is daunting. How and where do we begin? Universities, research institutions, think tanks, and even religious institutions have become so dependent on corporate largesse that their objectivity is in question. Truth and objectivity are ephemeral as knowledge is embedded in social, economic, political, and cultural contexts. Are there institutions that are not co-opted or corrupted by the present system so that they can participate in a discussion? How can a process that will last a decade or more be sustained? How can the process be made truly participatory? How can it be made democratic? How can power be shared, not exercised, something essential to the process and vision of sustainability? How can we learn new modes of speaking, learning, and interacting to make the process effective? It requires that the people in power learn to listen and respond rather than dominate conversations.

Creating a personal or even an institutional or community vision of a more sustainable future is, relatively, the easy part. What is infinitely more difficult, and what is often overlooked, is describing and creating the process for achieving a vision that is the product of truly public discussion and debate. How do the process and the resulting product become authentic by being inclusive? How do we build trust across race, ethnicity, class, sexual orientation, gender, and age? How can we cut across the factors, such as unequal power distribution, age, ethnicity, and race that often have hindered rather than helped to foster dialogue and action? How will such a dialogue be sustained among people already too busy dealing with survival or securing tenure? How do we manage a project that on the one hand has such clear goals, yet on the other hand has such ambiguous and ambitious outcomes? How do we overcome the forces that push towards short-term thinking?

All of the experiments in sustainability, large and small, must be examined, and we must learn from their successes and failures. We also must see how they interact and form a whole. Using the vision as a guide, we will need to build new systems that reflect a view of the world that prioritizes social justice, equality, and environmental soundness. We can look ahead, testing ideas against the vision. At the same time, we must engage in "back casting" as if we were archaeologists reconstructing the past from shards, looking back from the vision to the present. It helps to avoid being caught in our present mindsets. Both approaches will help to identify paths and pitfalls.

SOME MODEST PROPOSALS

Duke University historian Lawrence Goodwyn argues, "The first thing we need to do is license in people a degree of doubt and curiosity. . . . We live in a damaged culture, and, people are inhibited more than intimidated. Getting rid of complacency means expanding our curiosity. Then we need to encourage an insurgent temperament."

Sustainability concerns issues of justice and equity as well as the environment. Accepting this fact, colleges and universities can model some of their behavior in the shorter term to demonstrate their understanding of this case. Colleges and universities can develop participatory processes for envisioning a different society, both within their institutions and the communities to which they have obligations. They can begin the process of introspection in order to develop an understanding of the barriers to being more effective educators and researchers for sustainability. They can focus attention on the nature of the changes needed for sustainability both institutionally and in the society as a whole. They can demonstrate concern for justice by undertaking activities to make work satisfying and equitable as well as guaranteeing a living wage for workers. They can contribute to the development of neighborhoods not only for faculty but also for workers and residents, both low and high income. They can foster learning toward sustainability for all members of the institution, albeit imperfectly at the start. They can greatly reduce their ecological footprints through building design and maintenance, energy conservation, purchasing, and the like. As large institutional investors, they can exercise their obligations of ownership in corporations.

They can engage corporations in discussions of the externalities they generate that are contrary to a search for sustainability and through the voting of their proxies on issues of corporate governance as well as social and environmental concerns. Similarly, investments in community development should be consonant with sustainability. A new fiduciary duty that is farseeing requires that political, environmental, cultural, and social issues be integrated into investment decisions. Research shows that companies that act in accordance with good corporate governance standards, including awareness of their impacts on society, are likely to perform better and offer greater shareholder value. Finally, these steps are small but visible ones on a long road. Rabbi Tarphon preached centuries ago, "It is not your obligation to complete the task [of perfecting the world], but neither are you free to desist [from doing all you can]!"

REFERENCE

Bok, D. (1990). *Universities and the future of America.* North Carolina: Duke University Press.

CHAPTER 2

Education for a Transition to Sustainability

Kenneth Geiser

The transition to a sustainable society requires the active participation of all who promote environmental protection, social justice, and an economy that values and protects health. Progressive political leaders, visionary business interests, nongovernment advocacy groups and community-based civil society organizations drive the effort. The education and training required to be an effective advocate for a sustainable future is often learned on the job and through direct personal experience. Universities can play an important role in such education by providing students with a broader awareness, values clarification, technical and historical information, personal and professional skills, and an opportunity to share experiences. Such education fits the conventional individual development model that forms the basis of most degree-oriented higher education curricula.

However, universities also can provide training, skill building, and values development for communities of professionals and citizens who currently are engaged in ongoing campaigns and struggles. This kind of education differs from traditional learner-based training because it focuses on groups of people and seeks to form and sustain activist organizations capable of leveraging social and economic change. While there are many examples of this kind of education, it is a less conventional model for higher education institutions.

WHAT'S THE UNIVERSITY UP TO?

The University of Massachusetts Lowell, in its attempts to promote its stated mission of "sustainable regional economic and social development," has amassed a broad body of experience in educating communities of people seeking a transition to a more sustainable future. This chapter will focus on three examples conducted by the Massachusetts Toxics Use Reduction Institute and the Lowell Center for Sustainable Production in which I have had the opportunity to participate.

The Massachusetts Toxics Use Reduction Institute was established on the Lowell campus as a part of Massachusetts' state pollution prevention program. As part of its charge, the Institute was required to provide training programs for professionals who are required to assist state environmental agencies in reducing the industrial use of toxic chemicals and the generation of hazardous wastes. The Institute developed and frequently offered a fourteen-week training course that graduated a group of more than five hundred professionals who have gone on to form a special professional organization, the Toxics Use Reduction Planners Association.

The university's Lowell Center for Sustainable Production teamed up with the Center for Clean Products and Clean Technologies at the University of Tennessee to develop and offer a training program for national environmental advocacy organizations on the concepts and techniques of cleaner production. After two years, this training led to cleaner production advocacy in the national environmental justice movement and a new international nongovernmental organization called Clean Production Action.

During this period, the Lowell Center and the Toxics Use Reduction Institute designed a special training program for international, nongovernment environmental advocacy activists to develop their awareness and skills in promoting cleaner industrial production technologies and processes. This training formed the basis for the establishment of a new international advocacy network called the Global Alliance for Incinerator Alternatives (GAIA), which today has members in thirty countries throughout the world.

Each of these training programs has sought to increase awareness, skills, and substantive knowledge that would help participants increase the effectiveness of their advocacy. In each case, the training has led to the formation of new concepts and new organizations that today actively promote sustainable solutions.

What can be learned from these initiatives? What has succeeded? What lines must be carefully constructed to separate education for change from its direct advocacy? How best can a university dedicated to a sustainable future use its educational mission to help form viable communities of people capable of promoting that mission?

EDUCATION FOR SUSTAINABLE DEVELOPMENT

Education for sustainable development came out of the international movement for sustainable development. Beginning in 1987, the concept of sustainable development was discussed and negotiated in a series of preparatory meetings for the United Nations Conference on Environment and Development. Education was considered a fundamental factor in promoting sustainable development, and a framework for education for sustainable development was written into Chapter 36 of the "Agenda 21" strategy adopted at the Rio de Janeiro Conference in 1992.

This strategy involved three priorities: expansion of basic education to all children; reorientation of current education to embrace the concepts of sustainable development; and raising public awareness.

The priorities of Agenda 21 quickly found resonance among academic leaders in institutions of higher education, and there soon followed a series of university/educator conferences, several of which generated finely crafted declarations. The themes that ran through the Talloires Declaration of 1990, the Halifax Declaration of 1992, and the University Charter for Sustainable Development of 1994 all stressed the critical role higher education institutions play not only in shaping future generations but also in directly affecting the environment through their physical facilities and resource throughput. Many of these early programs focused on the environmental aspects of higher education campuses. These programs, often called "greening the campus," were fueled by a combination of students, faculty, and administrators reexamining the physical plant in terms of energy and resource use, waste generation, landscape management, commuting and transportation requirements, and local impacts on neighborhoods and habitats.

In addition, these discussions often focused on the need to reorient educational curricula and teaching. More specialized conferences followed with new teaching manuals, toolkits, and model curricula and redesigned texts and exercises that presented lessons about sustainability. Quite rapidly, a new specialty arose commonly referred to as Education for Sustainable Development.

Education for Sustainable Development has involved awareness raising, capacity building, curriculum development, program reorientation, teacher training, and field-based learning. Through seminars, workshops, and conferences, hundreds of academics and college-level instructors have contributed to a growing body of materials and experiences that have attempted to link the concepts of sustainable development to traditional disciplines and conventional classroom, laboratory, and field based settings. Often it has required new course development; even more often it has required reorganizing, modifying, and reorienting conventional courses.

Education for Sustainable Development has sought to:

- Increase environmental literacy. Curricula have integrated aspects of biology, ecology, geology, and atmospheric sciences into basic sciences, engineering, social sciences, and the humanities.
- Integrate social, economic, and environmental values. Courses are designed to interweave the biophysical sciences with the social sciences such that poverty, equity, justice, and politics are rooted in objective environmental conditions.
- Focus globally and internationally. The international and planetary dimensions of social and environmental problems are presented as a means of linking local and global conditions.

- Raise awareness of environmental limits and threats. Most coursework presents a picture of a limited planet with finite resources that are seriously stressed by human population and technologies.
- Build skills and capacity for analysis and intervention. Courses included methods for measuring and monitoring environmental and social conditions and models for analysis, evaluation, and prediction.

Education for Sustainable Development has become a movement in its own right with annual conferences, model curricula, a loose network of professional peers, and a specialized journal, the *International Journal of Sustainability in Higher Education*. The International Association of Universities has launched a Global Higher Education for Sustainability Partnership to promote Education for Sustainable Development on campuses around the world; and a new Association of University Leaders for a Sustainable Future has emerged. The movement has many examples of success, with scores of well-committed campuses and campus leaders as well as a strong presence in various international meetings. Indeed, the United Nations has designated the decade 2005 to 2014 to be the Decade of Education for Sustainable Development.

EDUCATION FOR A TRANSITION TO SUSTAINABILITY

Education for Sustainable Development has provided a significant step forward in training college-based students in the wider world of environmental and social conditions and needs. However, most of the programs have remained campus based and focused on college-enrolled students. Students may do field work off campus in community or professional settings, but the programs are generally viewed as preparing college students for future work, rather than supporting those who already are engaged. The majority of these programs have not often reached out to noncollege professionals, practitioners, and activists who currently are busy with promoting sustainability. Reaching these people requires different programs and different curricula. Heavily occupied professionals and activists have minimal time to attend university classes; they learn best when directly engaged in ongoing work and campaigns; they demand practical and pragmatic knowledge that can be used in current contexts; they are action oriented and see their work as changing existing programs, policies, or practices. Beyond Education for Sustainable Development, education for a transition to sustainability must be integrated into the daily needs of professionals and activists to act on and engage in.

This strategy is not opposed to Education for Sustainable Development. Indeed, education for those currently promoting sustainability needs to include all of the basic elements of Education for Sustainable Development. However, that education should be different in tone and immediacy and more deliberately designed in order to build a collective capacity for affecting the changes instigated by those who are presently involved in the transition.

Conventional higher education prepares the learner as a future participant. Education for a transition to sustainability is best focused on the learner within the context of current and ongoing work and struggle. Curriculum needs to address strategies and tactics. Case studies and concrete examples need to provide replicable examples and practical lessons. Instructors often need to have had direct experience in and be capable of modeling as well as teaching desired skills.

Conventional higher education focuses centrally on the individual as the learner. Professionals and activists promoting sustainability are usually engaged in collective actions. The context involves informal networks, loose associations and coalitions, more formal organizations, or existing institutions and corporations. Education for a transition to sustainability needs to respect and build towards social and collective responses. Teaching is best done in groups. Interpersonal and organizational skills need to be addressed.

Conventional higher education relies on transferring a body of traditional knowledge. Those promoting sustainable forms and practices are often engaged in creating a future that is largely undefined and uncharted. Education for a transition to sustainability needs to respect ambiguity and uncertainty and promote critical thinking, creativity, and flexibility. Participants need to learn how to reexamine and deconstruct conventional concepts and practices. A focus on building self-confidence and collective empowerment is important. Teaching needs to be interactive and engage participants in creating new concepts and new frameworks that create positive venues for social change.

Over the last decade, work on education for a transition to sustainability has developed and matured at the University of Massachusetts Lowell. From the university's early origins training a workforce for the textile industry of the Merrimack Valley, it has a long tradition of direct practical education that has immediate application in meeting current needs and solving contemporary problems. When the university attracted a group of academics and professionals to work on the environmental aspects of industrial production and community organization, it was natural that the orientation would be towards practitioners and activists currently engaged in change.

We did not set out to develop a unique educational approach—certainly not something with a label like education for a transition to sustainability. Rather we developed and refined a set of approaches that only in hindsight can be seen as evolving into an educational strategy. However, through our collective work and our earnest conviction to use education to advance social change, we created a legacy that is worth more careful reflection here.

This work has evolved out of several centers and academic departments at the university, and there are significant variations among the initiatives. Here I am offering a description of only three initiatives that grew out of the Toxics Use Reduction Institute and the Lowell Center for Sustainable Production. The reason for selecting these three is because I have had some personal involvement with each of them.

TRAINING PROFESSIONALS FOR TOXICS USE REDUCTION

In 1990, the Massachusetts Toxics Use Reduction Institute (TURI) was established at the University of Lowell (later renamed as the University of Massachusetts Lowell). The Institute was a unique program at the university. Unlike other campus-based centers, the Institute was established at Lowell by legislative mandate as a part of the state's Toxics Use Reduction Program. Enacted in 1989, the Toxics Use Reduction Act was one of the nation's leading state pollution prevention laws with a mandate to cut the generation of hazardous wastes in the state's industries by 50 percent over a ten-year period.

The Toxics Use Reduction Program aimed to meet its objectives by placing new responsibilities on both industry and government agencies. Toxics use reduction was a new (and controversial) idea that focused directly on reducing or eliminating toxic chemical hazards in production processes rather than simply managing chemical exposures. The law required that the state's largest industrial generators of hazardous wastes annually report on the toxic and hazardous chemicals that they used and pay a graduated fee based on the size of the firm and number of toxic chemicals used. In addition, each production facility was responsible for preparing a facility toxics use reduction plan to analyze and describe how the facility could reduce or eliminate the use of the targeted chemicals. The plans were to be reviewed and updated every other year. For its part, the state regulatory agency was required to create a special division to collect the annual data from the firms and to assure that the facilities complied with the planning and fee requirements. In addition, the state set up two nonregulatory divisions to provide technical assistance to the firms. The Office of Technical Assistance provided professional technical assistance and technical workshops for facility managers while the Toxics Use Reduction Institute provided professional training, research, and laboratory testing on alternative materials and technologies, and library and Internet information resources.

One aspect of the Toxics Use Reduction Act required that the toxics use reduction facility plans be certified by a trained and licensed toxics use reduction planner. The responsibility for training these professionals was given to the Institute. Formally, the Institute was to design and offer training for professionals from across the state who wished to sit for the state exam and acquire their license to certify the facility plans. At first, the Institute staff assumed that they could easily develop this training by adapting currently available curricula, but a brief survey revealed that there were no relevant curricula. With this recognition, the staff set out on a six-month effort to design and pilot a training program that covered topics ranging from industrial process characterization to environmental and occupational hazard recognition, technology assessment, and financial analysis; and included the procedural and legal aspects of compliance.

The first class brought together thirty-two industrial managers, health and safety professionals, and private consultants for a once-a-week, fourteen-week training program. The program was designed to be immediately practical and learner centered with a fictitious case exercise organized as a small group activity that ran for several weeks. A final day-long field visit to a participating facility was included. Beyond toxics use reduction, the curriculum introduced new concepts such as materials accounting, materials balances, and full-cost accounting. Over the subsequent several years, the training was adapted, altered, and presented in many simultaneous sessions at facilities across the state. While Institute staff taught the initial courses, it soon became apparent that professionals whom they recognized as business peers better addressed the industry-based participants. Recognizing this fact, several of the early participants were recruited as trainers, and soon professionals from Massachusetts industries largely taught the courses. Each year, nearly 100 graduates sat for the state examinations with 75 to 85 percent successfully completing the tests.

In order to maintain certification, licensed toxics use reduction planners were required to accrue continuing education credits over the two-year periods of the license. The Institute staff soon recognized that this requirement not only provided a means of continually updating and upgrading the planners knowledge and skills but also provided a means of keeping the planners connected to each other and aware of their common work and mission. The focus of the growing number of course graduates who were professionally engaging state industries led to a loose network of people trading information, tips on practice, and recommendations for business contacts.

By 1994, the numbers of licensed toxics use reduction planners had grown to more than 400 and at the close of one of the continuing education training conferences a group of the planners met to establish a loose professional organization that became known as the Toxics Use Reduction Planners Association (TURPA). TURPA was formed as a dues-supported organization independent of the university and the Institute with an elected board of directors and small group of presiding officers.

TURPA became an independent constituency for the state program. Beyond its efforts to provide advice and support to its members, the association provided periodic input and advice to those who managed the Toxics Use Reduction Program, sought to raise public visibility for toxics use reduction and supported the state program before the state legislature. Although an active proponent of less hazardous forms of industrial production, TURPA has not expanded its advocacy to encompass a broader vision of sustainability. However, as an organization of technical professionals with a new language and body of skills, it has been an important contributor to the state's success in reducing its hazardous wastes by 57 percent (well beyond the 50 percent goal set by the law).

TRAINING ENVIRONMENTAL LEADERS
FOR CLEANER PRODUCTION

Toxics use reduction and pollution prevention were innovative new concepts for environmental management in the United States. However, parallel initiatives in Europe and in other parts of the world took a somewhat different direction. The work that emerged in Europe during the early 1990s was often called "cleaner production" and involved not only waste and pollution reduction but energy and water conservation as well as a comprehensive focus on the environmental hazards of products across their entire life cycle. The concept initially arose in Sweden, Denmark, and the Netherlands, spread across Europe, and was soon adopted by the Industry and Environment Office of the United Nations Environment Program (UNEP). In 1989, the Industry and Environment Office established a Cleaner Production Program based in Paris that was designed to promote the ideas of environmentally sensitive production technologies and processes throughout industrializing countries as a means of advancing economic development without degrading environmental resources.

By the mid-1990s, cleaner production programs in Europe and in several industrializing countries were rapidly growing, and a small collection of corporate managers were vocal leaders in promoting the concepts. Cleaner production had been fully embraced at the United Nations Conference on Environment and Development held in Rio de Janeiro in 1992 and adopted directly into the conference's final "Agenda 21" planning document. However, the ideas were much slower to emerge in the United States where a more limited pollution prevention concept was better understood and implemented.

By the mid-1990s, the Toxics Use Reduction Institute had assisted in the development of a second university center called the Lowell Center for Sustainable Production, to carry out a wider range of work relative to sustainability within the United States and abroad. The staff at both centers was aware of the ongoing work on cleaner production in Europe and at the United Nations. As director, I had been invited by UNEP to serve on the core advisory committee for the Cleaner Production Program, and I had attended and spoken at several of the UNEP conferences on cleaner production. In addition, the director of the Institute's training programs also had attended the European conferences and was active in helping UNEP set up cleaner production technical assistance centers in several industrializing countries.

In 1994, the Institute staff conducted a short training program for environmental leaders on the techniques of toxics use reduction, and they repeated it in 1996. It became clear through this program that environmental activists in the United States could become valuable promoters of the broader concepts of cleaner production; however, they were largely uninformed about the international initiatives.

An unexpected opportunity, made possible by a private foundation director, brought together staff from the Lowell Center and the Center for Clean Products and Processes at the University of Tennessee Knoxville to plan a training program on cleaner production for environmental leaders from across the country. A small planning body involving staff from the two universities and several leading environmental organizations was assembled. After rather intensive preparations over a six-month period, a three-day training program was convened at Knoxville in Spring 1998.

More than 70 participants came to this first training to hear about the concepts of cleaner production and toxics use reduction and to develop skills in production characterization, materials accounting, facility assessment, product labeling, and life cycle assessment. Like the training program developed for the toxics use reduction planners, this curriculum included small group exercises and case studies as well as lectures and guided discussions. In addition, the course focused specifically on strategies, tactics, and organizational development issues to build cleaner production into ongoing campaigns. The training in Tennessee was followed by a second session in Detroit in 1999, which brought together another 60 activists with a similar curriculum, although this time several graduates of the earlier program were invited to provide training sessions as well.

Among those attending the Detroit session were several leaders of the national environmental justice movement who were quite enthusiastic about the solution-focused aspects of cleaner production. Locked in painful struggles to reveal the disproportionate exposures to hazards and the elevated risks of low-income communities and communities of color, the forward-looking future-directed vision of cleaner and safer industries was highly attractive to these seminal leaders. Soon thereafter, the idea of cleaner production began to appear in the literature and campaign work in the environmental justice movement. A hearing before the U.S. Senate Judiciary Committee in 1999 featured several environmental justice leaders speaking on cleaner production as a solution to low-income community industrial development. The Black Environmental Justice Coalition adopted cleaner production as one of its principle objectives and the Deep South Center for Environmental Justice followed by convening a statewide conference on cleaner production.

Meanwhile, others who attended the two training conferences maintained a continuing dialogue on the principles and tools of cleaner production. These discussions revealed a pervasive need for technical assistance and backup for activists promoting new industrial processes or chemical constituents of products. In 2000, these discussions led to the establishment of a technical assistance organization called Clean Production Action, which maintained a small staff of technical experts with specialties in industrial processes, chemical substitution, and product stewardship.

The work of the environmental justice movement and Clean Production Action in promoting cleaner production as a positive strategy for sustainability has roots in the cleaner production training offered by the Lowell and Tennessee institutions. Indeed, while both leaders in the environmental justice movement and the staff at Clean Production Action maintain working relations with staff at the university, their advocacy is independent of the university. The educational focus on awareness raising, new concepts, skill development, and organization building has merged comfortably into the dedication, strategic sophistication, and ingenuity of the activists who attended. The results have been a broader, more positive orientation toward advocacy for sustainability.

INTERNATIONAL TRAINING FOR CLEAN PRODUCTION

Information about the training offered by the Institute and the Lowell Center about toxics use reduction and cleaner production filtered out internationally, and in 1999 the centers were approached by representatives of two environmental organizations with a request to host an international training program for environmental leaders from industrializing countries. A small planning group was assembled from university staff and representatives of the environmental organizations. It was decided to build the participation around activists who were engaged in local struggles to clean up waste sites and oppose worrisome hazardous waste disposal technologies such as unmanaged land disposal and incineration. Staff at the Lowell Center took the lead and organized a 10-day training program on how to turn the oppositional struggles around waste disposal into promotional struggles for cleaner production systems that reduced the generation of hazardous wastes. Sections were developed on clean production principles, production characterization, materials accounting, energy conservation, facility planning, toxics use reduction, community recycling, and local mobilization. Again, the training was group focused, with special attention to strategic and organizational development. A special field trip was planned to provide participants with an inside look at an electroplating shop that had both older technologies and newer, cleaner production technologies.

In June 1999, the training opened with 35 well-selected participants from 22 countries in attendance. The summer schedule of the training permitted the participants to use the unoccupied university dorms for housing, and the university classrooms served as workshop sites. For trainers, the organizers employed a combination of university faculty, Institute staff, professional toxics use reduction planners, and environmental leaders from around the country.

The group that assembled at Lowell for the international training was highly motivated; individuals met nightly to begin to explore ways to network and follow up after the training to support one another and to expand the number of people who might benefit. In so doing, the group drafted a loose association, which was tentatively called Global Anti-Incinerator Alliance, or GAIA, in respect for the mythical Greek goddess of the earth. Following the Lowell training, the participants used the Internet to maintain contact, to recruit new participants, and to develop plans for a larger meeting where the GAIA organization could be launched.

Six months later, a founding conference was held at Johannesburg, South Africa, for formally establishing the organization GAIA, which now had an alternative name: the Global Alliance for Incinerator Alternatives, which provided a positive twist on the original negative terminology.

GAIA grew rapidly over the next year, and by 2001 the new organization was seeking to host another international training program for new members of the Alliance. Respecting the need to locate the meeting in industrializing countries, it was decided to host it in Thailand. The GAIA coordinators then asked the Lowell Center to co-host the training and to send staff to Thailand. Co-hosting was easy, but the distance meant that only one university staff member was able to go to assist in the training. Therefore, much of the training was delivered quite successfully by those who had participated in previous trainings. The Thai program drew 38 environmental leaders from both developed and developing countries around the world and another 25 non-English-speaking leaders from local organizations throughout Thailand. The subject matter now included cleaner production principles, production characterization, materials accounting, energy conservation, toxics use reduction, waste management, community recycling, local mobilization, and international networking.

Today, GAIA involves organizations from more than 30 countries, and training conferences have continued in Eastern Europe and Asia. The organization has grown well beyond its initial roots, and the university is uninvolved in its advocacy work; but the role of the university in providing that original foundation is well recognized, and cleaner production continues to be a central organizing theme in GAIA's efforts to promote more sustainable approaches to waste and pollution management.

ADVANCING EDUCATION FOR A TRANSITION TO SUSTAINABILITY

Sustainable development is both a goal and a process. It involves new forms of social and economic development for industrializing countries, and it involves shifting the current social and economic patterns of industrialized countries. Getting to a more sustainable social and economic structure requires changes: personal, social, and political. These changes do not come easily, and higher education can play an important role in facilitating the process. Universities engage in preparing future generations, and the values and knowledge imparted to young people can become the dominant values of the future society. Education for Sustainable Development has created a new educational strategy for preparing students who are capable of envisioning a more equitable and just global society capable of living within environmental limits. However, higher education institutions can participate even more directly in supporting those who are currently involved in shaping that future. By reaching out to currently active practitioners and activists, the resources of higher education institutions can be made available to those who have immediate needs for skills and knowledge because their daily struggles starkly reveal their need to know.

Educating professionals and activists involves providing awareness, knowledge, and tools. It need not draw the institution hosting the training directly into the advocacy. Higher education institutions are not organized to conduct advocacy. Indeed, strong advocacy for even laudable concepts such as sustainability can reduce the legitimacy of a teaching institution as a place of self-exploration and learning. However, higher education can reach out more directly to assure that those who do work directly for social and economic change are well versed and well prepared for their engagements.

The training programs designed and provided by the Toxics Use Reduction Institute and the Lowell Center for Sustainable Production demonstrate how university resources can be directly employed to support active professionals and activists. It is important that the educational programs for professionals and activists who promote a transition to sustainability are not bound by the conventional practices of higher education. These programs need to be practical and strategic. They need to respect and utilize the social context of the participants, and they need to promote critical thinking that encourages creativity and new and untried concepts. Such education needs to be seen as a foundation and a wellspring of resources for those who are promoting a transition to sustainability. Higher education institutions with educational programs that both prepare students for the future and equip professionals and activists for their present work and struggles can enhance the transition to sustainability.

CHAPTER 3

Beyond Disciplines: Integrating Academia, Operations, and Community for Campuswide Education for Sustainability

Robert Koester, James Eflin,
and John Vann

Academic institutions can play a major role in helping society pursue sustainability. They can do this obviously through education, but also by following sustainable best practices in their operations and by working with campuswide, local, state and/or regional communities in outreach activities. In education, institutions of higher learning must move beyond the narrowly defined, discipline-specific models that have typified the modern university over the last 150 years. Sustainable development itself encompasses an integrative view of how economies and societies bring about equitable growth and development that recognizes their interdependencies within the biophysical systems of the earth. Hence, a model to guide Education for Sustainability (EFS)[1] must draw on this integrative nature, and suggest an approach to restructuring the ways in which the educational arena is constituted. In operations, institutions of higher learning must enhance their own facilities' performances in demonstrably sustainable ways. Operations comprise physical facilities management, classroom management, materials flow, energy use, and transportation, to name a few. Such efforts in themselves are, by definition, educational, but more importantly they yield long-term economic and environmental benefits. In community outreach, institutions of higher learning must acknowledge their physiographic settings and seek to

---

[1] There remains a debate on terminology that seems to span the Atlantic. "Education for Sustainability" appears to be more widely accepted in the United States, while "Education for Sustainable Development" has greater support in Europe. However, the two terms are largely interchangeable in practice. See Huckle and Sterling, 1996; PCSD, 1994.

connect with their many public constituencies. In fact, community outreach activities can bring together faculty, students, staff, and community members to address issues of economic, environmental, and social equity within the immediate region and in the larger world. In short, Education for Sustainability must include all members of the institution's communities: students, faculties, operations personnel, and members of the general public. This chapter discusses the integrative ways that these functions have been pursued at Ball State University, a nationally recognized leader in Education for Sustainability.

Colleges and universities are concentrations of people with high commitment to developing and applying intellectual talent to formally categorized areas of academic pursuit (Kleniewski & Wooding, 2002). Conventionally, those areas of academic pursuit—traditionally defined disciplines, fields of inquiry, professional career tracks—have become narrowly defined and ever more specialized. And although such specialization has been an efficient means to advance knowledge and refine the production of goods and services in market societies, the categorical isolation inherently risks fragmentation of human activity, compromising the cooperative behavior which is so vital to the long-term survival of the biophysical environment of which we are a part and upon which we so fundamentally depend.

Since at least the 1970s, there has been a growing advocacy for achieving more integration of human endeavors, drawing on a holistic approach to inter-actions; the many inter-, intra-, cross-, multi-, and trans-disciplinary terminologies that reflect this interest, however, have come to symbolize the difficulty of grappling with this pursuit. Epistemically, we must move beyond narrow ways of knowing and acting, and push toward a conception of a metaphysically different "whole": the university.

This chapter takes this starting point as the (r)evolutionary first step in advancing a methodology in Education for Sustainability via the actual management of the academic institution itself. Often known as the "greening of the campus," this attention to adopting more sustainable practices is increasingly being addressed (Clark, 2000; Creighton, 1998; Keniry, 1995; Orr, 1992); given the short time frame since the inception of this movement, it should prove helpful to all institutions to reflect on the track record of others in the pursuit of such sustainable practices. Ball State University stands out as a leader in this movement and as a case study, provides a sampling of the inherent complexities, successful outcomes, and occasional failures encountered as an institution seeks to "become a sustainable university."

BACKGROUND: ORIGINS OF THE GREENING MOVEMENT AT BALL STATE UNIVERSITY

For more than a dozen years, momentum has been building at Ball State University; this work has transitioned from an early interest in campus greening to a more fully engaged emphasis on sustainability in all its dimensions. Many initiatives, from the early work of the greening of the campus to the more recent efforts that align with the rubric of "sustainability," have been shared in the five differing published proceedings from the Greening of the Campus conference series hosted by Ball State University starting in 1996 (Koester, 1996-2003). These initiatives continue to mature as they embrace more closely the spirit of sustainability, with its emphases on more than the singular environmental criteria. This section outlines the early efforts and initial outcomes, while critiquing that early period of tentative first steps as contrasted to the more robust, self-reflective approach needed for campuswide sustainable development.

An institution is both constrained and enabled by the historical contexts in which it finds itself. Ball State is no different and has had to take into account both fiscal and political cultures in trying to gauge what will work and what will not.[2] What has worked at this midsized, state-supported, Midwestern comprehensive university may or may not be practical at institutions that are smaller—or larger, or privately supported—with their differing infrastructural trappings.

The impetus for greening initiatives at Ball State was an early commitment by the university's provost. The stage was set when he named members to the first Green Committee (Green-1) in April, 1991; he charged the group with formulating recommendations that, if implemented, would "raise environmental consciousness in our student body, foster conviction in the students regarding these issues, and empower them with understandings of how they might channel their awareness . . . to shape the future" (Koester, 1991, p. 1).

In December 1991, Green-1 delivered in its report a total of 35 recommendations, of which some 20 have been subsequently implemented. Based on implications for time and resource needs, *The Green Committee Report* categorized recommendations in three broad groupings, each of which addressed both the Institutional and Physiographic contextual settings (see Table 1); the categories were:

> *Immediately doable at little or no cost.* These items would involve little or no capital expenditure and could be acted upon quickly. For example, the provost dedicated his 1992-93 lecture series to green issues, and established "Green" for Green summer faculty development workshops for infusing environmental education into existing course offerings (see further discussion below).
>
> *Capital investment or endowments requiring lead time to implement and more substantial investment of resources.* These items would require

---

[2] Ball State University is situated on 940 acres of contiguous land in Muncie, Indiana. It is a comprehensive doctoral institution serving approximately 19,000 students (45 percent male, 55 percent female). Seven academic colleges offer 120 undergraduate programs, 80 master's programs, and 20 doctoral programs. Approximately 1,300 faculty and professional personnel and 1,500 support personnel compose the employee base. The university maintains 62 buildings with a total of 5,875,000 square feet.

Table 1. Recommendations of the Green 1 Report (Koester, 1991)

I. Immediate implementation at minimal expense		II. Capital investment or endowment		III. Structural change
A. The institutional setting	B. The physiographic setting	A. The Institutional setting	B. The physiographic setting	A. The institutional setting
1. University mission statement	1. Model environmental practices	1. CESAR*—Staff, operational budget	1. CESAR*—Building addition	1. Interdisciplinary teaching, research and service
2. Information clearinghouse	2. Model environmental policies	2. Distinguished and endowed chairs		
3. External/community research opportunities	3. Campus settings as environmental teaching tools	3. International connections		
4. Faculty convocations on curriculum development	4. Promotional efforts	4. Collaborative study of earth systems		
5. Faculty research and teaching incentives	5. Physical plant teaching and research	5. Expanded number of graduate assistantships		
6. Faculty/staff reward system	6. Property manager for outlying properties			
7. Environmental studies options	7. Kiosk information			
8. Environmental ethics course	8. Database access			
9. Line-item financial support for student organizations	9. Forestation committee			
10. Counseling for prospective graduate students	10. Recycling			
11. Environmental studies graduate assistantships	11. Campus parking			
12. International connections	12. Program units and individuals			
13. Student affairs	13. Campus planning			
14. Enhanced collaborative faculty efforts				
15. Enhanced faculty research opportunities				

*Center for Environmental Studies and Applied Research.

careful planning, sufficient resources, and formal institutional support. They included the creation of a new course on environmental ethics, support for student recycling activities, and stimulation of campuswide faculty involvement by participation in the first of what has become a series of Greening of the Campus conferences.

Structural change requiring substantial capital investment and long-term planning. These items would involve a transformation of institutional culture in the management of on- and off-campus properties. A recent development in this area (some twelve years later) is the creation of a new Field Station and Environmental Education Center (FSEEC), which will integrate operational management of five off-campus properties (field areas) totaling nearly four hundred acres. The effort includes participation by the College of Architecture and Planning Land Design Institute in devising the site-development criteria and green-building design schemes for FSEEC.

OUTCOMES:
DETAILED DISCUSSION OF TWO INITIATIVES

Significant actions were undertaken by the university to capture the spirit of the original Green Report; two notable efforts included creation of the "Green" for Green summer workshops for faculty development and the initiation of the Greening of the Campus conferences for intercollegial networking.

"Green" for Green Summer Workshops

Developing a diverse faculty who are conversant in environmental complexities and sustainability necessitates committing development resources (time and funding). The solution used at Ball State is an annual summer faculty development workshop, called "Green" for Green. It was initiated in 1992 to increase the number of faculty who are literate in the critical issues:

> The Committee recommends that summer funding be provided to enable faculty to modify course syllabus materials, engage in readings and conduct research necessary to find a more inclusive environmental view in course offerings. (Koester, 1991, p. 13)

The rationale for this initiative was recognition that college faculty often find it difficult to step outside of their disciplines and investigate how environmentally related materials might affect the content of their courses. Further, faculties often are not given encouragement or, more importantly, formal recognition for taking such initiative. "Green" for Green was conceived to eliminate the sense of risk and uncertainty and thereby build a cadre of faculty who engage with collaborative potential on campus greening ideas, specifically through developing curriculum content that incorporates environmental (and more recently, sustainability) themes within their respective disciplines. Participants are compensated with modest financial stipends. Thus was born the financial "green" reward for faculty to gain skills, training, and expertise to develop ideas that benefit the campus with green environmental outcomes. In retrospect, this aligns perfectly with the fourth tenet of the *Talloires Declaration,* mandating that a university "Foster Environmental Literacy For All" (see discussion below).

Since its inception, "Green" for Green has been directed toward faculty; a mechanism for formal and continual support of professional and other staff remains to be attained. Applicants from disciplines conventionally outside the environmental fields are given the strongest encouragement to participate; most recently, only new faculty hires (e.g., those who joined the university within the last two or three academic years) were eligible for participation. Participants received a $500 stipend for attending the 15- to 20-hour workshop; they agreed to develop curriculum content for one or more of their courses, which incorporated environmental themes in the context of their disciplines. Workshop funding supports participation of up to 20 persons, plus a stipend for one or more faculty instructors/coordinators.

During its first nine offerings, the course content was tailored for a broad introduction to environmental issues, patterned in ways that resembled the course content of an introductory environmental science class. That is, the focus of "Green" for Green expanded environmental literacy among the faculty population. With greater urgency by the end of the first decade, increasing integration of community personnel from outside the university contributed to the learning experience, drawing expertise from resource management agencies to help enliven the workshop and provide increased linkages between the university and surrounding communities. This fact also was a response to a growing university commitment to service learning.

Greening of the Campus Conferences

In the early 1990s, a small but growing focus on campus greening was beginning its sweep through institutions of higher education, but the movement needed a forum for discussion. Beginning in 1996, Green-1 set in motion what has become five international Greening of the Campus conferences. Each conference had an organizing theme that drew attention to the complexity of issues involved in the greening movement. Each conference featured keynote speakers prominent in the fields of curriculum development, campus management, societal concern for the environment, and, more recently, the complex social, environmental, and economic aspects of sustainability. Technical papers, workshops, and panel sessions, have been structured as well, to provide participants a full range of experience during the conference and to facilitate networking and colleague interaction. The conferences aim to draw the full mix of university community sectors—private and public, small and large, liberal arts and research-based institutions—and play to the variety of audience members, from students, faculty, and administrators to facilities and operations managers, procurement officers, and community outreach program developers.

In the course of these five offerings, conference themes have shifted. The first conference was an introductory exposure to general campus-greening issues. The technical papers ranged from large-scale initiatives to specific technical guidance regarding recycling and landscape management. Workshop presentations were offered to facilitate peer-to-peer educational transfer at student, faculty, and professional personnel levels. The conference themes have moved since then to basic "issues and challenges," to "next steps" of mobilization, to engaging the relation of "theory and reality," to drawing the greening movement "into the mainstream," and most recently, using the conference as an opportunity for participants to "connect to place"; this latter focus included local field trips and hands-on activities using the Ball State University campus. Approximately 250 people have attended each conference. Keynote presenters have included a broad range of notable, internationally recognized leaders in their fields; their presentations have ranged from campus-specific facilities design and management to sweeping overviews of the interaction of societies, ecologies, and economies (see Table 2). Others have shared cutting-edge work in such areas as biomimicry and species extinction.

Perhaps of most importance is that over this sequence of conferences, the nature of discussion and presentation of content have shifted dramatically. Initially, much emphasis was placed on recycling and facilities/grounds management, with the attention to curriculum occurring mostly at the scale of particular course offerings or unique experiments within a course. More recently, the nature of discussion has been built around larger curricular intervention, including major and minor degree offerings, use of the university's economic power as a lever to change markets, examination and modeling of the throughput of resources, inventorying the net impact of campuses on their immediate communities (and ecological systems more generally) and exploration of the political dimensions of on-campus/off-campus initiatives.

OUTCOMES:
TRANSITIONING TO SUSTAINABILITY

Ten years after it was written, the *Green Committee Report* and the body of resulting initiatives continue to serve as a case of "best practice;" the work is summarized in a comprehensive assessment of campus sustainability programs prepared by Glasser and Nixon (2002) as a framework that could serve other institutions in their journey. More recently, however, our university adopted a frame of reference already in use by many institutions, and as a result we have unleashed a more comprehensive approach to Education for Sustainability.

Table 2. Keynote Speakers for the Greening of Campus Conferences

Keynote speaker (alphabetical by last name) and date	Affiliation or background	Keynote presentation (title)
Janine Benyus 2001	Author of *Biomimicry: Innovation Inspired by Nature*	The Lotus and the Peacock: Biomimicry and the Art of Well-Adapted Design
Robert Tree Cody 1996	Native American performance artist	Grandmother Earth
Anthony Cortese 2001	President, Second Nature; founder and managing director of the Consortium for Environmental Education in Medicine	Accelerating the Transition to Sustainability Through Higher Education
Robert Costanza 1999	Professor and Director, Institute for Ecological Economics, University of Maryland, College Park, MD	Integrating Ecology and Economics to Design a Sustainable World and Campus
Randy Croxton 1996	Croxton Collaborative Architects, New York, NY	Translating Sustainability Methods, Objectives and Values at Campus Scale
John DiBiaggio 2001	President, Tufts University, Cambridge, MA	Citizenship and Sustainability: A Vision for Higher Education
Christine Ervin 2003	President and CEO, U.S. Green Building Council, and board officer for the Energy Trust of Oregon	Higher Education and High Performance Green Buildings: A Perfect Match
Pliny Fisk III 2003	Co-Direct, Center for Maximum Potential Building Systems, Austin, TX	The Emergence of Life-Cycle Space in Planning and Community Development
Susan Flader 1999	Professor of History, University of Missouri, Columbia, MO	Toward a Land Ethic: The Legacy of Aldo Leopold
Hillary French 1999	Vice President for Research, WorldWatch Institute, Washington, DC	Global Eco-Politics in the New Millennium: The Role of Universities
Hazel Henderson 1997	Independent futurist, worldwide columnist, and consultant on sustainable development	Educating for Our Global Future
L. Hunter Lovins 1996	President and Executive Director, Rocky Mountain Institute, Snowmass, CO	How Not to Parachute More Cats

Table 2. (Cont'd.)

Keynote speaker (alphabetical by last name) and date	Affiliation or background	Keynote presentation (title)
Richard Norgaard 2001	President, International Society for Ecological Economics, and Professor of Energy and Resource Economics, University of California, Berkeley	An Ecological Economics of Sustainability
Michael Ogden 2003	Founding Director, Natural Systems International, a leading engineer in the design and project management of onsite natural wastewater treatment systems	Water Use in a Sustainable (Campus) Environment
Sabin O'Hara 1997	Professor of Economics at Rensselaer Polytechnic Institute, Troy, NY	Talking Green: Development as Discourse on the College Campus and Beyond
Howard R. Oliver 1997	Institute of Hydrology, Wallingford, England, and the Natural Environment Research Council	Environmental Concern Programs in the United Kingdom
David Orr (five keynot addresses) 1996, 1997, 1999, 2001, 2003	Professor and chair, Environmental Studies Program, Oberlin College, Oberlin, OH	Ecological Design and the Next Revolution (1996); Green Design/Green Education (1997); Beyond Greening the Campus (1999); Greening the Campus: The Next Phase (2001); The Nature of Design: Ecology, Culture and Human Intention (2003)
George Page 1996	Director of Science and Nature History Programming at Thirteen/ WNET, New York City, NY	Politics, Power, and the Earth
Sara Parkin 1997	Director of Forum for the Future	Globally Responsible Citizenship: The Learning Agenda
John Perlin 2001	Author of *A Forest Journey: The Role of Wood in the Development of Civilization; A Golden Thread: 2,500 Years of Solar Architecture and Technology,* and *From Space to Earth: The Story of Solar Electricity*	A Forest Journey

Table 2. (Cont'd.)

Keynote speaker (alphabetical by last name) and date	Affiliation or background	Keynote presentation (title)
David Quammen (three keynote addresses) 1996, 2001, 2003	Author and former correspondent, *Outside* magazine	The Song of the Dodo: Global Patterns of Species Extinction; The Improbable Lion; Man-Eating Predators and the Food Chain of Power and Glory (2003)
John Ryan 1999	Research Director, Northwest Environment Watch, Seattle, WA	The Seven Sustainable Wonders of the World, or The Dalai Lama vs. Baywatch
Jane Shaw 2003	Senior Associate, Political Economy Research Center (PERC)	Environmental Problems— Market Failure or a Failure to Have Markets?
Sharon Stine 1997	Professor of Landscape Architecture, California State Polytechnic University, Pomona, CA	Connecting Sustainability to Daily Life on Campus
Mathis Wackernagel 2003	Former director of the Indicators Program at Redefining Progress, San Francisco, CA, and developer of the widely-used sustainability measure, the "Ecological Footprint"	Our Global Footprint: Getting Real Here and Now

On Earth Day 1999, Ball State University became a signatory to the *Talloires Declaration.*

The Talloires Declaration, Green 2, and the Council on the Environment

Upon a recommendation by the provost, with the support of former members of Green-1, and a new core of faculty who advocated sustainability initiatives, our president became convinced that Ball State University should formally express its commitment to the sustainability movement. Originated in 1990, the *Talloires Declaration* commits the signatory institutions, through their respective lead administrators, to environmental stewardship and an acknowledgment of the role that universities play by being exemplars of best practices in society. They include husbanding resources, meeting the needs of society, and fulfilling the mission of academia to educate future generations. By signing the document, Ball State's president set in motion the planning needed to take the next steps in advancing campus greening initiatives. During 2000, the provost worked with a core group of faculty to reconstitute the Green-1 committee with a new appointment of members to Green Committee 2 (Green-2). And, in the spirit of sustainability as outlined in the tenets of the *Talloires Declaration*, the committee was structured to include members from all quarters of the campus (students, faculty, and staff), as well as community leaders from the East Central Indiana region. It is strongly recommended to other institutions that an inclusive base of stakeholders be involved in such efforts to promote Education for Sustainability.

Green-2 was structured around the ten tenets of the *Talloires Declaration* (Eflin, 2001); nine of them focus on particular action areas and constituency groups within academic institutions, while the tenth calls for creation of a secretariat to facilitate implementation and oversee and maintain its continuity. Subcommittees within Green-2 were identified by the key topical focus of each of the tenets: 1) Increase awareness of environmentally sustainable development, 2) Create an institutional culture of sustainability, 3) Educate for environmentally responsible citizenship, 4) Foster environmental literacy for all, 5) Practice institutional ecology, 6) Involve all stakeholders, 7) Collaborate for interdisciplinary approaches, 8) Enhance capacity of primary and secondary schools, 9) Broaden service and outreach nationally and internationally, 10) Maintain the movement. Following six months of planning, the provost appointed 94 members and in September 2000, Green-2 began its work.

In March 2001, after 2,000 person-hours of effort, Green-2 delivered its final report. It included 186 recommendations; 10 were prioritized as most worthy of initial implementation. Acknowledging the need for ongoing administrative support as prescribed in the *Talloires Declaration,* Green-2 recommended that a Ball State University Council on the Environment (COTE) be created and supported by a permanently staffed operational secretariat. The provost designated the Center for Energy Research/Education/Service (CERES) to provide this base, appointing its director as Chair of COTE. In addition, the provost appointed a Green Initiatives Coordinator, charged with programmatic origination and campus networking; and a Green Funding Specialist, charged with collaborating with all constituencies in seeking outside funding for program development with the support of COTE.

Council on the Environment[3]

In structuring COTE, it was recognized that all quarters of the university and the surrounding community needed to be given voice and continuing

[3] See www.bsu.edu/cote

representation. COTE is intended to serve as a forum—a clearinghouse for sustainability initiatives campuswide. Appointees include faculty and professional staff, representatives from each of the seven colleges, each of five vice presidential areas, student representatives, and members from the regional community.

Since its inception in the fall of 2001, COTE has met once a month during each academic year and adopted a specific structure of operation which itself reflects the history of the greening activities at Ball State University. At each meeting, the work of the council is structured according to a tripartite categorization; that which we can *celebrate,* we can *facilitate,* and we can *anticipate.* The council adopted a mission statement and prepared a Ball State University Statement on Sustainability (www.bsu.edu/sustainability/), which was endorsed by senior staff, academic deans, and members of the university senate, and thereafter accepted by the University Board of Trustees. The intent of the statement is to focus the university community on its role in exercising stewardship over its resources as it educates students so that, as stated in the original Green-1 committee charge, students can "foster conviction in students regarding these issues and empower them with understandings of how they might channel their awareness . . . to shape the future" (Koester, 1991, p. 5).

OUTCOMES: THE GREENING MOVEMENT MOVES INTO A NEW ERA

Ball State's greening efforts continue to mature beyond the more narrow environmental themes with growing adoption of efforts that emphasize the broader concept of sustainability. Some of these transformations are the direct result of Green-1, Green-2, and COTE actions; others are more a by-product of the climate of interest that continues to develop campuswide. A selection of these initiatives is discussed here, including a transformation of the "Green" for Green summer workshops, the introduction of a curriculum innovation in Education for Sustainability; and the use of campus-based research to advance understandings of how campuses affect environment.

"Green" for Green Goes Sustainable

In response to the Green-2 Report, the focus of "Green" for Green workshops has been directed more toward Education for Sustainability, rather than their previous emphasis exclusively on environmental issues. This effort was reflected in the adoption of a new workshop title: "Lighten Up! A Workshop in Sustainable Living." Under this approach, the green outcomes that each participant expected to return to the university or local community include: 1) Incorporating some environmental focus in one or more classes that each instruct ("greening the curriculum"), 2) Helping their respective department or academic unit to lower its environmental impacts in its operations or policies ("greening campus operations"), or 3) Carrying the message of environmental sustainability to a broader audience through community outreach projects ("greening the community"). This approach to capturing the spirit of Education for Sustainability may be readily adopted for use by other educational institutions.

To extend the "Green" for Green outreach, workshop facilitators involve key community leaders who are engaged in environmental or sustainability initiatives (e.g., Indiana Department of Natural Resources, the solid waste district, the area's recycling agency, the local chapter of the Audubon Society, a local land trust, and local community environmental outreach/education programs). This involvement has successfully engaged workshop participants, helping them learn more about local resources (natural and cultural), and has had the secondary benefit of increasing participation by local community leaders in campus environment or sustainability initiatives.

To date, more than 230 faculty have participated in the "Green" for Green workshops, representing more than 20 percent of all faculty members at Ball State University. These participants have come from 40 of the university's 46 academic departments or schools and each of the university's seven academic colleges. Additionally, two participants from the university's laboratory school (K-12) and six members of the professional staff have participated in the workshops. Assessment responses by workshop participants suggest that this learning opportunity has been life transforming; most participants indicate their wish to participate again and that they have made major adjustments in their own living.

To ensure that individual learning and life transformation are returned to the campus or community requires some accountability. While the "Green" for Green model has been successful in its mission and its impact on a substantial percentage of Ball State University faculties, there remains much opportunity to refine its content as well as tighten its connection with campus greening and sustainable development initiatives. Finding ways to hold faculty accountable for what they gain and stressing the need for their individual development to bear fruit—inside the classroom, inside their academic unit, inside their local community—requires a concerted effort and support from many levels of the institution.

Curriculum Innovations in Education for Sustainability

Education for Sustainability must fundamentally include curriculum transformation. Building on existing curricula by crossing and combining conventional disciplines is one way to build the foundation upon which to create a more stand-alone program that is centrally focused on sustainability as the core concept (NCSE, 2003; Orr, 1994; PCSD, 1994).

Disciplines, departments, or comparably named units are structured to meet the programmatic needs of university education that derive from a Kantian tradition in education, one that compartmentalizes knowledge and thereby narrows the missions of academic programs to fit into these compartments. Sustainability does not fit within this tradition, as it cuts across the lines of conventional knowledge categories; it is instead situated within a different educational meta-system. Sustainability embraces nonhuman systems, but acknowledges the importance of human-created systems as well. Hence, Education for Sustainability must address both biophysical systems (of which humans are a part) and socio-cultural systems—based on humans, but also dependent on their linkages with the biophysical systems (and limits) of the universe.

Creating interdisciplinary approaches to EFS curricula can benefit from innovative combinations of existing programs or courses. An example from Ball State University shows potentials for creating an EFS curriculum that primarily uses existing courses, which are supplemented by a limited number of new courses. One aspect of this model acknowledges the need to create "minor" programs of study that afford students opportunities to pursue curriculum in sustainable practices that complements their "major" program of pursuit. At Ball State University, it took the form of an intertwined "suite" of programs called the Clustered Minors in Environmentally Sustainable Practices (hereafter, Clustered Minors). Originated in 1998, the program currently offers five academic minors, each requiring completion of 24 semester credit hours of coursework, which students may pursue in conjunction with their principal or major program of study. These minors are: The Environmental Context for Business; The Environmental Contexts in Healthcare; Environmental Policy; Sustainable Land Systems; Technology and the Environment. Additional minors in Environment and the Arts, Environment and Communications, and Environment and Literature have been proposed; to date, they are in development stages only.

A second aspect of this model focuses on individual courses. For fiscal and political reasons, the Clustered Minors program did not attempt to develop a lengthy number of new courses. Rather, it built on existing courses that complement EFS and thereby required development of only a few new courses as cornerstones to the sustainability mission. The potential for creating such programs exists at any educational institution, drawing on the historically specific nature of existing curricula, programs, and faculty expertise. The program at Ball State University emerged as a suite of new courses that reflect the individual teaching emphases of their respective "champions"—individuals who took the leadership in promoting sustainability education from within their primary academic discipline.

The target of the Clustered Minors experience is a "closing" (or capstone) course, ID 400: Creating a Sustainable Future. The course was intended to bring together participants from each of the minors. ID 400 follows completion of an "anchor" course that is unique to and focused on the context of each minor, a course that provides a solid integration of ideas about sustainability in reference to the thrust of that minor; the course is usually taught by one of the champions. Before taking either of these courses, students are introduced to the "three-legged stool" of sustainability—ecology, economics, and social equity—by completing three "core" courses (BIO 216: Ecology, ECON 311: Environmental Economics, and PHIL 230: Environmental Ethics). Each of the core courses existed prior to the creation of the Clustered Minors; importantly, the Clustered Minors program attempted to integrate them into a coherent context of sustainability. A series of directed or selected electives was chosen from existing courses in the undergraduate catalog to round out each minor.

In November 2002, the Clustered Minors program was recognized nationally as a model curriculum by the Sustainable Buildings Industry Council, which awarded Ball State University the Council's Best Practice Sustainability Award for Sustainable Design Curriculum. The program has received recognition by Second Nature, Campus Ecology, and at numerous international, national, and regional conferences. Revisions to the program are being considered to broaden its appeal to a wider audience of students. Those who have participated to date have shown great enthusiasm and dedication. What remains is to find a means to expose a greater number of students to the concepts of sustainability; initiatives are underway to create an introductory course in sustainability and to infuse sustainability into the universitywide core curriculum taken by all undergraduates.

Campus-Based Sustainability Research

EFS approaches both formal and informal learning and reaches across the community spectrum. It starts with curriculum, but builds on other learning experiences too. In the community of an institution of higher education, the learning clientele includes both the students and the staff. In any EFS curriculum, it is insufficient to allow students to become entirely passive in their exposure to sustainability. They must have opportunities to actively learn about sustainability and must embrace participatory change. Students must be drawn into sustainability through participation in the very systems that are to be transformed. So, too, staff must be drawn into the mission of building the sustainable institution through a forum of participation in which their voices count.

As David Orr notes in *Ecological Literacy* (1992), using the local campus environment is one of the best ways to encourage student and staff participation. First, it offers an immediate environmental experience (especially for students who are not originally from the local area). Second, it offers the opportunity for students to give back to the community that supports them, empowering them with a sense of civic engagement; equally, there are powerful opportunities to learn how campus and local community blend into one another. Third, the physical campus on which the educational institution is situated offers an instructive setting to apply the principles of sustainability.

Conceptualizing the academic institution as an ecosystem has merit in terms of exposing students and staff to thinking about the function of an institution of higher education beyond the immediately intuitive delivery system of education. Like any other institution—governmental jurisdiction, commercial corporation, or household—an educational institution represents a system of flows involving pathways of material, energy, and information that mimic the structural interconnections and ecological energetics within a biological ecosystem or within the metabolism of an organism. Using this understanding, frameworks of Industrial Ecology may be applied to the university as a system (Ehrenfeld, 2002; Frosch, 1995). Achieving a more sustainable path is the goal in any industrial ecology; therefore, understanding the institutional ecology can serve as a framework for the university community to pursue a more sustainable path.

At Ball State University, instructors have used a variety of courses and collaborative research projects to immerse students and staff in various experiences that are directed toward applying principles of sustainability. Students engaged in such projects, either through course work or as research assistants, become empowered as collaborative stakeholders (with the faculty and staff) through hands-on learning. A multitude of systems that function to ensure the operation of a university, often below the surface or behind the scenes, can serve as a very fruitful experiential base.

An example of campus-based sustainability research is an ongoing project that began as a series of course projects and has been continued with external funding—the AT&T Foundation's Industrial Ecology Faculty Fellowship—and with internal funding through the university Honors College Undergraduate Student Fellowship and via a CERES Faculty Fellowship. In this applied research project, the 940-acre campus is viewed as an ecosystem, and the material flows that are part of the day-to-day campus operations are conceived as its metabolism. Borrowing from Industrial Ecology, the institutional ecology of the university is being modeled to give campus stakeholders both a better understanding of the environmental impact of university operations and some power to undertake corrective actions to reduce the institution's footprint. Ultimately, the resulting material flow analyses (MFA) are intended to become part of the accounting and operating systems for the university.

Other Campus-Based Programmatic Efforts

A faculty member who is given two-course equivalent assigned time as a release from teaching to pursue green initiatives staffs the Green Initiatives Coordinator position. Activities have included writing a green column for the university's internal news bulletin, giving approximately 20 guest lectures per academic year in various classes, working on COTE committees, helping to draft position statements, pursuing green purchasing options for the campus, communicating with local media, initiating recycling programs in sports facilities, and working with student groups and community constituents. Currently, the coordinator position, while resulting from a recommendation of the Green-2 Report, is not a formal position within the university structure, but is administered on an ad hoc basis year by year. This fact has resulted in some uncertainty, as release time is renegotiated each academic year. In addition, the informal basis of the position results in less leverage within the university hierarchy than might be possible with formal authority and budgetary control.

Since the *Green-2 Report,* Ball State students have been vigorous in their pursuit of sustainability. They have worked with the community on projects, such as a local community garden, river overlooks, and bikeways. As a direct result of reading the *Green-2 Report,* they founded a new organization, Ball State Students for a Sustainable Campus. As a follow-on to a project proposed in ID 400: Creating a Sustainable Future, two recent graduates worked on a special project that resulted in a sustainability plan for the university's Dining Services. It is a comprehensive plan that addresses everything from food purchasing to cleaning to the use of recyclable and china dinnerware. A student representative to the Student Government Association is currently drafting legislation to reflect student support for a stronger recycling program on campus.

Facilities management has also demonstrated a zeal for pursuing sustainable practices. Some of them have devolved from Green-2 initiatives, such as the purchase of hybrid electric cars as part of the university's fleet, some at the instigation of the Green Initiatives Coordinator, such as the separation of recyclables from the stands after football and basketball games, and some from the commitment of sustainability champions among the facilities personnel. Examples include the planting of prairies on some university properties; the increased use of perennial plants for landscaping purposes, especially cultivars of species native to the Midwest, which tend to be low maintenance; the recycling of all fluorescent light tubes; the increased usage of occupancy sensors for lighting control; the use of variable speed motors and bamboo flooring; and the use of 20 percent biodiesel fuel in university vehicles.

REFLECTIONS ON THE BALL STATE EXPERIENCE: THE FRUSTRATIONS AND THE SUCCESSES

On the face of it, the balance sheet for initiating, promoting, and developing sustainable campus practices at Ball State University shows positive outcomes. Thirteen years after the appointment of Green-1, many innovative programs have been instigated, leading to nationwide and international attention about the commitment of our institution to Education for Sustainability. Many of the outcomes reported above are explained more fully on the COTE and CERES Web sites.[4]

And although the Council on the Environment, with the support of its administrative secretariat and the active involvement of its Green Initiatives Coordinator and Green Funding Specialist, has made some concrete achievements, others are largely symbolic. For example, while the Ball State University Sustainability

---

[4] See www.bsu.edu/ceres and www.bsu.edu/cote

Statement has been approved by senior staff, academic deans, and the University Senate and has been accepted by the Board of Trustees, most rank-and-file faculty and staff members are still not fully aware of its existence. It has not sufficiently permeated the organization yet as a unifying ethic to guide decision making across diverse operational units, nor has there been additional directives from senior administrators instructing multiple units to more fully engage the sustainability theme.

The organizational structure of the university is such that it does not represent one monolithic entity, but rather multiple, relatively independent subunits. For example, Dining Services, Libraries, and Residence Life (student housing) all operate in relatively autonomous ways. Because of this fragmentation, success in promulgating sustainable practices in one part of the university structure does not transfer readily to other units in the university. Rather, the challenge continues for COTE to penetrate, again and again, the decision-making psyche of each unit across the university.

Primary control of sustainable retrofits within academic buildings resides with the academic deans or other administrative leaders who have primary usage of those buildings. Consequently, while installation of occupancy sensors for lighting control may be approved for one building, another dean's approval must be garnered for installation in his or her building. The same holds true for curricular change; each college must be approached, encouraged, and facilitated separately.

The ways that expenditures are budgeted and performance is evaluated affect incentives for adopting innovations that can improve energy expenditures. At Ball State University, electricity is paid for centrally, but individual operational units pay for retrofits and light bulbs. For example, Dining Services must pay to retrofit its lighting systems, but does not pay the electric bills for (nor can it capture the energy savings by making changes to) existing (often inefficient) systems. Consequently, there is only a financial penalty rather than a net benefit for Dining Services to institute changes in its lighting systems and/or purchase more efficient bulbs. Without a unifying top-down administrative directive to adopt the sustainability ethic, the situation is not likely to change, especially when each unit is evaluated on the basis of its financial performance and not its sustainability performance.

While this sort of institutional change continues to be slow in coming, champions have emerged across the campus as they spontaneously adopt sustainable innovations. Student members of the Paper Reduction Committee (a subcommittee of the Natural Resources Club) read the recommendations in the *Green-2 Committee Report,* including one for the establishment of a student sustainability organization. On its own, the group founded the Ball State University Students for a Sustainable Campus. Similarly, a faculty member in the Department of Accounting who had served on one of the Green-2 subcommittees introduced a module on sustainability reporting in two of her courses and is now publishing in that topical area. One of the consumer behavior professors now requires sustainability topics for course projects. All corporations tracked in a marketing management course are now ones that publish sustainability reports. An English professor who requires sustainability topics for writing assignments in her course has developed a semester-long workshop on the environmental literature of Indiana; others in her department, following participation in "Green" for Green workshops, use environmental and sustainability themes in their introductory expository writing courses. The facilities manager for Student Housing has initiated numerous sustainable retrofits for the residence halls. One of the university purchasing agents identified sources of 100 percent post-consumer-content recycled paper and distributed samples to members of COTE. The supervisor of grounds initiated a trash audit of academic buildings. The director of the 10 Freshmen Connection Communities[5] decided that each must conduct a sustainability project. Many faculty members have invited the Green Initiatives Coordinator to make presentations in their classes. The Associate Vice President for Facilities Planning and Management sat in on a new course on renewable energy and sustainable technology and then initiated a test utilizing 20 percent biodiesel fuel in university buses and trucks.

Slowly, sustainability initiatives are spreading at the grassroots level as word-of-mouth and local initiatives provide the impetus for change. The future is not grim; it is just clouded by the ever-present conflicting priorities of the disparate institutional agendas of the hierarchically organized subunits of the academic community. This conflict of mindsets reflects the situation in American society more broadly.

CONCLUSIONS:
APPLICATIONS TO OTHER INSTITUTIONS

The lessons learned at Ball State University suggest that movements forward in the campus greening movement—and toward Education for Sustainability in general—will continue to require dedication by change agents. But colleges and universities have a collective record of being progressive in the advancement of knowledge. Significantly, it is not only from the grassroots of students or faculty incentives that this movement is growing; often, it takes an "angel in the administration" to activate the initial push for change. Increasingly, sustainability within academia is gaining the attention and support of upper administrators (Clark, 2000). The Association of University Leaders for a Sustainable Future (ULSF) continues to be a leading advocate for advancing the movement at the top end, while the National Wildlife Federation's Campus Ecology program

---

[5] Each Freshmen Connection community is composed of students who reside within the same halls and take classes together.

promotes the efforts from the bottom up. Other initiatives, including the Higher Education Network for Sustainability and the Environment (HENSE), Second Nature, and the Education for Sustainability Western Network, offer support for those seeking to participate in this emerging movement. A promising new development has been the creation of the National Council for Science and the Environment, which held the third annual National Conference on Science, Policy and the Environment in January 2003, with the theme "Education for a Sustainable and Secure Future." Similarly, the Society for College and University Planning sponsored a nationwide teleconference, "Got Sustainability? Plan for It!" in October 2003. More people at more institutions are seeing the connections and seeking to embrace Education for Sustainability (Bartlett & Chase, 2004).

But the lessons learned also suggest that it is important not to see campus greening and Education for Sustainability from within the old trappings that delayed its inception: territorial, discipline bound, inflexible, and uncompromising (Anderson, 2003).

Integration of the key elements of sustainability within an institution of higher education, or any institution, for that matter, requires an ongoing and recursive learning about how to move toward a lasting set of practices that take the institution into partnership, connected and revealed as intricately woven into a fabric of ecosystem-wide interdependence. The commitment to endure by embracing these connections is one of hope and transcendence; it is one that we need to embrace for institutional change to move beyond discipline.

REFERENCES

Anderson, R. (2003). A call for systemic change, Plenary lecture at the 3rd National Conference on Science, Policy and the Environment: Education for a sustainable and secure future, Washington, DC, January 31, 2003. Internet document retrievable at http://www.NCSEonline.org/NCSEconference/2003conference/page.cfm?FID=2504 Accessed October 9, 2003.

Bartlett, P., & Chase, G. W. (Eds.). (2004). *Sustainability on campus: Stories and strategies for change.* Cambridge: MIT Press.

Clark, C. S. (2000). Campuses stainability. *AGB Priorities, 14*: 1-15. (AGB is the Association of Governing Boards.)

Creighton, S. H. (1998). *Greening the ivory tower: Improving the environmental track record of universities, colleges and other institutions.* Cambridge: MIT Press.

Ehrenfeld, J. R. (2002). Industrial ecology: Coming of age. *Environmental Science & Technology,* July 1, 281-285A.

Eflin, J. (2001). Addressing the Challenge of the Talloires Declaration at Ball State University, *The Declaration, 4*(2), 1, 19-20.

Frosch, R. A. (1995). Industrial ecology: Adapting technology for a sustainable world. *Environment, 37*(10), 16-24, 34-38.

Glasser, H., & Nixon, A. (2002). From the state of the world to the state of the academy: Campus sustainability assessment—A bright star on the horizon. *The Declaration, 6*(1), 6-10.

Huckle, J., & Sterling, S. (1996). *Education for sustainability.* London: Earthscan Publications.

Keniry, J. (1995). *Ecodemia: Campus environmental stewardship at the turn of the 21st century.* Washington: National Wildlife Federation.

Kleniewski, N., & Wooding, J. (2002). Building bridges: Sustainable development, interdisciplinary programs and the university. In J. L. Pyle & R. Forrant (Eds.), *Globalization, universities and issues of sustainable human development* (pp. 212-232). Northampton, MA: Edward Elgar.

Koester, R. J. (Ed.). (1991). *Final report: The "Green" committee on environmental studies,* Muncie, IN: Ball State University. Internet document retrievable at http://www.bsu.edu/provost/ceres/g2/0main/#green1

Koester, R. J. (Ed.). (1996-2003). *Proceedings, greening of the campus conferences I-V.* Muncie, IN: Ball State University.

McIntosh, M., Cacciola, K., Clermont, S., & Keniry, J. (2001). *State of the campus environment: A national report card on environmental performance and sustainability in higher education.* Washington: National Wildlife Federation.

NCSE (National Council for Science and the Environment). (2003). *Recommendations for education for a sustainable and secure future,* D. E. Blockstein & J. Greene (Eds.). Washington: National Council for Science and the Environment. Internet document retrievable at www.ncseonline.org/NCSEconference/2003Conference/ Accessed September 7, 2003.

Orr, D. (1992). *Ecological literacy: Education and the transition to a postmodern world.* Albany: State University of New York Press.

Orr, D. W. (1994). *Earth in mind: On education, environment, and the human prospect.* Washington and Covelo, CA: Island Press.

Orr, D. W. (2003). Remarks made during the teleconference, "Got Sustainability? Plan for It!" produced by Society for College and University Planning, October 9, 2003.

PCSD (President's Council on Sustainable Development). (1994). *Education for sustainability: An agenda for action,* Report of the National Forum on Partnerships Supporting Education about the Environment, San Francisco, 1994, Washington, U.S. Government Printing Office. Internet document retrievable at www.gcrio.org/edu/pcsd/toc.html Accessed September 27, 2003.

CHAPTER 4

The Role of the Humanities and Social Sciences in Education for Sustainable Development

Daniel Egan, Vanessa Gray, Whitley Kaufman, and Chad Montrie

This chapter is grounded in our collective experience of making sustainable development a major theme in our teaching. The four of us, all faculty in the humanities and social sciences at the University of Massachusetts Lowell (UML), support fully our university's public commitment to sustainable development as a central element of its mission. We have found, however, that education for sustainable development has been limited by the assumption that the meaning of sustainability is self-evident and universal. Our experience has led us to recognize that we cannot successfully teach about sustainable development without first addressing the meaning of the concept itself. We argue here, from the perspective of our own disciplines, that sustainability is fundamentally a moral and political question. Many corporations are embracing themes related to sustainable development in order to demonstrate that they are good corporate citizens; at the other end of the spectrum is a radical social ecology that sees capitalism as inherently unsustainable. Education for sustainable development must first acknowledge the value-laden nature of the concept, and then make explicit the particular values that are to be taught. Only after an ongoing social dialogue can we arrive at a consensus on a working definition of sustainable development. This is a task for which the humanities and social sciences can make a major contribution.

CHAD MONTRIE: A HISTORIAN'S PERSPECTIVE

Oftentimes, as a historian, I am challenged to defend the utility and social relevance of my discipline. This is a challenge put to me by the general public, students, and other academics, including members of the community educating and building toward "sustainable development." Most people recognize that study of the past is somehow important but rarely think of it when dealing with the present. Last year, for example, I traveled to a meeting of state university faculty on environmental initiatives and found myself the only historian among the many hundreds of people talking about toxics reduction, green campuses, and the like. During one session, I suggested that we could use the insight of more scholars from the humanities and social sciences. A political scientist from my own campus then made a more eloquently impassioned plea for incorporating both areas of study into the various environmental programs. Participants nodded their heads in agreement, but the commitment ended there.

Why, then, is study of the past important? And more to the point here, what is the role of historical interpretation in the larger project of sustainable development, particularly educating for sustainability? First, studying the past can, depending on the quality and intent of a given investigation or interpretation, provide a better understanding of the present. In fact, I would argue that we cannot understand who, what, and where we are without knowledge of who and what came before us. As Karl Marx once wrote, the traditions of dead generations weigh like a nightmare upon the living. We, and the society around us, are products of the past, whether we want to be or not. Because the past is always with us, weighing us down so to speak, circumscribing our choices, we must either work within the constraints it imposes (which requires understanding) or at least be fully aware of them if we seek to chart a new path, free of the old shackles.

As for sustainable development, it is simply impossible to have a full understanding of interrelated economic and environmental problems without knowing their history. Study of the past, for example, puts the ongoing industrial transformation of nature by people in perspective, situating it as part of a larger process of change and continuity over time. In this way, historical investigation can draw attention to aspects of modern environmental problems that were previously unseen in the usual myopia of the present. It can also give them a new significance, making clearer the shaping force of political structures, economic systems, and cultural frames. And finally, while this does not exhaust the contributions of the discipline, historical knowledge can provide us with a better sense of what can and should be done about the development problems we face. It can make more evident the ways in which apparently obvious solutions are unworkable or need to be modified, and perhaps suggest other responses yet unconsidered.

For our students—whether they are enrolled in environmental studies or science programs, exploring a minor interest, or merely fulfilling a general education requirement—a history course that sheds light on modern economic and environmental problems is critical to their full understanding of sustainable development. It is also essential to students' future participation in solving problems that arise. To send graduates out into the world to monitor water quality, plan urban development, design production processes, or whatever they choose to do, without a historical sensibility, is to do them a great disservice. It also impedes the larger effort of building a sustainable society. When an engineer, public official, or activist confronts the issues of toxics, brown fields, or genetic modification of crops without some inkling of the historical and social factors that have shaped them, they are crippled in making an adequately sophisticated response. We cannot expect our graduates to be the generation that finally begins to reorganize society on a sustainable basis if they are not properly trained for that task.

One practical example of the application of these abstract arguments is the debate over strip mining for coal in Appalachia. At present, coal is the primary source of energy for running our factories and illuminating, heating, and cooling our homes. Most of that coal comes from strip mines, many of which are located in the coalfields stretching from northern Alabama to Pennsylvania. The coal operators and energy conglomerates who own these mines insist that the mineral does and must continue to play a critical role in supplying our energy needs as a nation. They claim that strip mining can be done in an environmentally sound way, by restoring the landscape to an equivalent or sometimes better condition than before the blasting and digging started. In Appalachia, where flat land is at a premium, the former mine sites can also be used to build hospitals, schools, and prisons (although stability of the repacked ground has proven to be a problem for this purpose). Finally, the operators maintain, stripping provides badly needed jobs, and that stricter regulations or tighter enforcement of existing control legislation threaten those employment opportunities.

On the other side of the debate, some residents of the Appalachian coalfields vehemently object to strip mining. Active mines and the many poorly reclaimed sites cause erosion and siltation of streams, they say, which harms aquatic life and, along with more rapid surface runoff, exacerbates flooding. Acid mine drainage pollutes groundwater, deforestation removes important wildlife habitat, and unstable slopes and "valley fills" also threaten disastrous landslides. Pointing to the economics of stripping, critics claim that coal companies and energy conglomerates have not been known to give back as much as they take from the region. Their payrolls are relatively small and tax payments insufficient to sustain local and state infrastructure and services. Meanwhile, the coal surface mining industry ruins good farmland and destroys the scenery that would draw tourists and help alleviate the region's chronic unemployment problem.

Looking to history for insight on this, it becomes clear that addressing the concerns of besieged coal companies and strip mining opponents is not simply a matter of technical or regulatory action. For decades, the coal industry has been steadily, and very intentionally, mechanizing operations and shedding jobs. Surface mining was and is particularly attractive to mining companies because it so dramatically lowers labor costs, requiring considerably fewer miners per ton of coal extracted than deep mining. In West Virginia, for example, there were 100,000 union miners at midcentury, but now there are less than 19,000 miners in the state, and only about half of those are members of the United Mine Workers of America (Vollers, 1999). This decline has not caused a drop in production, however, which has continued to rise. At the same time, the shift to strip mining has had a dramatic impact on the environment, affecting the land, forest, and streams of Appalachia. Evidence of this damage is scattered all about the region, in abandoned and so-called reclaimed mine sites, as well as in scientific studies and reports, congressional hearing testimony, and newspaper exposés. And yet, despite the environmental degradation and economic harm, current regulatory legislation for surface coal mining is undeniably weak and poorly enforced. The question is, why? And what can be done to address these economic and environmental problems? To begin to answer those questions, we must turn to the discipline of history.

If the issue of strip mining were presented in the classroom, and discussion of the history behind the dispute between the industry and its opponents was omitted, our presentation would be incomplete. Students would miss the opportunity to investigate the decades-long degradation of the environment and chronic unemployment caused by stripping as well as the ease with which coal operators have avoided meaningful regulation. This fact would make it impossible for them to weigh the validity of the claims both sides now make and determine the best course of action in the future. Yet in programs dedicated to instructing students about sustainability, that is often how we engage current economic and environmental problems when we neglect to make the humanities and social sciences prominent parts of that course of study.

DANIEL EGAN: A SOCIOLOGIST'S PERSPECTIVE

In many ways, sociology is ideally suited as a means of teaching undergraduates the concept of sustainability. Sociology emerged during the 19th and early 20th centuries as a response to massive social upheavals that began in Western Europe centuries ago and that have since become the characteristic features of modern society. Karl Marx examined how the development of capitalism enforced the brutal subordination of all social relationships to the cash nexus, which led to such unsustainable conditions as alienated labor, class inequality, and ecological destruction. Max Weber's critique of the "iron cage" of bureaucracy pointed out that while modern society was impossible without the thorough rationalization of all social institutions, such rationalization inevitably resulted in a dehumanized world in which all moral or social responsibilities are constrained by the goal of efficiency. Emile Durkheim argued that traditional forms of community, characterized by what he called a strong "collective conscience," have largely given way to more fragmented moral systems that emphasize individual rights at the expense of collective responsibilities, thereby making social disintegration more likely. While the specific events that stimulated the rise of sociology have receded into the past, the problems that sociology was designed to answer are still the defining problems of contemporary society.

In addition, from its origins a fundamental component of sociology has been a commitment to progress. While this commitment has taken many forms, such as Marx's revolutionary praxis and Durkheim's conservative program of moral education, sociology is a science that not only sees progress as a defining feature of modern society but also sees as its goal the creation of solutions to the problems it uncovers. C. Wright Mills (1959) wrote that sociology should help people see the personal troubles in their daily lives as public issues, rather than viewing unemployment, poor housing conditions, boring work, and so on as purely individual failures. Mills saw the job of the sociologist as helping people understand how these personal troubles are the result of the historical period and the social institutions in which they live. Once this "sociological imagination" has been cultivated, there can emerge active "publics" capable of changing history and social structure to produce a more liberating, fulfilling life. This dialectic of biography, history, and structure is particularly relevant for education for sustainability. It asks us to see the social forces that construct the types of problems people face, the possible solutions available to them, and the central role that people play in creating and shaping their world.

Sociology would thus appear to be an ideal setting from which to convey to undergraduates the ecological, social, and economic goals of sustainable development. Indeed, one could argue that sustainability is the very core of sociology in both its substance and its methodology. However, there are a number of problems that sociologists must face in this project. First, most undergraduates enter the university without any prior exposure to the sociological perspective. Because sociology is unfamiliar territory, the value of sociology has to be demonstrated to them. This fact puts an extra burden on sociology that other disciplines do not face. This is a specific example of a more general identity crisis that sociology faces among the public; I have lost count over the years of the number of times that people, upon learning that I am a sociologist, ask if I have an LICSW or tell me that some family member is also a social worker. Despite the central role that questions of public policy play in sociology, the profile of sociologists as participants in political debates is understated. If there is confusion over what sociologists do, then their effectiveness in educating for sustainability will necessarily be problematic.

In addition, we must be aware that what we teach and what students hear may be two different things. All of my classes are organized explicitly around Mills' dialectical framework and present a critical political economy approach to understanding U.S. and global capitalism. Students readily accept the substantive details of this perspective—they have no problem seeing how the corporate pursuit of profit devastates workers, communities, and the environment, for this is consistent with the reality of their lives—but I have found that the broader meaning of these details is much harder to grasp. Students hear what I present in the classroom through social filters constructed by media, economic, family and other social institutions. The biggest challenge I face in my teaching is to prevent students from breaking down the systematic critique I present in class to fit into the more individualized market culture in which they live. For example, when I ask students to use Marx's analysis of the labor process to analyze their own experience as workers, I am regularly chagrined to find that the lesson many students draw from this analysis of exploitation is that they hope to escape this in the future by being the boss! Given the reality of their class situation, they have taken away something very concrete from my class; it is just not exactly what I was hoping for.

The fact that even the most passive students play this active role in processing what is presented in the classroom means that sustainability cannot be presented to students as if it is an objective set of socially responsible criteria for economic activity. The term is a contested terrain that reflects a particular balance of political forces, and any process of education for sustainable development must make this recognition a central feature. The problem with the term "sustainable development," I believe, is that it is so broad that it opens itself up to reinterpretation through the cultural filters referred to above. Sustainability encompasses both the mission of UML and, more specifically, the work of the Committee on Industrial Theory and Assessment (CITA), as well as efforts by corporations and their political allies to put a "green" face on their activity. While we may argue, convincingly I believe, that the latter is simply a political strategy developed over the last thirty years or so to maintain corporate hegemony in the face of challenges from social movements, we must recognize that the culture in which students hear our words is more supportive of the latter interpretation of sustainability. Thus, we cannot say "sustainability" and expect that students will hear what we want them to hear. What I take from this is the central role that language and values must play in our teaching. The political uses of language have to be directly acknowledged and addressed if our sense of sustainability is to prevail. This approach would mean making explicit the class forces that seek to socialize the costs of their profit-seeking behavior and identifying how the call for sustainable development has been co-opted by these forces to ensure their continued domination. Only then can we hope to successfully present a counter-hegemonic understanding of sustainability.

VANESSA GRAY: A POLITICAL SCIENTIST'S PERSPECTIVE

Like history and sociology, political science brings a unique perspective and valuable specialized knowledge to discussions of sustainability. In addition, political scientists have written more textbooks, taught more courses, and generated more research in environmental studies than their colleagues in the humanities or the other social sciences. Not all of the work in environmental politics helps educate for sustainability, but political science's longstanding, focused attention on environmental topics has yielded meaningful insights. The pedagogy for helping students to grasp those insights is a rapidly advancing subfield of political science. A superb example of this literature is a volume edited by Michael Maniates, *Encountering Global Environmental Politics: Teaching, Learning, and Empowering Knowledge,* published in 2003 by Rowman & Littlefield. Given that senior scholars in my field have written extensively on sustainability education, my goal in this section is merely to give a personal account of some of the challenges I face in teaching global environmental politics.

I often use definitions as a starting point in my course. Political analysis, like other rigorous inquiry, begins with an effort to make definitions explicit and to clearly delineate the object of discussion. When students hear competing definitions and are encouraged to come up with their own definitions, they may fret about not having a simple term they can memorize in order to get a good grade. Nevertheless, they are usually quick to grasp the political content of definitions (as in, one person's terrorist may be another person's freedom fighter).

The term "sustainable" is ripe for such scrutiny. I provide students with background information on how the term has been used over time. For example, *ecological* sustainability was an incipient concept championed at the 1972 United Nations Conference on the Human Environment in Stockholm. In contrast, the broader term of "sustainable development" emerged out of UN proceedings in the 1980s in which the developing nations had a greater voice. The definition of sustainable development that was enshrined in the resulting Brundtland report— "development that seeks to meet the needs and aspirations of the present without compromising the ability to meet those of the future"—leaves wide room for interpretation. Whose needs and what kind of aspirations are we talking about? In my upper-level seminar, I find it relatively easy to elicit discussion along those lines.

Insisting on clear definitions is but one skill that political science can offer students to help them think critically about sustainability issues. Another skill is to identify conflicts of interest. "Who wins?" and "who loses?" are the time-honored questions of my discipline. When two Latin Americanists, a political scientist, and a tropical biologist, applied those questions to the prevailing usage of the term "sustainability" in the early 1990s, they demonstrated that the concept's slipperiness allowed it to be appropriated by economic interests in ways that eviscerated both its ecological content and its intellectual integrity (Redford & Sanderson, 1992). Soon even strip mining companies, as Chad Montrie notes above, were embracing the notion of sustainability. Consequently, when my students and I talk about "sustainability," from the very outset we are looking for competing claims about what should be sustained. Is it the use of a certain resource by a specific group of humans? A way of life for a particular group of us? Robust populations of other species? I seek to guide the discussion toward which groups or individuals benefit from a particular definition or policy, and who is likely to bear the costs of a particular policy carried out in the name of sustainability.

Most of my students can easily recognize the conflict of interest inherent in, say, a research program on the health of marine ecosystems that is funded by the shrimp industry. Students find it harder to analyze cases in which conflicts arise between two "good causes," such as when the self-determination of an indigenous group undermines the protection of an endangered species. But that is precisely what political scientists do: we assume that competing interests are ever-present and that tradeoffs are unavoidable. Unfortunately, a good strategy for attaining one sustainability goal will not necessarily advance other sustainability goals. Worse, research on sustainable development projects in South America's tropical forests shows how easily sustainability goals collide. The evidence suggests that it is exceedingly difficult to raise the living standards of forest dwellers or to harvest forest products without seriously endangering local plant and animal communities.

Thus, in the real world, the highly desirable goals of alleviating poverty, maintaining indigenous traditions, and protecting biodiversity are rarely achieved concurrently. When a time horizon is introduced—for how long do we hope to sustain such-and-such?—still more conflicts of interest emerge. For example, the residents of a settlement inside a protected area may currently practice environmental stewardship, but one cannot guarantee that it will always be thus—that is, without denying that community its right to self-determination and autonomy.

In my classes, we use the word "stakeholder" to describe the parties relevant to a given environmental issue, but all stakeholders are not alike, nor is the political arena a level playing field. Indeed, the political scientist cares not just about conflict but also about power. I highlight for students the huge differences in the relative capacity of different groups to defend their interests and the way that power differentials help to explain environmental outcomes. For example, an impoverished indigenous tribe in the Ecuadoran Amazon has limited power vis-a-vis the transnational oil company drilling in the vicinity. The national government, strapped for foreign exchange and rife with corruption, is also ill-equipped to compete with the oil firm or to advance state interests. Meanwhile, the local wildlife may have no defenders at all. In such a scenario, it is no surprise whose interests ultimately prevail. If the indigenous group joins forces with a transnational activist network, the picture may change somewhat. The group will now have more information, resources, and avenues for expressing its position, but nevertheless, only in rare cases will the tribe succeed at protecting its lands and culture from despoliation.

I also encourage students to examine the motivations behind a self-proclaimed sustainability effort. Is a particular attempt at sustainability being pursued in response to political pressure? Because key stakeholders have embraced certain scientific concepts? Or perhaps because they are committed to social justice goals? Or are they motivated primarily by aesthetic preferences? Or security concerns? When students are required to tease out answers to these questions, they can observe how underlying motivations tend to shape outcomes.

Moreover, they frequently insert their own opinion of what should be done in a given situation. I try to get them, in their writing assignments and in class discussions, outside their own opinions enough to be able to recognize what motivates *their* views as well as the positions of others. To identify the material interests, values, and emotions behind support or opposition to a given sustainability effort is to engage in a form of political analysis.

I do not teach my students that every situation has to be a zero-sum game in which one side's gain results in a commensurate loss for the other side; but I do encourage skepticism regarding the win-win scenarios heralded by some sustainability advocates. For students of politics, the world has never been a place where all good things go together. We are trained to seek out the ways in which a policy (or the status quo) favors some interests while disadvantaging others, typically the poor and powerless. Thanks to the efforts of ecocentric environmentalists and animal welfare advocates, some of us are now more conscious of the interests of nonhuman nature. Another goal of mine, when selecting readings and designing activities, is to raise students' awareness that nonhuman interests exist.

By providing students with repeated opportunities for analyzing the positions of multiple stakeholders on a wide range of issues, I am also trying to get them to think beyond simple binary oppositions like "people vs. nature" or "rich vs. poor." I want them to be able to perceive nuances such as the winners among nonhuman species or the losers among business interests. In my opinion, this kind of political analysis is an acquired skill of tremendous value. Some students gravitate to it quite naturally. Throughout the semester, I employ numerous methods to engage everyone in this kind of analysis in the hope that they will continue to apply it after the course is over. I suspect that my success is limited, but not nil.

Analyzing sustainability topics from this perspective can evoke lively and deep class discussions. But it can also dishearten students. One of my greatest concerns in teaching global environmental politics is that if I successfully convince students of how grave and how complex the ecological crisis is, I will contribute to their passivity or even nihilism. For that reason, I design my course to go beyond defining and deconstructing environmental problems and dedicate almost half the semester to examining possible remedies. Finding good course materials on activities that offer hope of alleviating the ecological crisis, however, is far from easy. History offers mostly examples of failures to mitigate ecological damage, and an understanding of the global political economy reveals mostly obstacles to substantive change.

The recent political science literature demonstrates the difficulty of implementing environmental policy at every level, from local regulations to international treaties. Worse, collaborative research between political and natural scientists shows a lack of positive biophysical outcomes, even in cases where the political obstacles were overcome. On the rare occasion of success, such as the Montreal Protocol on ozone, the full story reveals progress that is limited and difficult to replicate. (The dominant manufacturer of ozone-destroying chemicals had already developed an affordable substitute and was therefore keen on international sanctions against producers using anything but the new substitute. Moreover, the treaty's loopholes allow massive production of CFCs by Third World industrial giants, and a thriving contraband trade exists, in which U.S. consumers play a key role.)

The news from comparative political scientists offers no panaceas either. Are strong civil societies and democratization the answer? Yes and no. While transparent, responsive institutions and empowered communities are excellent checks on some environmental abuses, the record shows that voters only respond to dramatic crises, not the creeping scourge of environmental degradation. Nor have high levels of citizen empowerment and environmental concern, such as in Japan and Scandinavia, been sufficient to change unsustainable consumption patterns. Environmental outrage helped bring down authoritarian regimes in the USSR and Eastern Europe, but since then, environmentalism has had little impact in that part of the world. Finally, some notable examples of successful sustainability policies come from authoritarian regimes (China's one-child policy, Cuba's shift away from an oil-dependent economy, and Thailand's ban on disposable plastics are examples).

Where does this leave us? Has the political scientist anything hopeful to share with students who are learning about sustainability? My answer is an emphatic yes. If our project is to promote genuine and enduring social change in the form of a more ecologically sustainable society, then understanding what has not worked and what is unlikely to work is an indispensable step. I assign case studies that illuminate the pitfalls of the pass-a-law approach and cautionary tales that tend to temper zeal for extreme measures. We also read about and discuss our complicity as consumers, voters, and taxpayers. In addition, I use case studies as a partial antidote to the human tendency to reinvent wheels, and I try to drum it into students' heads that much is already known about sustainability-related topics in other societies, academic disciplines, and periods in history. Most important, the final portion of my course consists of student presentations on hopeful alternatives.

For their projects, I provide students with a list of examples of current efforts—from around the globe and close to home—that arguably make a contribution to remedying the ecological crisis. Students choose a topic that interests them, learn about it, identify stakeholder positions and motivations, and then teach the rest of us about their remedy. Students find they have to scour various sources to locate information on their topic and they often have to rely entirely on primary sources. That information is sparse and contested provides students with additional opportunities for political analysis. Some of the topics my students have made presentations on include: the voluntary simplicity movement in the United States, local community-supported agriculture, the campaign of the Colombian Uwá against Occidental Petroleum, the Italy-based "slow food" movement, the Merrimac River cleanup, the amazingly sustainable city of Curitiba, Brazil, forensic genetics' role in prosecuting illegal whaling, the Chipko campaign to save forests in India, transnational law enforcement efforts to curb Freon smuggling, and hybrid automobiles.

In teaching my course in global environmental politics, I attempt to bring the best of my discipline to the task of educating for sustainability. It is only one course. As part of a broader interest in sustainability education, I am collaborating with colleagues from other disciplines at my university. Our goal is to raise student awareness of existing sustainability courses and activities at UML, offer new courses on the topic, and ultimately provide students in the social sciences and humanities with an integrated education in sustainability issues. Needless to say, political skills and insights are highly useful to this endeavor, too.

WHITLEY KAUFMAN:
A PHILOSOPHER'S PERSPECTIVE

The task of educating students on the topic of values and morality in general has largely fallen to the field of philosophy in modern times. Most other disciplines have tended either to aspire to the status of the neutral, objective value-free sciences, or evade issues of values altogether. It thus becomes an important task of both philosophy and the humanities in general to address such questions as sustainability in the university from the perspective of value theory and indeed the broader question of the place of values in education and in public discussion generally. For a discussion of sustainability is inextricably entwined with questions of moral value, no matter how hard one tries to present a neutral definition of the idea.

Consider the World Commission on Environment and Development's definition of "sustainability:" "Humanity has the ability to make development sustainable—to ensure that it meets the needs of the present without compromising the ability of future generations to meet their own needs." It can hardly be questioned that such a shift in priorities is a welcome one: a call for attention to the long-term effects of our current practices, a shift away from short-term thinking. Far too many of our current practices are unsustainable in the strict sense; they cannot be kept up at current rates for very long. Noteworthy, for example, is overfishing, where virtually every major commercial fish species is being removed at a faster rate than it can reproduce. Numerous other examples are available, such as agricultural practices that result in topsoil erosion, such that on world farmland, the rate of soil erosion is 30 times higher than the rate of soil formation (Eisenberg, 1998, p. 30). A coordinated effort to address such practices is in our own best interests, even aside from the interests of future generations.

There is then at least a relatively clear and uncontroversial core meaning of unsustainable: a practice that cannot be continued at the same rate very long before destroying the resources on which it depends is clearly unsustainable.

Nor do we need to appeal to much more than the student's (and society's) economic self-interest in order to motivate a shift away from such practices. However, things get much muddier very quickly. Take the issue of renewable versus nonrenewable energy sources. By a strict definition, a renewable source of energy is (or at least can be) exploited in a sustainable way, whereas a nonrenewable source (such as fossil fuels) cannot be. But such a position leads to unacceptable implications: shall we cease immediately (or even gradually) the use of oil and coal? The question is not just the massive economic disruption such a shift would cause. More fundamentally, what is wrong with using a resource even if it is unrenewable? The removal of coal and oil deposits in itself (that is, if a minimally polluting way of utilizing them could be found) will not substantially impair the functioning of the ecosystem nor human ability to survive (unlike say the destruction of topsoil), nor even the aesthetic or spiritual values of nature for future generations. Moreover, that an energy source is wholly renewable and sustainable does not necessarily make it desirable: consider the use of dams to generate hydroelectric power. Such a use is renewable yet extremely destructive from an ecological standpoint.

The larger difficulty with presenting the concept of sustainability to students, I would suggest, is a lack of attention to or even an avoidance of the more difficult and controversial value questions regarding our relation to the environment. The concept of sustainability can be all things to all people because of deliberate ambiguity as to the ethical basis of the concept. For some, sustainability has a wholly pragmatic, prudential sense: it counsels us not to be foolishly shortsighted, but to attend to the long-term implications of our actions. A slightly more demanding interpretation of sustainability defines it as applying specifically to issues of intergenerational justice. That is, our primary duty is to ensure the availability of resources for future generations; a practice that may be sustainable for our lifetimes may not be prudent for the indefinite future. Indeed, in this view even a practice that can be sustained indefinitely in an economic sense might be impermissible because it is unsustainable in a moral, aesthetic, or spiritual sense (e.g., because it eliminates species which are of little importance biologically or economically).

Other advocates of sustainability, however, interpret the concept in an even more rigorous and demanding sense, as requiring *intra*generational justice as well as intergenerational justice. That is, some have read the World Commission definition as a mandate to meet the needs of all people at the present, while also ensuring that the needs of future generations are not compromised. While this is no doubt reading more into the definition than the World Commission intended, still other groups have explicitly endorsed social justice as a key component of sustainability. Thus the World Business Council for Sustainable Development has defined the concept as the "integration of economic development with environmental protection and social equity" (Payne & Raiborn, 2003, p. 373). Of course, the introduction of social justice issues into the teaching of sustainability would oblige the teacher and the student to inquire into highly controversial questions about the current distribution of wealth and resources in the world. How, for example, should we respond to the enormous gap in lifestyle between the wealthy countries and the poor ones? Should we try to raise the level of welfare of poor countries until it reaches that of the wealthy ones, even at a substantial cost to the environment? Or should we require that wealthy countries reduce their impact on the environment, perhaps lowering living standards substantially as a result?

The sustainability rubric thus encompasses an enormous range of meanings, from the minimally demanding interpretation in terms of economic sustainability, to the interpretation in terms of social justice, or even to the maximally demanding position of ecocentrism, in which moral duties are owed directly to nature or its component parts: animals, plants, species, even inanimate objects such as rivers. (The most minimalistic interpretation I have seen is contained in the "Dow Jones Sustainability Index," which creates financial products "linked to economic, environmental, and social criteria," but always with a "clear focus on long-term shareholder value creation," i.e., profit (see http://www.sustainability-index.com/). But we cannot effectively educate students in the idea of sustainability without attempting to resolve or unify these widely divergent possible interpretations. How can we reconcile the competing values of economic sustainability, environmental protection, social justice, and direct obligations to nature? There can be no formula for resolving them; there is no substitute for entering into a debate about balancing fundamental values. But this debate is just what the discussion about sustainability has seemed to lack so far, or even to deliberately avoid. And this is where I see the role of the humanities in the university as having special importance. This brings us to a discussion of the teaching of values in the humanities.

In the 20th century, two distinct trends contributed to an increasing reluctance in the university to teach values. One is the rise of the movement called positivism, in which the goal was to emulate science in every discipline by adhering to a strict distinction between facts (considered objective) and values (considered subjective). The rise of the social sciences in particular reflects a concern to follow a neutral and value-free study of human beings. To discuss or debate values, in this view, would be unscientific; one can do no more than record values or preferences as simply given facts about human beings. The other trend is the political theory known as liberal pluralism, of which John Rawls is the most well-known advocate. In this view, a liberal democratic society is one in which each individual chooses his ultimate values for himself, and no one imposes values on anyone else. In the liberal society, the goal is a state that is neutral between competing ultimate values. As Rawls says, in a democracy, citizens "cannot reach agreement or even approach mutual understanding on the basis of their irreconcilable comprehensive doctrines" (Rawls, 1999, p. 132). Remarkably, both of these philosophies end up with the same position: that the notion of truth or falsity in the area of values must be abandoned. Thus, for Rawls the idea of "truth or right [must] be replaced by an idea of the politically reasonable."

The result is that for the better part of a century, university professors have become increasingly uncomfortable with the idea of teaching values in the classroom. Social goals became increasingly focused on economic growth as a means of avoiding difficult questions of values; the idea was to satisfy as many preferences as possible rather than have to make difficult choices about which values are to outweigh others. Indeed, this emphasis on relentless social and economic growth is no doubt partly to blame for our current environmental crisis. However, it appears that we are now finally emerging from this positivist/pluralist consensus, and from the naïve idea that growth is the solution to all our problems or a way of avoiding difficult tradeoffs and choices (indeed, as we recognize that uncontrolled growth itself is part of the problem).

As we move beyond the idea of value subjectivity, it will be the humanities that will have to lead the way toward a renewed emphasis on moral education in the university. Such an education takes many forms, including the explicit consideration of moral theories and moral principles as takes place in an ethics class, the historical training in the cultural and religious traditions that have shaped our current debate, and the implicit consideration of values that is so central in the encounter with great works of literature. However, to abandon the Pluralist Model in which values are irredeemably subjective and private, does not entail going to the opposite extreme according to which values are fixed and determinate, and need simply to be instilled in youths (call this the Authoritative Model). An alternative to these two extremes might be named the Deliberative Model, in which values are chosen through a process of open discussion aimed at reaching democratic consensus. In this view, values are objective and rational in that they can be the subject of reasoned debate; yet they are not the sort of thing that can be simply read off the structure of the world like a law of nature. Values are a product of individual commitment, but that commitment always takes place within a social and cultural context, and values are constantly subject to development and renegotiation within a community.

It is the humanities that provide the ideal forum in which to raise and debate such questions, and the humanities departments in the universities must thus play a central role in the debate over sustainability. The very concept of sustainability is at best a starting point for consideration of the multiple conflicting values at stake: the standard of living of the current generation, social justice, preservation of resources for future generations, and respect for other living things and for the integrity of ecosystems. A central goal must be the developing of habits essential to citizenship in a democracy: the willingness to engage in good faith in debates about values, even ultimate values, the resistance to dogmatism of all sorts, the virtues of intellectual humility as well as moral commitment, and respect for other citizens as equal participants in the construction of the good society. All of these habits will be essential to the debate over sustainable development, a debate that is only beginning.

CONCLUSION

Our narratives provide strong experiential support for giving to the humanities and social sciences a major role in education for sustainable development. If the university is going to make sustainable development a central part of its mission, there must be an explicit discussion of the values that inform sustainability and, more specifically, what *type* of sustainability is to lie at the heart of this mission. Making the concept of sustainability problematic raises the potential for considerable conflict within the university, as there will necessarily be a range of perspectives on what sustainable development means. In the absence of such a struggle over the nature of sustainability, however, its educational value will be minimized; without addressing the moral and political context of sustainability, we will be left with a collection of technological fixes that can be easily absorbed by the same economic system that produced the problems of ecological destruction, economic insecurity, and social inequality that sustainable development is supposed to resolve.

In order for sustainable development to be a central theme in the university and not just one of many ideas students encounter in their education, it must be presented in an integrated format that extends throughout students' tenure at the university. If students encounter sustainability here and there, depending upon the particular professor or course, then it will be relatively easy for students to compartmentalize what they learn in that course. After all, if a university is a great marketplace of ideas, then students should expect to encounter diverse ideas and approaches; why should sustainability be expected to assume a privileged role in their lives as students and citizens? An important step to encourage both students and faculty to engage in a dialogue about the meaning of sustainable development is to promote and develop a cross- and interdisciplinary curriculum.

REFERENCES

Eisenberg, E. (1998). *The ecology of Eden.* New York: Vintage.

Mills, C. W. (1959). *The sociological imagination.* New York: Oxford University Press.

Payne, D., & Rayborne, C. (2003). Sustainable development: The ethics supports the economics. In T. Easton & T. Goldfarb (Eds.), *Taking sides: Clashing views on controversial environmental issues* (pp. 372-381). New York: McGraw Hill.

Rawls, J. (2001). *The law of peoples.* Cambridge: Harvard University Press.

Redford, K., & Sanderson, S. (1992). The brief, barren marriage of biodiversity and sustainability. *Bulletin of the Ecological Society of America, 73*(1), 36-39.

Vollers, M. (1999). Razing Appalachia. *Mother Jones, 24,* July/August, 36-43.

CHAPTER 5

Teaching Sustainability: The Case of the Incredible Shrinking Professor

Elisabeth M. Hamin

Teaching sustainability, it seems to me, is different than many of the topics we teach at a university. Unlike biology, say, which creates biologists, or planning which creates planners, there is not profession of "sustainer." As David Orr notes, achieving sustainability in the postmodern world will require an "active, competent citizenry" (1992, p. 30), demonstrating "civic virtue, a high degree of ecological literacy, and ecological competence throughout the population" (1992, p. 31). The pedagogic goal is to encourage a world view, one in which students will become citizen activists for sustainability after they graduate, whether in the civic sphere or by bringing sustainability criteria to bear on their work. Because sustainability is very complex, these citizens need to be able to acknowledge the insufficiency of what they will know and not be paralyzed by it. Instead, they will need to turn to others to form groups of inquirers who can research multiple aspects of a question and together have a chance of seeing a broader picture of the complex designs of the world and the opportunities for sustainability. Sustainability will be achieved only through communities of learners and activists, and this is what a curriculum in sustainability must model. Empowerment cannot be only an academic concept described in the class, but must also be experienced by the students within the class. Only by making teaching approaches consistent and coherent with teaching substance on this topic will we create the communities and citizens we need for the future.

I have taught a course entitled *Sustainable Communities* once a year for six years. The course has been taught as a collaboration with a former colleague, Rob Thompson, and as a sole instructor course; taught primarily as a lecture series, and more recently as a regular seminar; taught to undergraduates and graduate students; taught primarily to planning students; and taught to primarily environmental studies students. I have tried out a variety of books and varied the ratios of lecture to in-class exercises and discussion, over time moving further and further from lecture-based content. The course has sometimes utilized regular research reports for students to further investigate one topic of their own choosing and sometimes had the whole class work together on a campus greening project. Clearly, I have struggled and experimented with the course over its life. While these variations certainly are not efficient in terms of class preparation time, they do give me a better base from which to write this chapter, and have kept the course overall fresh for me each year.

The one thing that has stayed steady over the years is the focus of the class. The goal of my particular course is to give students a chance to investigate ways to integrate sustainability into the structure of the built environment and introduce ways to undertake community development that are alternatives to market-driven economic development. The focus of the course is on actions that can take place at the site, community and regional scale, rather than national or international policies, although one cannot effectively address the local without some discussion of the national and the global. But I am convinced of the value of focusing student discussion on local activities because these are often implementable and because it is at the local level that most people are actually involved and where they typically can make the most difference. My goal with this course is to graduate citizens who recognize the applicability and importance of sustainability criteria in a wide range of settings, whether as volunteers or within their employment, and feel empowered to begin to address them. It is developing ways of viewing the world, rather than accumulating quickly forgotten facts and theories, although certainly some of this learning goes on.

Let me make this more concrete by describing the general principles that underlay my particular take on sustainability and that are introduced in the first few weeks of the course. Most students enter the course having been raised on a steady diet of television nature shows describing human devastation to the tropics, science projects on what goes into landfills, and bad news about global warming. As a result, I spend little time preaching to the choir about global environmental degradation. What is less obvious to most students is that there cannot be just environmental solutions; that sustainability is a three-legged stool, which also requires improvements to economy and equity to allow fundamental changes in the world (Campbell, 1996, p. 276). Thus, the "three-e" approach is central to all inquiries and, even as we talk about solar energy for instance, we think about how it can be more accessible to those with fewer resources, how it can be made in ways perhaps less dependent on traditional profit motives and more based in the community, but still improving lives. Throughout the course, as we discuss alternative building techniques, infrastructural technologies, and social structures, we try to find the holy grail— policies which achieve the nexus of the three e's: improving equity, ecology, and economy all at the same time. This approach accords well with what Orr (1992, p. 39) calls the epistemology of sustainability, which centers on interrelatedness—the connections between viewer and viewed, indigenous and colonial, air and water, human and nature.

The second key point that must be made early is a contested point. I present the idea that sustainability is not about individual lifestyles. I personally am not interested in persuading students to recycle; I am interested in getting them to identify what will have to change so that everyone recycles or, better yet, so that businesses make less trash in the first place. The course may incidentally change students' individual choices, and that is great. When I compost, for instance, it is not for the joy of composting, but out of a desire to live coherently and not be hypocritical; the course tends to keep me honest and keep sustainability in the forefront of my mind. I hope it does the same for the students. But I am personally not sanguine that as a society we will get the majority of people to do things that are less convenient or more expensive on a daily basis over the long haul just because those actions are more ecological or socially beneficial. Instead, doing the right thing needs to become easy and the wrong thing hard; we need to build into our physical structures and delivery mechanisms resource efficiency, social and distributional equity, and prevention of ecological harm. In many ways, I see this as prerequisite for changing the underlying values of the average citizen— only by doing the right thing will people learn the value of the right thing. I acknowledge that this notion creates a political circle. Without widely held values that support sustainability, how can we force sustainability onto the political agenda? Without experience of the values of sustainable policies, how can we get citizens to prefer them? I am glad that I need not resolve these dilemmas to teach the course or to take action. My job, as I see it, is to assist in widening awareness of the values of sustainability and the existing and (re)emerging technologies that help us in that direction. From there, it is our future leaders, our students, who must develop those alternatives, publicize them, and get them to become standard rather than alternative.

A key point for the course is that this "enstructuration" approach removes a certain piety from discussions; it is not about "greener than thou," and I tell students this right up front. I admit to having bought disposable diapers at Wal-Mart. That always appears to be comforting to the "less evolved" in the class, who are, after all, in some ways more important to reach than the already converted, and minimizes moralizing and judgments that I prefer not to enter the classroom. Similarly, when we talk policy, sometimes we judge policy benefits by whether they would convince the Sopranos of television fame, or someone's SUV-driving mother, as examples of those whom policies have to persuade to do the right thing. This has a way of keeping the course real, although it makes policy design that much harder.

An interesting point is that a colleague of mine, Professor John Gerber in Plant and Soil Sciences at the University of Massachusetts, has begun offering an undergraduate course on sustainability that takes exactly the opposite perspective. His entire course is structured around providing students with the space and time to evaluate their own values and actions as well as how they support the planet or increase global and local harm. The argument here is that change will come only through individual choices and beliefs. If I were to design a curriculum on sustainability, this sort of contrast is exactly what I would try to encourage.[1]

At a certain level, once these core principles are clear, my main role in the class is done. The rest of the course becomes interesting iterations of examining policies and designs to implement these key principles (enstructuration and the three-e's). The challenge in the course design then becomes to find our way through the variety of technologies and approaches that could be included under the rubric of sustainable communities. These options can and have ranged from power sources to building materials to neighborhood and city design; from household economies to community-supported agriculture; from community gardens to the consequences of genetically modified crops on organic agriculture; to the implications for butterflies and Nigerian farmers from Monsanto's policies. We can discuss organizing for campus change, for civic change, for opposing the World Trade Organization or for creating community food banks and alternative currencies. We can discuss the connections between corporate manufacturing decisions and municipal solid waste, and William McDonough's efforts to create safe, recyclable materials, for instance, and the principles of waste reduction. We could talk about how power is generated and the relative benefits of being on the national grid or off of it. You see the problem—the issues that local sustainability brings up are so broad, so interconnected, so interesting, that it is quite difficult to place boundaries on the topic. It is this very breadth that has structured my pedagogic response—the incredible shrinking professor.

The implementation of sustainability principles in the world covers such a breadth of material that certainly I, as a limited human being, cannot profess expertise over all of it. Yet I am loathe to tell students that we will discuss only these certain aspects of sustainability because that is all I can say that I really know, when there is this whole relevant universe out there that the students are often more interested in than my particular area of city planning. Were there a curriculum on sustainability, the problem might be addressed. But at this university today, there are few courses where that is the main topic, although certainly in many courses ecological and social innovations come up. Facing the limits of my knowledge has been a humbling, but also enlightening, experience. My response has been to structure the course so that students can follow their own interests and learn from each other.

Let us return for a moment to how our university graduates may be implementing sustainability. Will any individual have sufficient knowledge or political power to determine appropriate policies, particularly as citizen activists? No, clearly not. Instead, the way policies change and in particular the

---

[1] Details on Gerber's class are available at: http://www.umass.edu/umext/jgerber/sustliving.htm

way sustainability will get built into existing practices is by citizens working together, researching new topics and learning from each other. Implementing sustainability at the local level will require citizen learning communities, empowered to explore alternatives, learn from each other, and press for implementation of new approaches. Will these citizens have a professor telling them what to do, what to know, what to read? Again, obviously not. Given this fact, it is unclear to me why we should model that experience in the classroom when it so clearly will not be the conditions of their lives. Classic instructional style may make sense where there is a clear body of knowledge that builds into a relatively coherent whole, but sustainability studies are not that. So alternative learning models that facilitate development of shared learning appear necessary.[2]

I try to be very explicit about the pedagogy of the course so that students will not be surprised and frustrated when I don't behave like a "real professor." In the syllabus, for example, I include this paragraph:

> In keeping with the ideals of sustainability and community action, I have designed the teaching approach (pedagogy, for those comfortable with that word) to emphasize student initiative and peer learning. Generally, I expect to lead discussion on the frameworks and conceptual questions. Student presentations will describe particular techniques for increasing community sustainability. . . . My hope is that we can model the same values implicit in the sustainable communities movement—grassroots, collaborative decision making in a locally-situated framework that nevertheless considers more global concerns.

I talk about it the first day of class, in a gentle effort to get students to shift their expectations. I also talk about it the last day of class, reminding them that peer learning and collaboration as they experienced it in the course is likely to be the way they will be successful in activism for the structural changes that we have investigated throughout the semester. I should say that while this overall pedagogy has been well received by many students, for others it is quite annoying. For example, in a recent evaluation, a student identified himself [3] as a "consumer" of classes and suggested that if students could get refunds, he would ask for it, since the professor did not contribute substantially to his knowledge (i.e., accumulation of facts). Indeed, a student looking for what Donald Finkel (2000) calls "The Great Teacher," one who lectures authoritatively and engagingly, will be dissatisfied, and this does constitute a certain percentage of the students who preregister for the class. Fortunately, for a larger percentage of the students, the

---

[2] The approach I describe here has clear resonance with learning communities and shares many assumptions and goals with them. However, learning communities are usually understood to be residential or at least to flow through coherent curriculum (Shapiro & Levine, 1999), and my single class does not achieve that. Still, creating residentially based communities of learning based on a shared interest in sustainability could be a very powerful technique, much more so than my one class.

[3] I am not certain the writer was a he, but the language choices appeared to be gendered male.

pedagogy seems to work, and evaluations have suggested over and over again that students value having had discussion opportunities, and while experiencing occasional frustration when peers do a poor job of leading learning, nevertheless most students appreciate the course design.

Within the course, there are several methods I have used to develop rapport and empowerment among students. First is having a student lead particular class readings. I have tried assigning discussion leadership for general readings and for particular case studies and find the case studies to clearly and positively contribute to the development of a participatory class culture. Having students lead regular course readings is less clear, as students are often presenting information they are not all that comfortable with and, as a result, the presentations are not routinely successful. Not surprisingly, students seem to prefer to lead discussions that focus on why a group did something and its outcomes, rather than a lecture on, say, alternative economies. This is particularly true for undergraduates; were I to teach a primarily graduate student course, I might return to having students lead topical discussion rather than focusing on cases. Even within the case studies, I have found it helpful to clearly identify the key questions I hope each discussion leader will address. An example is the book *Ecology of Hope* (Bernard & Young, 1997), which describes various resource-based communities and their efforts to use community organization to regain or retain control over their natural and economic resources. This book was quite popular for its focus on what is actually being done now, and students seemed pleased to present these cases, although it needs to be supplemented with urban material to appeal to a broad spectrum of students and their likely future work.

Another approach I have used is to align students into reading groups. I assign groups of three or four students who share a general interest, and they are supposed to help each other write their papers. I assign to the students within the reading group dates that drafts are due, and days when comments are due back; only after that does the paper go to me. The response to this varies a great deal by the particular personality of the students and for some groups has worked very well and for others created just an empty exercise. For motivated groups of graduate students, this approach seemed quite successful, and having them help each other with papers changed the sense of a competitive classroom into a cooperative one. For undergraduates, the sincerity with which they undertake their peer reading has varied significantly. To encourage seriousness about it, at the end of the semester, I give students a chance to rate each other regarding the helpfulness of comments received from team members. To encourage students to take this seriously, I allot a small percent of the grade for it.

To facilitate research skills and provide students with experience investigating a topic on which they often know very, very little, I also assign a research paper. The students choose the topic, although often I bring in a list of topics from previous years plus things I have been wondering about. One student in the class thereby becomes the class expert on solar heating for homes, another the expert on community gardens for immigrant neighborhoods, while a third can tell us about community currencies. As discussion progresses, students can contribute from their new area of expertise. A risk is that these topics can feel scattershot and unrelated. To address this factor, I group the presentations into shared themes.

The first set of techniques I described develops a sense of community, and the second set develops empowerment to learn through research. A third key principle is that of engagement. For this, the approach I have used is a project to green the campus. Work at the campus level has several advantages. It is the area the students know best, particularly the undergraduates, and are the most invested in. It is also a big, complex institutional environment and gives students a taste of how difficult the real world can be. But administrations can be responsive to students in ways that are difficult to mirror in some external community of which the students are not members. While I was at Iowa State University, students gathered baseline indicators for what we hoped would provide guidance for projects in subsequent years. (I subsequently left that university, so that effort did not directly continue.) At the University of Massachusetts, students chose instead to undertake specific projects such as researching how to increase recycling in the dorms and how to better include alternative transportation in the campus plan. In all cases, I let students discuss what project they want to undertake for the campus greening, vote if consensus is taking too long, and overall they must provide their own direction. This aspect is part of the discipline of empowering students—I would have preferred that last year's students do an indicators project, but there was not support among the class members for it, so I had to live out my principles and shut up. In retrospect, the indicators project was a much better way to start, and I may step in and insist on it as this year's project.

Ideally, each class lays a foundation that the next class can build on, so that over the years there is sufficient follow-up and depth to actuate real campus change. Doing a campus greening project well requires great dedication on the part of the instructor, as many people spread throughout the university system have to be contacted, such as operations and procurement departments, power and water plants, and so forth, to develop an understanding of how a university operates and what is its current status. But doing it well has the potential to combine all of the various desired characteristics of community, empowerment, and engagement, and can create long-term change. And of the methods I have used in the class, this one, with its opportunity for actually changing the world, means the most to students. This sort of engaged service work, assuming sufficient support by the university or the department for the instructor to succeed, is central to really optimizing a course based on sustainability principles.

The premise of this chapter has been simple. The pedagogy of teaching sustainability needs to cohere with the principles of the topic. Students must take control of the class, just as in life they will have to take control of their communities and workplaces. This suggests that the role of the instructor is large at the beginning of the course in setting frames of inquiry and readings, identifying appropriate styles of discussion and comments that do not connect to the course's themes, assuring contributions by the shyer members of the class. But as students master these ideas and skills and the course progresses, the sign of success is how often the professor can keep her or his mouth shut, to borrow Finkel's (2000) phrase. In sustainability studies, the professor should, over time, shrink from expert to revered member of the inquiring community.

REFERENCES

Bernard, T., & Young, J. (1997). *The ecology of hope.* Gabriola Island, BC: New Society.

Campbell, S. (1996). Green Cities, Growing Cities, Just Cities? *Journal of the American Planning Association, 62*(3), 296-312.

Finkel, D. (2000). *Teaching with your mouth shut.* Portsmouth, NH: Boynton Cook.

Orr, D. (1992). *Ecological literacy: Education and the transition to a postmodern world.* Albany: SUNY Press.

Shapiro, N., & Levine, J. (1999). *Creating learning communities: A practical guide to winning support, organizing for change, and implementing programs.* San Francisco: Jossey-Bass.

CHAPTER 6

Strategies Used to Embed Concepts of Sustainable Development in the Curriculum

Linda L. Lowry and Judy K. Flohr

This chapter illuminates the experiential pedagogy that was used to embed concepts of sustainability in the curriculum of the Department of Hospitality and Tourism Management (HTM) at the University of Massachusetts Amherst and clarifies the educational benefits that students gained from the process. The primary vehicle for discovery and reflection is Community-based research (CBR). The impetus for this form of experiential teaching and learning came from the management academy's need to grow leaders who could solve problems and manage diverse peoples and situations in an increasingly complex world. The issue of sustainable tourism development was selected as the context for exploration as it is a serious challenge facing "destination communities" and countries.

The origins of the department go back to 1938, making it one of the oldest hospitality and tourism programs in the country. Since its inception, the department has evolved to accommodate the changing nature of its industries and to best prepare students for careers in their chosen fields. Today, with approximately 500 students in its undergraduate and graduate curricula, the program is among the most respected in the world, earning a fourth-place ranking in the 1996 *Gourman Report: A Rating of Undergraduate Degree Programs in American and International Universities.*

Its mission, "to teach, advance, and support the practice and management of the hospitality and tourism industries," reflects and addresses the needs of its multiple constituencies: 1) Educating students at the undergraduate and graduate levels so they can succeed as professionals capable of providing innovative leadership in changing environments, 2) Advancing the state of knowledge in the industries through original and adaptive research and scholarship, 3) Serving the industries through programs on and off campus that are designed to advance and renew the education of those practicing in the fields, and 4) Supporting the University of Massachusetts by participating in its governing bodies and serving the state public at large.

The department's international ranking is an indicator of its ability to successfully serve multiple constituencies while simultaneously adhering to the more traditional roles of teaching, research, and service. In addition, the Hospitality and Tourism Management Department is keenly aware of the role of its industries in the economic health of communities, states, nations, and the world. In order to prepare its graduates to become successful leaders and managers in the 21st-first century, the curricular goals of the department are outcome-based and are built on the premise that successful leaders and managers must be able to communicate effectively, solve problems, think creatively, act strategically, and remain aware of the impact that our hospitality and tourism industries have on the economy and in sustainable community development.

We are not alone in our quest to better prepare tomorrow's leaders for the complex challenges they will face. As early as 1993, tourism educators noted that "for sustainable tourism to occur, it must be closely integrated with all other activities that occur in the host region" (McKercher's, 1993, p. 14) and that lack of environmental awareness would produce graduates with short-term attitudes toward tourism (Barron & Prideaux, 1998). By 2000, academics in the tourism discipline were discussing among themselves the need to couple the teaching of theories of sustainable tourism with the skill set that would be necessary to implement sustainable tourism development (i.e., the application of theory). Simultaneously, scholarly conversations and research focused on the ethical dimension of sustainable tourism development and the pedagogical challenges of teaching theory, instilling values, and developing skills that graduates could use to implement potentially controversial tourism development within a dynamic community setting (Jamal, 2004; Jurowski, 2002; Tribe, 2002).

FINDING BEST PRACTICES FOR TEACHING ABOUT SUSTAINABILITY

As a national leader in hospitality and tourism education, our response to the growing need for skilled tourism managers with expertise in sustainable development was to embed concepts of sustainable development in the curriculum of both undergraduate and graduate students. We knew that experiential learning was the key component of our strategy, and we had to make a conscious choice from among the prevailing experiential pedagogies. We also were mindful of the continuing debates over issues of accountability; the best practices of teaching and learning; the relationship between the academy and the community; meaningful assessment of teaching and learning; and the pressing need to educate students in such a way that they become critical thinkers, life-long learners, and engaged citizens.

Our strategy for embedding the concepts of sustainability in our curriculum was forged from this cacophony of voices. Pioneering faculty members at our institution and around the world were shifting their focus from traditional, lecture-based, teacher-centered learning to experientially based, student-centered learning. The landscape of experiential education (i.e., teaching) and experiential learning was varied. We recognized the following four challenges with experiential teaching and learning, and we wanted to select the best type of experiential learning for teaching sustainability: 1) Experiential teaching and learning requires more effort on the part of both faculty members and students, 2) It is difficult to assess its effectiveness on student learning, 3) There is minimal agreement on defining what counts as experiential education and experiential learning, and 4) There are minimal data to support best practices with regard to teaching sustainability.

We attempt here to share some of our findings, as we believe that those who teach sustainability theory that must then be operationalized into practice by our graduates will be compelled to find best practices for experiential teaching and learning.

EXPERIENTIAL EDUCATION AND LEARNING

Educational organizations associated with experiential education gave general definitions of experiential education and learning (Association for Experiential Education, 2002; International Consortium for Experiential Learning, 2000) and there was little difference between them. On the other hand, Itian's (1999) study looked at the various definitions and origins of experiential learning and experiential education and offered comprehensive definitions that reflect the paradigm shift in teaching and learning that is shaping today's universities and colleges. In his view, "experiential learning is best considered as the change in an individual that results from reflection on a direct experience and results in new abstractions and applications" (Itian, 1999, p. 92). What, then, were these forms of experiential teaching and learning, how had others defined them, and which one would be the best pedagogical choice for embedding sustainability in our curriculum? Three techniques associated with educational movements emerged: community service learning, community-based learning, and community-based research. We needed to determine whether there were differences among them.

Community Service Learning

Community Service Learning can be traced to the 1950s when the earliest service-learning definition was found in the publications of the Southern Regional Education Board (SREB). The impetus for the definition came from SREB members Bill Ramsey and Bob Sigmon who "were concerned with developing learning opportunities for students that were integrally connected to community development" . . . and they coined the term "service-learning" (Stanton, 2000, p. 5).

The National Service-Learning Clearinghouse (2003, p. 2) online resource entitled *Service-Learning Is . . .* from its self published 1994 book pointed out that there are different views on the nature of service learning and used differing sources to illuminate the various perspectives. Two were relevant to this study: the first had to do with the characteristics of service learning as described by the National Commission on Service Learning (2002) and the other was a definition of service learning by Eyler and Giles (1999). Both convey the benefits of student involvement in helping to determine and meet real, defined community needs as well as the learning and deeper understanding that occurs when students go through a cyclical process of action and reflection while simultaneously seeking to achieve real objectives for the community. The use of service learning as a pedagogy that connects community service with critical reflection continued to evolve as more faculty and students engaged in the process, and faculty have become proponents of its use as a tool for teaching critical inquiry and developing students who are more civic and socially minded (Campus Compact, 2003; Waldstein & Reiher, 2001).

Were there any dissenting voices? Eyler (2000, p. 3) painted a cautionary view of service learning and said that although service learning "appears to be ideally suited to help students develop a deeper understanding of subject matter, a practical knowledge of how community decision-making processes work, and strategies for transferring knowledge and problem-solving skills to new situations," there is a pressing need for a more rigorous, outcome-based assessment of the impact of service learning. As with any new philosophy or pedagogy, it must be tried, tested, and improved. On the other hand, when asked by the Campus Compact (2003, p. 1) about the direction of service learning and the public purposes of higher education, Ehrlich Award winner Dwight Giles said that the most innovative and groundbreaking work that is happening in campus/ community engagement is "best captured at the moment by the 'community-based research' emphasis. The cutting edge is where teaching, scholarship, and public service are connected and reciprocal."

Community-Based Learning and Community-Based Research

Differences between the academy's view of community-service learning and community-based learning seemed in some cases to be a matter of semantics, in others, a matter of politics. From the perspective of the authors of this study, community-based learning was the preferable term, as students were not simply providing a service for some group or organization. Instead, they were engaged in community-based learning that fit the competency-based, curricular goals of the

Hospitality and Tourism Management Department. More specifically, students worked in partnership with a community on specific research projects. As collaborative partnerships, research and planning are integral to sustainable tourism theory and sustainable tourism development; we needed to find out how CBR was different from traditional research practices carried out at institutes of higher education.

We found three key differentiating aspects that set CBR apart from traditional research, including the following: 1) the community, instead of the academy, initiates the research agenda (Axel-Lute, 1999; Chopyak, 1999; Sclove, Scammell, & Holland, 1998; Stoecker, 1999; Strand, Marullo, Cutforth, & Stoecker, 2003); 2) the community is involved in every step of the research process instead of commissioning the research project (Axel-Lute, 1999; Chopyak, 1999; Sclove, Scammell, & Holland, 1998; Stoecker, 1999; Strand, Marullo, Cutforth, & Stoecker, 2003); and 3) in many cases, the community uses the research in practical efforts to effect positive social change (Axel-Lute, 1999; Chopyak, 1999; Stoecker, 1999; Strand, Marullo, Cutforth, & Stoecker, 2003). In other words, the nontraditional role taken by academics and students in CBR is one of a collaborator who works with the community as a participant in the research process and who builds a relationship with community stakeholders through social interactions.

We were impressed by CBR as a particular type of experiential teaching and learning tool since it afforded students the opportunity to work with a community to collaboratively gain new knowledge and addressed the inherently complex issues surrounding sustainability while simultaneously working within the complicated dynamics of community stakeholder relationships.

STUDENTS AS THINKERS AND LEADERS

Could CBR, as a form of experiential learning, also transform students into engaged citizens who, as members of their own communities, would champion sustainable development? We found evidence to suggest that it could. Mitchell and Poutiatine (2001, pp. 179-180) discussed the challenges of training leaders and the desire of educational programs to "deliver a curriculum capable of inspiring students to personally transform into leaders" and said that "experiential methodology" . . . that places the learner as close as possible to the experience from which she or he is learning" is the key to leadership development in students. In addition, they found that experiential pedagogy that used group processes also developed leaders. When they used community-based research methodology, they found that "experiential learners developed an understanding of a subject by organizing knowledge around experience" (Mitchell & Poutiatine, 2001, p. 183) and that through this experiential research process, students learned "about leadership, teamwork, and themselves" (Mitchell & Poutiatine, 2001, p. 184).

Itian (1999, p. 94) said that "if we want to develop critically thinking, self-motivated, problem-solving individuals who participate actively in their communities, we must have an educational system and educational approaches that model and support this" and found that a team-based student research project in a community setting was an excellent example of experiential education. He reminded us that "as we move into the 21st century, it becomes increasingly clear that we must develop citizens who can actively participate in a democratic process and, in doing so, work toward creating a just and compassionate world" (Itian, 1999, p. 98).

EMBEDDING SUSTAINABLE DEVELOPMENT IN THE CURRICULUM: THREE EXAMPLES

The issue of sustainable development is particularly relevant to tourism management, and students within the discipline must develop the knowledge and skill sets to address its implementation in businesses, communities, and countries. The concept of sustainable development originated in the 1983 United Nation's first global task force that was convened to deal with issues of sustainability. It was further defined and given principles of application in the World Commission on Environment and Development, which is commonly know as the Brundtland Report. Sustainable tourism has been defined in many ways, and numerous tourism scholars have outlined the policy, planning, and development principles inherent in the practice of sustainable tourism development. However, two Canadian definitions captured the essence of sustainable tourism development that was embraced by the authors of this study (Gartner, 1996; Gunn, 1994; Harris, Griffin, & Williams, 2002; Harrison, 2000; Harrison & Husbands, 1996; Smith & Brent, 2001; Weaver & Lawton, 2002).

Rees (1989, p. 13) defined sustainable tourism development as "positive socioeconomic change that does not undermine the ecological and social systems upon which communities and society are dependent. Its successful implementation requires integrated policy, planning, and social learning processes; its political viability depends on the full support of the people it affects through their governments, their social institutions, and their private activities." Tourism Canada (1990, p. 179) adopted a vision of sustainable tourism development that leads to "the management of all resources in such a way that we [the tourism industry] can fulfill economic, social, and aesthetic needs while maintaining cultural integrity, essential ecological processes, biological diversity, and life support systems."

Strategies used by the Department of Hospitality and Tourism Management to embed concepts of sustainable development in the curriculum were best described in a case format. Three community-based research projects that occurred between 2000 and 2003 formed the basis for this case. More specifically, the case focused on three key areas that applied to each of the research projects.

They included designing a community-based research framework that grew from the needs of a community; conducting the research within courses that utilized student-centered, problem-based, experiential teaching and learning; and assessing the effectiveness of the research projects in terms of both student learning competencies as well as sustainable community development. We mindfully selected CBR, as previously described, as our experiential framework for teaching sustainable tourism development. While those outside the discipline of hospitality and tourism might not immediately make the same conclusion, we view sustainability, sustainable community development, and sustainable tourism development as inseparably entwined. All require careful examination of the environmental, social, and economic impacts their implementation will create, and all are affected by their particular social, cultural, physical, and political environment. All require the public will to make policies and enforce appropriate practices.

Some of the specific types of sustainable tourism development-related data that must be collected and analyzed include inventory of tourism attractions; visitor numbers; types of visitors; spending patterns of visitors; the potential of the area to influence their customer markets and economic base; and their natural, cultural, and financial resources. Other types of data include physical and social carrying capacities and the cultural capacity to make sound policies. Sustainability is socially constructed and, as such, is heavily influenced by various and often competing stakeholders.

Suffice it to say, just telling students that sustainable tourism development involves interaction with competing stakeholders is both necessary and desirable, and giving them various definitions and a list of the steps that a community must take in order to achieve sustainable development is almost a useless endeavor. While students might become convinced that sustainable development is a good objective and could pass a test on the definitions of sustainable tourism and the action steps to achieve it, they would neither have any practical ideas on how to help a community achieve sustainable development nor would they have the necessary skill set to affect the desired outcome. Understanding the uniqueness of place that each community possesses and the different set of circumstances, stakeholder interests, opportunities and challenges, resources, and so forth that it exhibits is a daunting task, let alone working as a coparticipant in a research project with members of its community who have different notions about the level of sustainable tourism development they wish to see implemented. Another challenge was convincing students that not only was research a type of experiential learning, but that it was fun to find out new information, turn it inside out to extract meaning and use it to solve problems for themselves and for others (Lowry, 1991). However, the most challenging obstacle that the authors faced in the CBR process was preparing students for chaos, the unexpected, the reality of politics, and the uncertainty inherent in living, working, and succeeding in a messy and complex world.

In the following community-based research projects, students were asked to use their knowledge of sustainable development and its importance to the well-being of communities as they worked with community partners to find sustainable tourism solutions and recommendations.

CBR Project 1: An Undergraduate Honors Thesis

The Tri-Community Area Chamber of Commerce approached the Hospitality and Tourism Management Department at the university in August 2000 about the possibility of conducting a study for the region. The Chamber had various expectations regarding the kind of information and analyses it required and wanted to coparticipate in the research process. In general, it wanted a profile of visitors and of the tourist-sector businesses as well as an assessment of the impacts of tourism on the Greater Sturbridge, Massachusetts area. Chamber leaders also wanted an assessment of the current and potential conditions for the development of a convention-sector market for their community. As they currently did not have any of this type of data, they envisioned this CBR project as a benchmark tourism study for the area that would provide valuable information for its various stakeholders. The Chamber, the general community, the business community, policy makers, and investors were the key stakeholders who would benefit from the study and using it, they could begin developing a responsible strategy for sustainable tourism development. When the Honors Student took on the project, he, his Thesis Chair, and the university also became stakeholders in the research process and outcomes produced.

The establishment of the research agenda, the methodological framework, and the survey instruments used were based on the various expectations of the Chamber; the private sector, which it serves; and the citizens of the community. It evolved through numerous meetings with the stakeholders and it included both the Honors Student and his Thesis Chair.

The objectives of the study were multifaceted and overlapping to a certain degree, and the results would be used to develop sustainable tourism in the Tri-County Area. All of the objectives involved the collection of primary data through face-to-face, in-depth interviews with both visitors and tourism-related business owners or managers. The specific objectives included the following: to assess selected aspects of the economic impact of tourism on the Greater Sturbridge area; to assess the current convention market conditions within the Greater Sturbridge area; to profile the visitors and businesses within the Greater Sturbridge area; to identify and classify the tourism-related businesses; and to create a study to serve as a model for future research or expanded investigation.

The Honors Student, a team of tourism students who were specifically trained to conduct intercept interviews for this project, the Honors Thesis Chair, and stakeholder groups in the community helped to collect the data. While the community stakeholders did not conduct the actual intercept interviews, they provided access to their places of business for the purpose of conducting the interviews. Each of the stakeholders was invested in the research project; was anxious to use the data to make planning, policy, and/or development decisions; and was committed to the success of the project.

The Honors Student entered and statistically analyzed the survey data and developed conclusions and recommendations. This CBR constituted his honors research and thesis. He gave a formal presentation summarizing his findings for the stakeholders who had participated in the project. An executive summary, produced by the chair of the thesis committee, was made available to the community through the Chamber of Commerce. The various stakeholders were pleased to participate and immediately began to use the findings and recommendations to inform their own strategy for sustainable tourism development.

CBR Project 2: A Junior-Level Class Project

The IBI Group (a consulting firm that held the contract for construction of a comprehensive traveler and tourism information system that would increase tourism, travel safety, and economic development in northwestern Massachusetts) approached the university's Hospitality and Tourism Management Department in August 2002 about conducting capacity-building research for their project. They had very clearly defined objectives and expectations and wanted students in the fall 2002 Tour Management class to help them build capacity for their database. The database of tourism attractions would be featured in a searchable format on their Web site. Visitors and potential visitors to the area could plan their own activities, map them, and in many cases book rooms or make dinner reservations. They viewed the situation as a win for themselves and for the students in the class. IBI obtained free labor from students who had an academic understanding of tourism capacity building, and the students engaged in experiential learning that was related to their discipline of study and helped with the new economic development initiative for northwestern Massachusetts.

The objectives of the project already had been established through a bid process and a series of meetings between the Franklin Country Chamber of Commerce, the Massachusetts Highway Department, and the IBI Group. The specifics of what the UMass Amherst class could and could not do, the time frame in which the research could occur, and the possible outcome were all arrived at through meetings with the IBI consultant who was responsible for the project and the professor who was responsible for the course.

The overall goals of the project were to increase the availability and quality of information available to the traveling public through a variety of modular, Web-based tools; to improve the experience of travelers already in the region; to encourage travelers to stay in the region longer; and to attract new visitors to the region. Capturing Interstate-91 corridor pass-through traffic was a goal and one of the instruments for achieving it was the development of a comprehensive

Web site (http://www.masscountryroads.com), which included information on attractions, lodging, dining, events, services, and so forth; recommended tours and itineraries; customized and printable itineraries; mapping and powerful mapping tools; e-marketing of local products; advertising and sponsorships. In general, the Web-based system would cater to the independent travel planner by providing an attractive image for the region and offer information, tools, and suggested itineraries.

Students were assigned to develop a tour itinerary for a weekend trip (two to three days) that catered to a specific market segment and showcased the attractions of the region. The tour was geared toward an independent traveler using the project Web site to plan a trip. Each of the 11 five-student teams was assigned a specific tour theme and demographic profile. They were told that their tours should incorporate the following elements: a brief overview that sells your tour; a tour narrative; attractions; special events (if any); lodging; dining in the area; and other noteworthy features or information. Student teams also were told to focus primarily on the Franklin County area; that their tours could be, but were not required to be, routed; and that they should not be over-planned (e.g., they should, where possible, include choices for attractions, dining, lodging, and so forth). The IBI Group consultant briefed the students on their role in the project and the specific parameters for the outcomes they produced and was available to them through e-mail; and he came to the class to check on their progress at the midpoint of the semester.

Student teams organized their own timetable and the roles of their individual team members. They collected as much secondary data as possible on the tourism inventory of the area, and then they ventured forth into the community to assess the quality and draw of the attractions, accommodations, food and beverage establishment, and so forth. From their composite resource inventories and their assessment of the quality and drawing power of these resources, they designed tour products for their assignment markets.

At the end of the semester, each of the student teams gave a formal presentation of its tour product for representatives of the Massachusetts Highway Department, the Greenfield Chamber of Commerce, and the IBI Group. Their database of the tourism capacity of the Franklin County region and the tour products they created were turned over to the IBI Group, who incorporated them into their own database, which was used to produce the traveler and tourism information system (http://www.masscountryroads.com). This was used as a tool for economic development and eventually sustainable tourism in the region.

CBR Project 3:
A Graduate-Level Industry Research Project

The Greater Northampton Chamber of Commerce came to the Hospitality and Tourism Management Department in May 2002, citing their need to develop a visitor profile for the community. In several meetings with a tourism professor, they discussed the type of information they wanted to collect, various ways to construct the survey instrument, potential questions to ask, and the best way to distribute the survey and ensure a sufficient response rate. Eventually the Tourism Committee of the Chamber established the objectives of the project and designed a survey instrument that could be used to build the visitor database and develop a visitor profile for the community. They devised a plan for distributing the survey and enlisted the help of thirteen different points-of-purchase and high-traffic locations in Northampton that would distribute and collect the self-administered surveys. They also created an incentive for visitors to complete the survey. After this phase of the project was completed and 2,972 surveys were collected, they approached the Hospitality and Tourism Management Department about the possibility of entering the data and analyzing the results. This phase of the project was suitable for a graduate-level industry project.

A graduate student in the department elected to undertake the data entry and statistical analysis of the data as a formalized Graduate-Level Industry Project. The Industry Project is a type of directed-research project that is one of the departmental options for its master's students. She completed her analysis of the data and her findings, conclusions, and recommendations formed the basis of a visitor profile for the community. The raw data became part of a visitor database for the Chamber. Her research report was given to the Tourism Committee of the Chamber, which used the information to inform its members and develop strategies for sustainable tourism development.

IMPLICATIONS AND CONCLUSIONS

The three projects varied in terms of inclusiveness and scope of work, and all used a CBR framework. The research process was guided through teamwork, and both leadership and communication skills were necessary ingredients for their success. There was a high degree of accountability on the part of all participants. In all three cases, students produced the research products that were needed by their community partners. The community partners were pleased with the students' work and enthusiastic about using the information to make critical decisions about sustainable tourism development.

Although students were able to participate only in limited phases of the sustainable tourism development process, they learned leadership skills, communications skills, the skills for critical analysis, and the ability to cope with the unexpected. They understood, from a practical perspective, how to work with communities to achieve sustainable development and the need for and challenge of building relationships. They gained a better understanding of the needs of other people, and they also reflected on their own experience and gained the confidence to solve problems and answer questions through the research process. Students also discovered that research can be fun, and it is often like a road trip—the experiences and sights along the way are often better than the destination.

We are reminded of the quote from Jacques de Bourbon-Busset: "What we want is not to guess at the probable future, but to prepare one that is desirable and perhaps even go that bit further and try to make the desirable future the probable one" (Müller, 2001, p. 61). Creating tomorrow's leaders and living in a sustainable environment do not happen by chance. The CBR projects conducted by the authors of this study and their students not only served specific needs of the community, they also helped students develop knowledge and skills that prepared them for active civic engagement. Simultaneously, they helped students develop knowledge and skills that prepared them for careers in tourism management; honed their awareness of the need for sustainable tourism planning and development; and gave them the tools to help communities achieve it. We found that the unique inclusiveness of the CBR model and its departure from the traditional research models gave it transformative power not only in assisting communities with sustainable development but also in shaping students' values.

Leaders creating a just and compassionate world are the cornerstones of sustainability. Not only had we found sources that enabled us to choose which form of experiential teaching and learning that would best serve our curricular needs, we also found a few sources that corroborated our own findings. Bradbury (2003, p. 1) found that "a growing number of corporations, especially multi-nationals, are embracing practices associated with sustainable development." Her work suggested that students who are exposed to the concept of sustainable development as it relates to their own lives and to the lives of other peoples and organizations become better systems thinkers. Pesonen also found that "environmental issues, as one dimension of corporate social responsibility, are an important element in the management of both private and public organizations" (2003, p. 1). In addition, she cited the increased demands from stakeholder groups regarding the environmental performance of a company's products and processes as a reason for integrating environmental sustainability issues into business school curricula.

Kearins and Springett (2003) suggested that pedagogy that uses critical theory is essential to environmental management and sustainability and cited specific skills such as reflexivity, critique, and social action/engagement, which are vital components of this type of pedagogy. Welsh and Murry (2003) also found that critical pedagogy that uses a collaborative approach and a real-world context empowers students to think about innovation from a sustainability perspective. Similar to these authors, Croy and Hall (2003) used CBR to help students learn research methods and carry out research projects that were needed by the community while simultaneously helping the community to develop tourism in a sustainable way.

Currently, one of the key areas of discussion among academics in the tourism field is the need for more community involvement in the process of sustainable tourism development (Hardy & Beeton, 2001; Hardy, Beeton, & Pearson, 2002; Liu, 2003). We believe that by continuing the practice of embedding sustainable development in our curriculum through the use of CBR as an experiential connection to a dynamic community, we will be able to fulfill our mission "to teach, advance, and support the practice and management of the hospitality and tourism industries" and continue to be one of the top departments of hospitality and tourism management in the nation.

REFERENCES

Association for Experiential Education. (2002). *Experiential education defined.* Retrieved September 15, 2003, from http://www.aee.org/ndef.html.

Axel-Lute, M. (1999, November/December). Town & gown: Making research serve communities' needs. *Shelterforce Online—The Journal of Affordable Housing and Community, 108.*

Barron, P., & Prideaux, B. (1998). Hospitality education in Tanzania: Is there a need to develop environmental awareness? *Journal of Sustainable Tourism, 6*(3), 224-237.

Bradbury, H. (2003). Sustaining inner and outer worlds: A whole-systems approach to developing sustainable business practices in management. *Journal of Management Education, 27*(2), 172-187.

Campus Compact. (2003). *The essential services learning resources brochure.* Retrieved September 15, 2003 from http://www.compact.org/faculty/SL-brochure.pdf.

Chopyak, J. (1999). Community-based research: Research for action. *The Evaluation Exchange, 5*(2/3), 14-15. Retrieved September 15, 2003, from http://gseweb.harvard.edu/~hfrp/~hfrp/eval/issue14/eval14/pdf.

Croy, W., & Hall, C. (2003). Developing a tourism knowledge: Educating the student, developing the rural area. *Journal of Teaching in Travel & Tourism, 3*(1), 3-24.

Eyler, J. (2000). Strategic directions for service-learning research, 2000). What do we most need to know about the impact of service-learning on student learning? [Special Issue]. *Michigan Journal of Community Service Learning.* Retrieved September 23, 2003, from http://www.umich.edu/~mjcsl/.

Eyler, J., & Giles, D. (1999). *Where's the learning in service-learning?* San Francisco: Jossey-Bass.

Gartner, W. (1996). *Tourism development: Principles, processes, and policies.* New York: Van Nostrand Reinhold.

Gourman, J. (1996). *The Gourman Report: A rating of graduate and professional programs in American and international universities* (7th Ed.). New Jersey: Princeton Review Publishing.

Gunn, C. (1994). *Tourism planning: Basics, concepts, cases* (3rd Ed.). Washington, DC: Taylor & Francis.

Hardy, A., & Beeton, R. (2001). Sustainable tourism or maintainable tourism: Managing resources for more than average outcomes. *Journal of Sustainable Tourism, 9*(3), 168-192.

Hardy, A., Beeton, R., & Pearson, L. (2002). Sustainable tourism: An overview of the concept and its position in relationship to conceptualizations of tourism. *Journal of Sustainable Tourism, 10*(6), 475-496.

Harris, R., Griffin, T., & Williams, P. (Eds.). (2002). *Sustainable tourism: A global perspective*. London: Butterworth Heinemann.

Harrison , L., & Husbands, W. (Eds.). (1996). *Practicing responsible tourism: International case studies in tourism planning, policy, and development*. New York: John Wiley & Sons.

Harrison, N. (2000). *Constructing sustainable development*. Albany, NY: State University of New York Press.

International Consortium for Experiential Learning. (2000). What is "experiential learning?" Retrieved September 15, 2003, from http://www.el.uct.ac.za/icel/.

Itian, C. (1999). Reasserting the philosophy of experiential education as a vehicle for change in the 21st century. *Journal of Experiential Education, 22*(2), 91-98.

Jamal, T. (2004). Virtue ethics and sustainable tourism pedagogy: Phronesis, principles and practice. *Journal of Sustainable Tourism, 12*(6), 530-545.

Jurowski, C. (2002). BEST think tanks and the development of curriculum modules for teaching sustainability principles. *Journal of Sustainable Tourism, 10*(6), 536-545.

Kearins, K., & Springett, D. (2003). Educating for sustainability: Developing critical skills. *Journal of Management Education, 27*(2), 188-204.

Liu, Z. (2003). Sustainable tourism development: A critique. *Journal of Sustainable Tourism, 11*(6), 459-475.

Lowry, L. (1991). Research & teaching: Not separate issues. *News & Views: The Newsletter of the International Society of Travel & Tourism Educator, 6*(1), 2.

McKercher, B. (1993). Some fundamental truths about tourism: Understanding tourism's social and environmental impacts. *Journal of Sustainable Tourism, 1*(1), 6-16.

Mitchell, M., & Poutiatine, M. (2001). Finding an experiential approach in graduate leadership curricula. *Journal of Experiential Education, 24*(3), 179-185.

Müller, H. (2001). Tourism and hospitality into the 21st century. In A. Lockwood & S. Medlik (Eds.), *Tourism and hospitality in the 21st century* (pp. 61-70). Oxford: Butterworth Heinemann.

National Commission on Service Learning. (2003). Defining service-learning. In *Learning in deed: The power of service-learning for American schools*. Scotts Valley, CA: Author. Available online: National Commission on Service-Learning Final Report. Retrieved September 27, 2003 from http://servicelearningcommission.org/slcommission/learningindeed.pdf.

National Service-Learning Clearinghouse. (2003). *Service-learning is . . .* Retrieved September 27, 2003 from http://www.servicelearning.org/article/archive/35.

Pesonen, H. (2003). Challenges of integrating environmental sustainability issues into business school curriculum: A case study from the University of Jyvaskyla, Finland. *Journal of Management Education, 27*(2), 158-171.

Rees, E. (1989). Defining sustainable development. *CHS Research Bulletin*, University of British Columbia, (May), 3.

Sclove, R., Scammell, M., & Holland, B. (1998). Community-based research in the United States: An introductory reconnaissance, including twelve organizational case studies and comparison with the Dutch science shops and the mainstream American research system—Executive summary (July). Amherst, MA: The Loka Institute. Retrieved September 6, 2003, from http://www.loka.org.

Service Connections. (2003). To the next level: Erlich Award winner discusses the future of the service learning movement. *Service Connections: The Newsletter of the Massachusetts Campus Compact, 8*(2).

Smith, V., & Brent, M. (Eds.). (2001). *Hosts and guests revisited: Tourism issues of the 21st century.* New York: Cognizant Communication Corporation.

Stanton, T. (2000). Linking service with academic study: Stanford's lessons in service-learning. university lecture, Vanderbilt University, February 10. Retrieved September 15, 2003, from http://www.el.uct.ac.za/sl/resources/tim-vdbyl-paper.PDF.

Stoecker, R. (1999, November/December). Roles for academics in research for social change. *Shelterforce Online—The Journal of Affordable Housing and Community, 108.* Retrieved September 27, 2003, from
http://www.nhi.org/online/issues/108/towngown.html.

Strand, K., Marullo, S., Cutforth, N., & Stoecker, R. (2003). *Community-based research and higher education: Principles and practices.* San Francisco: Jossey-Bass.

Tourism Canada. (1990). *An action strategy for sustainable tourism development: Globe '90.* Ottawa: Author.

Tribe, J. (2002). Education for ethical tourism action. *Journal of Sustainable Tourism, 10*(4), 309-324.

Waldstein, F., & Reiher, T. (2001). Service-learning and student's personal and civic development. *Journal of Experiential Education, 24*(1), 7-13.

Weaver, D., & Lawton, L. (2002). *Tourism management* (2nd ed.). Queensland: John Wiley & Sons Australia Ltd.

Welsh, M., & Murry, D. (2003). The ecollaborative: Teaching sustainability through critical pedagogy. *Journal of Management Education, 27*(2), 220-236.

World Commission on Environment and Development. (1987). *Our common future (The Brundtland Report).* London: Oxford University Press.

SECTION TWO:
The Regional and Global Fabric

CHAPTER 7

Building Sustainable Community/University Partnerships in a Metropolitan Setting*

Alan Bloomgarden, Mary Bombardier, Myrna M. Breitbart, Kiara Nagel, and Preston H. Smith II

The Pioneer Valley in Western Massachusetts is home to the Five College consortium, which includes three small private liberal arts colleges, Amherst, Mount Holyoke, and Smith Colleges; an innovative and experimental institution, Hampshire College; and the state's flagship campus, the University of Massachusetts at Amherst. For nearly 40 years, the consortium has served as a vehicle for collaboration and resource sharing among the five colleges, including in the field of community-based learning (CBL).

Interest in CBL intensified locally and nationally in the mid-1980s. Individual faculty and staff at each of the colleges began to adopt CBL into their teaching, research, and community service in the Pioneer Valley. Since each of the schools brings a unique culture and set of resources to community outreach and practice, the nature of conversations and the infrastructures developed to support such work looked very different from campus to campus. In 1995, the Five College CBL Committee, composed of faculty and directors of CBL programs, was formed to jointly gain more visibility and legitimacy for CBL work on the campuses and to address the weaknesses that prevented the work from having the most positive and sustainable impact on community needs.

*The authors express their gratitude to Sara Littlecrow Russell for her editorial contributions to this chapter.

Although some reciprocal projects had been created over the years between the area colleges and community organizations, up to that point the majority of relationships were imbalanced, providing more benefits to student learning and college public relations than to community organizations. Community partners faced constant requests from colleges for research sites, short-term internships or orientations to the community, yet our institutions remained ill-prepared and ill-equipped to respond to requests for sustained assistance. Poor communication among the colleges duplicated efforts and demanded even more from already overburdened community organizations.

In its first years, the CBL Committee hosted several faculty workshops, introducing concepts and successful models in CBL to encourage more faculty members to get involved and to foster relationships among them and non-profit leaders. In 1999-2000, Hampshire College hosted a Five College seminar funded by the Teagle Foundation, providing course development grants for faculty at all five institutions. Collaborative facilitation and teaching in the seminar helped to solidify common goals, yield future projects, and foster community/campus dialogue. In January 2001, a forum that was specially designed to further dialogue featured Ken Reardon, a professor of urban planning at Cornell University who has done groundbreaking work in this field (Reardon, 1994, 1998).

More than 50 community leaders came to Hampshire College's events venue, the Red Barn, to share with an equal number of faculty and staff from the colleges the message to "get our act together" with regard to collaboration. Carlos Vega of Nueva Esperanza, a community development corporation in Holyoke, recounted how he had spent many hours being interviewed by students not connected with each other or each other's work, who time and again reinvented their inquiry into Holyoke's history and the city's Latino community. While he generously provided the students with time as a long-term investment in his organization's relationship with the area colleges, when he asked the students for their papers at the end of the semester, "about half of them gave me the paper and the other half, I never saw again." Participants in the forum responded by calling for the design of more efficient and effective means of college and community interaction and greater transparency in the processes and opportunities for accessing college resources, such as internships, faculty research, and collaborative grants. We asked Nueva Esperanza and other community-based organizations (CBO's) how we might make better use of student research hours for community needs, without compromising students' achievement of their academic goals. Could such processes simultaneously value and strengthen the knowledge and skills of community leaders? Could we find ways to better coordinate the CBL efforts for a higher degree of community benefit? Ultimately, we were led to question what we were seeking to achieve by this college/community collaboration.

COMMUNITY/COLLEGE PARTNERSHIPS:
GUIDANCE FROM THE LITERATURE

Much of the literature on college/community partnerships begins by defending and promoting the idea of an "engaged" institution of higher learning and the practice of "civic responsibility" as an *institutional* rather than individual obligation to enhance community capacity (Dugery & Knowles, 2003; Holland, 2001; Ramaley, 2000). If one of the aims of a partnership is to enhance community capacity, we would ask, "capacity to do what?" Is the goal to enable community partners to enter more effectively into service-learning partnerships with institutions of higher learning or to meet some other criteria with respect to addressing critical local needs? Are those goals mutually exclusive or dependent upon one another? Literature on community/college partnerships is rarely explicit about the goals (suggesting mainly that partners agree on them). Yet goals can range from creating opportunities for students and faculty to become better citizens while communities better understand their problems, to striving for full-scale societal change and social justice.

Although there is little attention focused on specific goals, partnership literature does identify institutional practices that both create obstacles to and further college-community relationships (see for example, Leiderman et al., 2003; Perkins & Wandersman, 1990; Silka, 2001). For example, academic cultures that marginalize applied research and learning outside the classroom and the distinct cultures of institutions of higher education and the communities that surround them, are frequently cited as obstacles (Ramaley, 2000; Sandmann & Baker-Clark, 1997). Focusing our attention on the power and resource discrepancies between academic institutions and community entities, Compton critiques this idea of borders, believing that it obscures recognition of unequal distributions of resources and power among partners (2003, pp. 10-11).

Based on Cruz and Giles' understanding of partnerships as a means to a larger end—greater social justice—one of our goals is to increase community access to resources to address the inequities in resource distribution between colleges and community-based organizations serving low-income populations. Resonant with Cruz and Giles, we assess the success of partnerships by asking two key questions: Is the service, the learning, or the ability to address local needs better because of the partnership? And has the community identified more assets and acquired greater access to resources (Cruz & Giles, 2000, p. 31)? By attempting to correct the imbalance of resources in our partnership relationships, we consider how participatory regional community development might enable a community-defined agenda to emerge and accommodate diverse priorities among our CBO partners and among our diverse institutions of higher education.

Much of the literature focuses on markers of good CBL practice, such as relationship and trust building at all stages of the process (but especially in the earliest stage of partnership development); shared control of the partnership and its continual reassessment; respect for diverse knowledge (academic/theoretical vs. practical/experiential); accountability on the part of academic partners in working with the community; the integration of community partners into campus life and preparation of faculty and students for community-based work; a long-term sustainable commitment of resources and positive outcomes for all parties involved (Campus Compact, 2003).

The adoption of the these markers suggests that more institutions of higher education are seeking greater reciprocity and are abandoning the practice of imposing academic-defined problems on communities or utilizing the resources of community-based organizations without providing much in return. However, even this literature on relationship development tends to focus on the construction of limited partnerships between a single institution of higher education and a single (or a few) community-based organizations. In contrast, the Five College consortium is a "loose" collaboration in which institutions retain distinct authority over policies and the commitment of resources. The recent addition of Holyoke Community College (HCC) into this planning group introduces even more complexities for what has become known as the Holyoke Planning Network (HPN).

Currently, HPN involves six institutions of higher learning (all but one of which reside outside the geographic limits of the community) and a multitude of community-based organizations. As we move beyond a phase of initial relationship development to utilizing the best practices of CBL in the construction of alliances among the colleges and CBOs, this situation presents many challenges and opportunities. Addressing the power differentials in terms of access to resources occupies a considerable amount of our time even while we seek ways to generate more resources to address critical community needs. Our interest in considering how community/college partnerships might promote greater equalization of power and resources through joint research, projects, and social actions, leads us to the primary issues we address here:

- How do we build a regional coalition among institutions that support varying levels and types of activity in the city of Holyoke?
- How can we most effectively pursue institutional buy-in from institutions at different levels, through different processes, and within different time frames?
- How can partnerships promote the acquisition of resources for community partners and further community control of those resources while also promoting the campus acquisition of new knowledge and innovative pedagogical practices?
- How can we create mechanisms for college administrators, development officers, and potential partnership funders that acknowledge the provision of community resources that will enrich student learning and faculty research?

INITIAL EFFORTS TO FORGE
COLLEGE/COMMUNITY LINKAGES

Since addressing CBL problems of practice was a parallel priority to advancing CBL as a component of campus teaching and research, we began early on to design concrete projects that would create a more coordinated infrastructure among our institutions. They included coordinating training and transportation for students, creating community access and transportation to our campuses, and increasing outreach. As an additional measure, a CBL Web site was designed. Our next priority became the development and implementation of good practice with an appropriate subset of community partners.

Holyoke was the obvious location for our coordination efforts because it was the city where each of the Five Colleges and HCC had placed hundreds of student interns, launched several large research projects, and interviewed many community members and organizations. Countless research papers had been written about Holyoke on subjects as wide ranging as analyses of asthma prevalence and mental health issues, assessments of affordable housing and healthcare access, and investigations into the impact of systemic racism and multigenerational poverty. In spite of this research and the efforts of individuals on the various campuses to address the issue of reciprocity, Holyoke nonprofits continued to struggle for survival in an environment of fiscal cutbacks. At its most fundamental elements, the process of researching the Holyoke community remained inequitable.

Holyoke is a compelling place to research and serve because it is one of the poorest cities in Massachusetts, yet has many untapped assets. It currently provides jobs for many residents who live (and pay taxes) in bordering towns and is a resource to area colleges (who also do not pay taxes to the city). From our perspective, there was and is a potential for natural reciprocity, as yet unrealized. Area educational institutions already had a stake in Holyoke's economic health, and an economically healthy Holyoke would reward these institutions by greatly enhancing the colleges' attractiveness as institutions of higher learning. In a successful community/college partnership, we would play a crucial role in lending intellectual and human capital to economic development efforts. HPN's role would be to help our educational institutions understand that sharing resources with Holyoke's CBOs is working toward a common goal of revitalization, addressing the city's problems and building upon its assets.

Planning the Planners Network Conference

HPN wanted to evolve from holding seminars to effecting similar changes to what Ken Reardon and the University of Illinois had spearheaded in East St. Louis (Reardon, 1994, 1998). Reardon was also a member of the national steering committee of the Planners Network, an association of professionals, activists, academics, and students who use planning as a tool for strategically allocating resources to promote fundamental change at the urban basis of our political and economic systems. When he approached Hampshire College's Community Partnerships for Social Change Program (CPSC) to host the 2002 Planners Network conference in Western Massachusetts, CPSC director Mary Bombardier, Professor Myrna Breitbart, and CPSC Program Coordinator Kiara Nagel saw the conference as a springboard for current community-based learning efforts and as an opportunity to create an innovative model of accountability and collaboration among members of the academic community and representatives from the Holyoke nonprofit community.

With its strong history of social commitment, Hampshire College supported CPSC, to lead in the creation of this innovative model of educational partnership in conjunction with leaders from Holyoke's nonprofit community, the Holyoke Office of Planning, and faculty and staff from area colleges. Nueva Esperanza, a community development organization in Holyoke with a long-standing relationship to CPSC, was approached to be the lead community organization and work with academic partners to create a steering committee. The steering committee created a conference vision and planned the details for a national gathering in Holyoke.

From the outset, our organizing circle sought to break down traditional community/campus boundaries. We worked daily to develop a decision-making process that respected each person's opinions with equal weight without being influenced by the notions of status or power that exist in academia, city governments, and most nonprofits. Our meetings often began as brainstorming sessions and ended up as graphic depictions of the intense struggles that community leaders have faced in the last 20 years of working in Holyoke. These conversations were critical to rebuilding trust and establishing relationships among socially and economically disparate groups; they also forged a unified vision for change. Under this vision, we hoped to use the conference to:

- Explore new solutions to old problems, address barriers to change, and create a collaborative new vision for the city of Holyoke and its surroundings.
- Showcase Holyoke and the innovative work of community-based organizations, articulate their specific planning and organizing needs, and engage in dialogue about these self-identified needs with local and national consultants.
- Develop effective working relationships.

Conference Highlights

"New Visions for Historic Cities: Bridging Divides, Building Futures" took place in June 2002. It included no scholarly lectures or theoretical papers. Instead, there were vibrant panels, workshops, and activities, each carefully structured to balance the representation of academics and community organizers. A bus tour oriented participants to Holyoke and its diverse neighborhoods and issues. Site visits allowed participants to dialogue with community members and see innovative neighborhood projects firsthand. A local theater group performed a play on the industrial history of the city and its canals. A featured artist introduced the keynote speaker with a poem. A local teen sang the U.S. and Puerto Rican national anthems. Throughout the conference, national perspectives and issues were balanced by local ones, academic standpoints with community views. The dialogue was rich and multilayered. Late one evening, as an 11-piece salsa band played, the relationships that the conference had renewed and revisioned between the academic community and the people of Holyoke erupted into an enthusiastic intergenerational version of the Electric Slide, and the dance floor was filled with laughing steering-committee members, urban planners, college professors, students, teens, and Holyoke families.

The most important long-term effect of the conference was a powerful demonstration of coalition building supported at its foundation by a commitment to an equitable planning process. By collaboratively creating a conference of many voices, the very planning process presented a model for how we wanted our academic institutions to engage with the Holyoke community. As such, the conference not only laid a foundation for increased cooperation among Hampshire, Mount Holyoke, Smith, Amherst and UMass Amherst, but also provided a model for these institutions to work collaboratively in the community of Holyoke.

The visible success of the National Planners Network conference inspired many people to harness the momentum and incorporate lessons into new models of community-based learning and partnerships. The steering committee continued to meet and was joined by representatives from other local colleges, the university, and Holyoke-based organizations. The profound and lasting partnerships with community-based organizations in South Holyoke have continued to evolve under the name of the HPN. As the Network seeks to secure funding and academic administrative commitments to this planning work, tension is fed by competition for resources, lack of focus, unclear priorities, and the dismal economic climate. The challenge of reconciling the priorities of academic institutions with those of the community still remains large and threatens the fragile trust that the conference planning was able to create.

As Five College CBL faculty and staff continued to explore metropolitan issues with community partners, questions of resources and institutional buy-in for enhanced community partnership in Holyoke came up in two related contexts. These contexts were the development of a HUD Community Outreach Partnership Center (COPC) grant and building the relationship between HCC and the Five College consortium.

THE HUD COPC PROPOSAL PROCESS

HPN began planning for a HUD COPC grant to focus our community/ university dialogue on the partnership goal of creating a permanent physical presence in Holyoke as a means to sustain reciprocal community and educational programming. From the perspective of community organizations, COPC funds and the accompanying structural relations between higher education and community partners mandated by the grant's operating environment (a solid, matching-funds supported infrastructure) promised real cash and partnership activities with equally real potential to address community challenges by building on Holyoke's assets. From the perspective of academic partners, a COPC framework promised a focal point for an institutional/city partnership on which we could further the wide range of small-scale partnership activities in which we were engaged. To HPN as a whole, the COPC was seen as a vehicle to overcome the geographic divide between Holyoke and our various institutional settings in Amherst, South Hadley, and Northampton. It could address the logistical and infrastructural challenges in our construction of programming for students, faculty, staff, and community members in Holyoke. We believed that Holyoke's demographics made the argument for external support in both the grant's and our own identified areas (education, economic development, and community capacity building) especially compelling to our institutions and prospective funding sources. We hoped to create a model similar to the outstanding UMass Lowell community outreach partnership center and to advocate for HPN faculty to be given release time to teach CBL courses and/or do community-based research in accordance with the needs of the Holyoke community.

In Fall 2002, we began the discussion of applying for the HUD COPC grant. Despite strong enthusiasm, we faced two major challenges. First, seeking institutional cash commitments to meet federal matching requirements would be difficult during a period of budget cutbacks, and some colleges were uncertain about institutional commitment to a college/community partnership with Holyoke. Second, we believed our consortial approach to a COPC grant would pose practical challenges to HUD grantors and invite skepticism. Yet we felt that our metropolitan approach to urban issues could better address community issues while providing a vehicle for academic institutions from more affluent towns and cities to share their resources with Holyoke. Under this model, metropolitan and regional collaboration held the promise of creating institutional/community partnerships that allowed institutions too small to independently venture large-scale community collaboration to pool intellectual, human, and financial resources.

In March 2003, HPN held a meeting to invite community-based organizations, social and governmental agencies, and additional educators to participate in this dialogue. Several community, public, and social agencies participated and seemed excited about the prospect of a more fruitful partnership. The meeting was successful in both communicating the potential of such a partnership and in yielding participation from previously external constituencies. HCC's role in HPN discussions had been rather limited, yet HCC made strides to connect with community-based organizations in Holyoke and sought greater cooperation with area academic institutions involved with Holyoke. Representatives from HCC and from their engaged community partners urged the HPN conveners to adjust both their perspective and language to reflect a strategic vision more inclusive of the efforts and goals of HCC in community partnership. The strong and welcome presence of HCC's direct participation in the March 2003 meeting and more indirectly through the circle of community partners with whom they were becoming actively engaged in a parallel process (the "Avanza" initiative, focused on Latino educational attainment in Holyoke) was a positive, if complicating, development. Through subsequent HPN "summit" meetings in April and May 2003, senior HCC administrators and community members worked hard to bridge historic differences and emerged with a renewed commitment to developing community leadership in educational support programming. As a result, HPN fully became a "six college" collaboration.

While it is unusual to found college/community partnership upon such a consortium, we believe that aiming to coordinate, clarify, and amplify partnership activity across institutional relationships is the best strategy for gaining significant metropolitan impact, despite a period of serious institutional and municipal budgetary constraints. The March 2003 meeting also yielded three core community-driven partnership foci for Holyoke—education, economic development, and capacity building for CBOs. Our COPC framework first connected existing community initiatives with existing college and university teaching, research, and service resources. In its second phase, these groups worked collaboratively to identify unmet community needs as well as potential community and higher education assets that could address those needs. In its third phase, a partnership framework would be constructed, which would allow these and additional collaborations to benefit the community and institutional partners in a more sustained, cost-effective, and mutually beneficial way.

We developed our COPC application by surveying our own institutions' commitments in Holyoke and proposing a COPC-supported framework that would improve Five College/Holyoke collaborations in relationship to these identified programmatic commitments. During our planning, HCC questioned where HPN's Five College participants stood in regard to their own institutional commitments, and it was revealed that senior Five College administrators were only sporadically involved. In response, the Five College staff and faculty worked to secure more explicit commitments from their senior administrators; however, both the economic climate and the lack of in-depth understanding of CBL on the part of administrators left us unable to secure sufficient high-level commitment to proceed with the 2003 COPC grant. This experience demonstrated to us the critical need to educate administrators about the dramatic successes of other

CBL work and to build a greater awareness of the value of CBL work on our respective campuses.

The HUD COPC Proposal Process Revisited

In Spring 2004, HPN members renewed the discussion of a HUD COPC grant. We had recently become aware that the Extension Office at the University of Massachusetts had hired a grant writer to write a COPC proposal. The grant writer originally sought to build a partnership with a rural county north of the university, but was interested in HPN's work in Holyoke. After an initial meeting with the Extension Office, HPN split into two working groups to decide which projects to include in the COPC proposal. It soon became clear that the amount of money was quite small in relation to our goals. Our CBO members felt that obtaining a COPC grant and spreading its resources equitably would attract more CBO interest and lend us greater credibility to apply for other grants. Mindful of past experience, HPN academic members concentrated on eliciting support from senior administrators. As a result, academic partners committed cash and in-kind resources such as significant time commitments from faculty and staff. These direct and indirect matching funds supported a strong COPC application.

RECENT HPN PROJECTS

The core areas that had been identified by the Holyoke community in March 2003 as focal points for partnership were education, economic development, and capacity-building. As HPN continued to focus on these areas, three projects emerged.

Grant-Writing Workshop in Holyoke

In February 2004, a grants-writing workshop for Holyoke CBOs was coordinated by Alan Bloomgarden, a member of HPN who worked as a development officer at Smith College. CBOs in Holyoke have been hard hit by the fiscal crisis in Massachusetts. In response to the desiccation of state government funds, Holyoke CBOs were turning to grants to prevent severe budget shortfalls. Aware of this circumstance, Bloomgarden organized a workshop for CBO personnel. By combining the assistance of the director of the Western Massachusetts Funders Resource Center in Springfield and the resources of the regional library of the Foundation Center, he hoped to assist Holyoke CBOs to gain better access to the resources that were available to them. Additionally, the development offices from the Five Colleges donated grant directories. Seventeen representatives from thirteen different Holyoke CBOs attended the workshop and deemed it to be very successful. Bloomgarden continues to provide voluntary development consulting to Holyoke CBOs and is a member of the Avanza Resource Development Team.

The Puerto Rican Studies Seminar

The second project originated when a nontraditional Mount Holyoke student who also worked for a community-based organization in Holyoke, expressed concern that faculty who taught CBL classes involving community partners in Holyoke did not know enough about Puerto Rican history, culture and politics, and therefore could not adequately prepare their students to work respectfully and productively in the city. In the 2003-04 academic year, HPN members began a monthly Puerto Rican Studies faculty seminar. The seminar was facilitated by a Puerto Rican Studies professor from the University of Massachusetts, the Director of an adult literacy and popular education CBO, the student from Mount Holyoke College who originated the idea, and Preston H. Smith II, the CBL director from Mount Holyoke College.

The seminar met once a month throughout the academic year and went to Puerto Rico for a week in January. This seminar was unique because it was attended by community members from three Holyoke CBOs and a community liaison representative from Holyoke's mayor's office, in addition to faculty from five of the six colleges. The fall seminar sessions concentrated on readings, films, and speakers both from the academic institutions and from the Puerto Rican community. The spring sessions focused on education, housing, economic development, and the work of Holyoke CBOs in these areas. The highlight was a trip to Puerto Rico in which three-quarters of the seminar participants were presented with an opportunity to understand the island side of the Puerto Rican transnational experience as well as an opportunity to make connections with Puerto Rican-based academic institutions and CBOs for future exchanges and reciprocal visits. The program and trip were immense successes, and the seminar continues to be offered.

The HPN Archive Project

The assistant director of community outreach at Amherst College and two Mount Holyoke CBL students coordinated the HPN Archives project. The project stemmed from the shared concern that academic studies of Holyoke's Puerto Rican community were not benefiting the city. HPN wanted to harvest the benefits of the research by collecting it and making it accessible to members of the Holyoke community. The archive team directed the collection of material and arranged for its deposit and management in the archives section of the Holyoke Public Library. A presentation of the project drew more than fifty people from the Puerto Rican community, elected and appointed officials in Holyoke, and senior administrators from the six colleges. The project was very well received, and the director of the oldest Puerto Rican CBO commented that the project was the first effort to recognize Latinos' contributions to the city of Holyoke.

CHALLENGES TO BUILDING A METROPOLITAN
COLLEGE/COMMUNITY PARTNERSHIP

The process of establishing legitimacy with our community partners was a complex and time-consuming collaboration that did not initially allow HPN sufficient time to simultaneously build legitimacy with our respective upper level administrations. When faculty and staff are unable to make meaningful commitments on behalf of their institutions, CBO partners are reluctant to invest in long-term and more productive partnerships and are understandably wary of overextending even short-term ones. For HPN to maximize the reciprocity in the relationships between the academic and community sides of the partnership, the institutional legitimacy of faculty and staff in HPN have to be examined against the goals of good partnership practice in Holyoke. This immediately raised the question of whether CBL faculty and staff have the authority to represent the priorities and goals of their institutions. For many, formalizing the HPN as a Holyoke/higher education partnership and obtaining official sanction for their work, represented not only a step toward attaining greater authority in representing their institutions but also was an important step toward greater legitimacy for CBL as a whole. Yet it is also significant that not all of the consortia partners were prepared to make this investment or fully acknowledge the HPN partnerships.

At this point, HPN is still educating senior administrative officials about the core of HPN's vision, while actively pursuing firm commitments to HPN from various deans and presidents. As necessary first steps toward this better practice, we want our respective administrations to see the wisdom in more long-term strategic partnership development and in the immediate investments of institutional and external resources. Administrations are understandably concerned with the matter of raising expectations in communities, yet do not fully appreciate that they are raised anyway whenever our students and faculty enter them to learn or do research. This nearsightedness enables the view that sharing resources is charity, rather than a component of regional partnership that serves both education and development simultaneously. In our outreach to senior officials, we must better communicate this formulation and learn to measure returns from community partnerships. Both efforts will assure them that expectations are being managed responsibly.

The challenge for CBL faculty and staff in working with community partners is to develop ways to adequately measure and articulate the benefits of community-based learning for both students and faculty and also to determine the true costs to a community organization that is accommodating CBL opportunities. On both sides, a fair accounting of the total resources required to create true community-based learning opportunities is a necessary prerequisite for equitable partnerships. We hope that providing administrators with an understanding of the benefits of CBL to their institutions and the related costs to the community will encourage them to commit resources to sustained partnerships. While HPN academic members have initiated the necessary dialogues, the process of building consensus among our institutional leaders for a plan of sustainable commitment to CBL pedagogy and a long-range, strategic community partnership with Holyoke, is ongoing.

CONCLUSION

In the coming years, CBL faculty and staff will work to demonstrate the academic contributions of past and present CBL work to senior administrative officials. They will also lobby for a permanent community partnership outreach center in Holyoke and work on innovative ways to demonstrate to these administrators that expanding the capacity and effectiveness of CBL opportunities in Holyoke will yield direct benefits to HPN's academic institutions and to the region surrounding these institutions.

As representatives of academic institutions, we must recognize that our fate is intrinsically tied to that of our neighboring communities, and that we share a responsibility for each other. Talk of social justice and social change is meaningless unless we work hard to overcome the barriers to justice and change in our own institutional settings, while at the same time striving to ensure the well-being and sustainability of our community partners. There simply is no room for principle without practice.

REFERENCES

Campus Compact. (2003). *Introduction to service-learning toolkit: Readings and resources for faculty* Providence, RI: Brown University.

Cruz, N. I., & Giles, D. E. (2000). Where's the community in service-learning research? *Michigan Journal of Community Service Learning*. Fall.

Compton, C. (2003). *Exploring the borderlands of university/community partnerships.* Unpublished thesis, Amherst, MA: Hampshire College.

Dugery, J., & Knowles, J. (Eds.). (2003). *University + community research partnerships: A new approach*. Charlottesville, VA: Pew Partnership for Civic Change.

Holland, B. A. (2001, March). *Characteristics of 'engaged institutions' and sustainable partnerships, and effective strategies for change.* (Monograph) Indianapolis: Office of University Partnerships, HUD at Indiana University—Purdue University at Indianapolis.

Leiderman, S., Furco, A., Zapf, J., & Goss, M. (2003). Building partnerships with college campuses: Community perspectives. Washington, DC: The Council of Independent Colleges.

Perkins, D. D., & Wandersman, A. (1990). You'll have to work to overcome our suspicions. In *Social policy: Community action*. Summer.

Ramaley, J. (2000). Embracing civic responsibility. In *AAHE Bulletin, 52,* 7.

Reardon, K. M. (1994). Undergraduate research in distressed urban communities: An undervalued form of service-learning. *Michigan Journal of Community Service Learning, 1,* 1.

Reardon, K. M. (1998). Enhancing the capacity of community-based organizations in east St. Louis. *Journal of Planning Education and Research, 17.*

Sandmann, L. R, & Baker-Clark, C. A. (1997). *Characteristics and principles of university-community partnerships: A delphi study.* Paper given at the Midwest Research-to-Practice Conference and Community Education. Michigan State University, October 15.

Silka, L. (2001). Addressing the Challenge of Community Collaborations. In *Approaches to sustainable development: The public university in the regional economy.* Amherst, MA: University of Massachusetts Press.

CHAPTER 8

Education for Sustainability: Preserve Good Ideas—Recycle Them

Linda Silka, Priscilla Geigis, and Will Snyder

At the heart of sustainability is the familiar theme that we should "reduce, reuse, recycle." This advice reminds us of the importance of not discarding materials after a single use but instead, continually seeking ways that materials can be productively reused and recycled. We are reminded of the need to move beyond the throwaway culture that we have become. To perhaps a surprising extent, this same theme of reuse and recycle also emerges in discussions on education for sustainability. In the case of education, however, it is the recycling and reusing of ideas, curricula, and best practices that is important, and it is the failure to draw upon past insights that is lamented. The waste is pointed to when each group, organization, and community individually reinvents the wheel, and, in so doing, fails to reuse hard-won insights from the past.

Yet just as it has turned out that there are many complications to the task of recycling materials, it also is the case that recycling ideas is complex and confronts us with difficult and sometimes perplexing choices. In the case of both materials and ideas, we need to look closely at these complexities. By doing so, we can perhaps see our way to better strategies for recycling and reuse while avoiding some of the problems that have plagued past efforts. As we shall see in this chapter, the steps to recycling ideas are not as simple as they might seem. To examine some of these issues, we will consider Massachusetts' efforts at education for sustainability that have taken place under the umbrella of community preservation. These complexities go to the very heart of many of the themes raised in the Committee on Industrial Theory and Assessment's Education for Sustainability Conference.

COMMUNITY PRESERVATION AS AN ALTERNATIVE
TO SMART GROWTH

In the late 1990s the state of Massachusetts began its community preservation initiative as a way to focus attention on sustainability. Legislation was passed that called for tying together initiatives on housing, historic preservation, transportation, open space, and the environment, thereby "preserving and enhancing the quality of life in Massachusetts, community by community and watershed by watershed." Under the Community Preservation Act, Massachusetts cities and towns could pass a local property tax surcharge, enabling them to tap a state fund for preserving open space, creating affordable housing and the like, and communities could access a variety of state technical resources to help them tackle the complex links between various community preservation issues. Much of what is called smart growth in other states took the form of community preservation in Massachusetts, but with important differences. Full details of the Community Preservation Initiative can be found in Geigis, Hamin, and Silka (2005).

Why community preservation? Massachusetts was grappling with the question of how to organize an approach to smart growth that would reflect the political realities of the state—where most political decisions are made at the local level—and that would be consistent with strong environmental practices. In Massachusetts, individual communities control much of the planning agenda; there is little regional authority of the sort that makes collaborative smart-growth planning feasible in other states. Community preservation also reflects the fact that Massachusetts is close to build-out; that is, nearly all land in eastern Massachusetts is already under development. The population from 1950 to 2000 increased statewide by a mere 28 percent, yet during that same period the consumption of land for development increased an astonishing 188 percent (Geigis & Silka, 2003). As a result, many communities have little remaining in the way of untapped land. Community leaders have begun to realize that alternative routes to development are needed if the quality of life in their communities is to be preserved. Much of the decision making on these routes is in the hands of citizen planners. That is, smart growth specialists are not the people who will be responsible for preserving communities in the face of these limits. Citizens will be. The question then becomes one of how sustainability in the form of community preservation can be made comprehensible to the diverse groups in which community decision making is invested (Hamin, Silka, & Geigis, in press).

Using the term "community preservation" instead of "smart growth" or even "sustainable development" was far from a case of simply old wine in new bottles. The term opened up a new set of connections and opportunities. In January 1999, the state had just appointed a new Secretary of Environmental Affairs, Robert Durand, who was creatively searching for ways to bring together the disparate efforts being undertaken by communities to address issues of environmental problems, open space, adaptive reuse, and the need for affordable housing. He recognized that, in the absence of more integrated approaches, efforts to address local problems would continue to be unsuccessful. Secretary Durand led the way to making community preservation the central theme of the work of Massachusetts' Executive Office of Environmental Affairs (EOEA) throughout his tenure. He originated and helped to pass the Community Preservation Act and reorganized the work within EOEA to reflect the importance of community preservation as a concept for sound, balanced planning by launching a statewide initiative to help communities address growth and development issues.

EDUCATION FOR SUSTAINABILITY:
THE COMMUNITY PRESERVATION INSTITUTE

EOEA consistently worked to bridge the gap between state efforts and those of local cities and towns, and EOEA created many different resources for communities struggling with issues of growth and development; these resources included build-out analyses, small- and large-scale summit meetings on key topics, and a Web site providing resources for pursuing community preservation. Still missing, EOEA found, were "education for sustainability," resources—resources that would assist communities in their examinations of these issues. The puzzle was how best to get education into the hands of the citizen leaders who would be responsible for many of the decisions about local development.

Four challenges confronted those who would design effective programs on education for sustainability: 1) the citizen leaders in Massachusetts cities and towns did not frame their work in terms of education for sustainability even though most observers would likely say that this is exactly the issue with which communities were grappling; 2) little in the way of a regional infrastructure existed that could bring communities together to share their understanding of sustainable development and act in concert on that understanding; 3) few trainings were available that were designed to meet the highly varied needs of adult citizen learners; and 4) even when such trainings were available, most communities had few resources to underwrite the efforts of their citizen leaders to become educated on community preservation. So, at the level of motivation, programs, and resources, there were daunting problems to overcome. Sustained problem-solving at the state level would be needed to come to terms with how the citizenry could become more informed and engaged.

To address these challenges, the Community Preservation Institute (CPI) was created, providing a forum for local leaders to gain greater understanding of growth issues as well as to gain greater confidence in their ability to address such issues (Geigis, Hamin, & Silka, 2005). Unique in its origin, design, outreach, and impact, the CPI training was tailored specifically to teach community leaders to consider development and growth pressures within the context of their community and to preserve community character. Various training models had been tried in our state; the question was: which elements could be recycled to fit in the new context? For example, the Citizens Planning and Training Collaborative (operated by the University of Massachusetts) represented a successful, practical program offering courses on individual subjects, including implementation of new laws and regulations. The Citizen Training approach, however, included little in the way of linkage between topics, nor was there much connection to an overarching theme such as community preservation. The CPI was designed to capitalize on the eagerness among adult learners to determine how everything fits into a wider context by providing a broader focus linking a variety of subjects, many of which involved issues that, in any given development decision, compete with each other.

The resulting nine-week, 25-hour evening curriculum, open to citizen planners throughout the Commonwealth and offered at various locations statewide, took up in an integrated fashion many of the issues that emerge when concerns about community preservation are raised. These issues include adaptive reuse, housing, open space, transportation, and community economic development; and participants were exposed to topics such as land acquisition, water protection, and historic preservation (Hamin, Silka, & Geigis, in press). Specialty sessions also were offered to reflect the uniqueness of each region in the state, and these classes included "Diversity in Community Preservation" at Lowell (Silka & Eady, in press), "Natural Resources as a Catalyst for Economic Development" at Dartmouth (Ryan & Bergeson, in press), "Creative Zoning" in Lowell (Wickersham & Wiggin, in press) and "Brownfields and Environmental Justice" in Boston (Eady, in press). Sessions were designed so that participants gained subject matter knowledge, developed coalition-building skills, and had opportunities to network with resource people within the UMass system, state agencies, and nonprofit groups. Participants were given tools and information to make decisions and were taught how to assist their constituent base in becoming educated about development that would help preserve the special character of their communities. Throughout, the CPI encouraged participants to become a part of a network of local leaders who "get it" when it comes to making decisions that promote sustainable development.

A regional perspective to addressing these issues also was incorporated into many of these classes in a variety of direct and indirect ways. The institute allowed students to see firsthand that many of their community's issues were not unlike those confronting their neighbors in adjacent communities. In the evening class on water, for example, regional solutions to local problems were introduced to point out that communities, through shared responsibility, could achieve better and more efficient protection of their increasingly scarce water resources. Attempts to strengthen the regional approaches were also made through shaping the class makeup so that the citizen leaders in each class of 25 were, on average, drawn from 20 different but adjacent communities.

The CPI was free. By being offered at no charge, it attracted local leaders from all over the state for this program that would have been prohibitively expensive if individuals or communities had been charged tuition. Few training programs underwrite their costs, and thus the institute was seen as a special opportunity provided by the state. To date, 252 alumni have graduated from the CPI, held on all five University of Massachusetts campuses. Detailed information about the training is available in the forthcoming book *Citizens as Planners* (Hamin, Silka, & Geigis, in press).

The institute filled a need for local leaders and, as described below, also served the more far-reaching goal of bringing researchers and policy-makers together. While different regional partnerships had emerged in Massachusetts— created to consider and address growth and development issues—none of the entities provided the kind of infrastructure and clearinghouse for local leaders that a joint initiative from EOEA and the University of Massachusetts could provide.

POLICY ARM AND EDUCATION ARM
WORKING TOGETHER

An important feature of the CPI was that its creation represented a joint venture between the EOEA (the state environmental agency) and the University of Massachusetts (the state research university). At the outset, these two entities were far from recognizing that any benefits might result from pooling their skills and resources. So, although developing the Institute was aimed initially at finding ways to provide customized education on sustainability for the citizen leaders of Massachusetts, it turned out that an equally important goal was having the joint development of this training engage EOEA and UMASS on the topic of sustainable development so that together they would generate new strategies, new programs, new research on sustainable development, and would continue to work together on other projects.

Community preservation provided an unparalleled opportunity for these two entities—the policy arm and the education arm of state government—to explore strategies each thought were crucial if citizens were to become engaged in community preservation. What evolved was a planning process that included joint decision making and joint discovery of research and policy skills within both branches of government as well as exploration of the different approaches on how citizen leaders can best guide their communities through the tangled set of issues confronting their localities as they grapple with issues of growth and development.

During the time EOEA and the University of Massachusetts planned the CPI, everything about the CPI as a possible educational resource came under scrutiny from these policy makers and research specialists: the topics each group regarded as essential to include, the format that each thought would be most effective at capturing research and producing action, how participants should be recruited, and how EOEA and UMASS should allocate responsibilities. Ultimately the process of reaching consensus on these issues made it clear to EOEA and UMASS that it would be valuable to emulate this team approach within the institute itself by having each class co-taught by two instructors. CPI participants received at least two different viewpoints on any given community preservation issue because for each individual class a university specialist was paired with a state agency policy maker or community leader as class facilitators. The result was that the CPI represented integrated training, bringing together both research and practice, both under the umbrella of community preservation and emphasizing local approaches tailored from a variety of ideas.

The successful collaboration in creating the institute led EOEA and UMASS to engage in additional ventures regarding sustainable development. In Spring 2003, the partnership launched *Community Preservation: YouthVisions*, a two-day, on-campus program designed to inform youth leaders about sustainable development using the Community Preservation curriculum model as a base. This initiative and the questions it raised are described below.

THE *YOUTHVISIONS* PILOT

Could the same "education for sustainability" approach essentially be reused and recycled for youth? *YouthVisions,* an outgrowth of the CPI, was an attempt to answer this question. After four successful semesters of offering the CPI, UMASS and EOEA turned their attention to youth, reasoning that the launch of a sustainable development pilot program for high school students could foster in young people a sense of place and a commitment to their communities during a crucial period when youth are beginning to assume more responsibility.

Using course topics and curricula from the institute, in Spring 2003, EOEA and UMASS created a two-day *Community Preservation: YouthVisions* program aimed at engaging youth in the sustainable development issues that now face Massachusetts cities and towns. For the pilot, teams of students and advisors from geographically diverse parts of the state were selected to take part. Participating schools/programs were: Quabbin Regional High School, Essex Agricultural High School, the Eagle Eye Institute in Somerville, and the River Ambassadors Program from Lowell. Twenty-five students participated in this diverse series of workshops, discussions, and interactive activities designed to help foster leadership and team-building skills as well as a better understanding of natural resource protection, land use, and community development. Through this program, students could learn what it means to belong to a community and what roles they could play in helping to preserve their own city or town and shape the future of development. Teams prepared and offered roundtable discussions concerning: suburban sprawl in the Quabbin area, river protection in Lowell, street tree protection in Somerville, and marine Geographical Information System (GIS) studies at Essex Agricultural High School.

YouthVisions included on- and off-campus field trips. Through hands-on lab applications, students learned about the important role of the GIS in growth planning decisions. Students also toured the university's extensive recycling facility, learning about its role in ensuring a sustainable university community. Additional off-campus trips brought students to Atkins Corner to learn about its future as a smart-growth designed village center and to the Sawmill River in Montague to examine the effects of development on ecological health and water quality.

At the conclusion of the conference, each of the five youth groups made brief presentations about what they learned during the two days and what actions they intended to take in their own communities as a result of the conference. It was clear that the participants were influenced not only by the curriculum but also by each other. Perhaps not surprisingly, one of the greatest contrasts occurred between the students from Somerville, an urban community flanking Boston, and those from Quabbin, a rural community in the middle of the state, as they discussed differing housing stock and transportation alternatives. If asked to create "the good city" at the end of the conference, no doubt their drawings would be influenced by their enhanced understanding of what makes a good community.

REUSING AND RECYCLING TRAINING INGREDIENTS

What did the *YouthVisions* experience suggest as important components for a program to effectively promote youth involvement in community preservation? To begin with, *YouthVisions* reused and adapted program designs and educator networks developed by other groups for two previously successful high school environmental programs, *Earth Connection* and *Envirothon*. Over the previous decade, hundreds of educators and youth in Massachusetts had been involved in these programs; tapping into their success, as described below, allowed the *YouthVision* planners to move forward quickly to design the program, invite participants, and hold the conference with the confidence that it would meet with approval from its intended audience. Part of the success, then, resulted from building on existing programs and collaborations. But, as we shall see later, *YouthVisions* also differed from these approaches in using the Community Preservation Institute as a model for identifying how sustainable development principles would be incorporated into the youth curriculum.

A community focus is central to community preservation but not to all youth environmental programs, so it was crucial to find students and advisors already familiar with community themes and their link to the environment. It turns out that the planners of *Envirothon* and *Earth Connection* had previously discovered ways to incorporate a community focus into their environmental initiatives. Since 1995, the Massachusetts *Envirothon*, the high school environmental competition, had included a community exploration component. High school teams learned about a current environmental issue (such as open space protection, stormwater management, or wetlands conservation) and were asked to investigate how the issue manifested itself in their own community. Through interviews, library research, and field work, student teams determined the critical concerns for their town and then developed a proposal aimed at addressing that concern. At the spring *Envirothon*, the teams presented their findings through a formal presentation to a panel of judges. Thus, the *Envirothon* presented themes that might be drawn upon and might resonate with existing groups.

Just as the previous themes provided important ideas that could be adapted and reused, so too did the format. *YouthVisions* used the *Envirothon/Earth Connection* model of an adult advisor with a small group of young people. At *Earth Connection*, teams involving four to eight young people with one or two advisors represented schools and community groups from diverse rural, suburban, and urban communities across the state. This model assumes that community projects for environmental improvement will benefit from the involvement of both youth and adults. The youth provide energy and new eyes. Adults provide experience, judgment, and knowledge of the community. The presence of youth in a project can encourage the whole community to think more about the future and the larger public interest.

YouthVisions also drew on *Earth Connection's* format of a two-day con-ference as a successful model for involving both high school educators and youth on community service and the environment. The *Earth Connection* conference, held on the UMASS Amherst campus annually for a number of years, included workshops on issues and skills for community environmental action and oppor-tunities to explore environmental teaching, research, and facilities management on campus.

Networking—among teachers, between high school participants and college age conference staff, and among the high school young people themselves—was another key feature of both *Earth Connection* and *Envirothon,* and these planners indicated to those preparing the *YouthVisions* conference how essential it was to build in networking and draw on existing networks. As a result, the *YouthVisions* conference was structured to maximize opportunities for young people and advisors to get to know each other. These efforts made at building in communication and networking (described below) apparently were successful. Meeting people from other communities was the most important *YouthVisions* benefit, according to youth participants.

An important networking feature was the roundtable session. *Earth Connection* developed a roundtable format that encouraged information sharing among young people, without the pressure of competition or adult evaluation. At *YouthVisions,* the roundtables allowed participants to communicate with each other one-on-one and learn about each other's communities and schools. Each team was asked to come to the conference prepared to lead a discussion on a topic of their choice. Students from Essex County demonstrated their GIS mapping work. Students from the Quabbin area presented their concerns about suburban sprawl. Youth groups from Lowell and Somerville talked about their work in river protection and street tree protection. Each team had a round table as its home base. At any given time during the session, half the team members were at the home table leading a conversation, and half were visiting other tables. The atmosphere was deliberately intended to be different from a poster session or a science fair: the emphasis in the *YouthVisions* roundtables was on informal conversation rather than on formal presentations, and for at least the first half of the session, there were no adults present. During the youth roundtable session, team advisors met separately to share ideas on how the program should grow.

Massachusetts communities are increasingly diverse. Issues of racial, ethnic, and class diversity continue to grow as challenges for American society and are connected with many issues of community preservation. A major benefit of bringing together these community-based urban youth groups with more suburban school-based classes and clubs is learning about diversity within projects that have youth empowerment and leadership as explicit goals. *YouthVisions* sought to include groups that represented both the ethnic and geographic diversity of Massachusetts classrooms and communities. In the end, the pilot included groups from among the most rural (Barre) and the most urban (Somerville) communities in the state and a majority of youth of color. It was clear from the final team presentations that significant bridges to understanding had been built among these communities. Rural and suburban teams voiced new understanding of the urban environment and admiration for the environmental improvement work being carried out by the urban teams.

As the description suggests, previous youth programs provided structures that could be drawn upon and recycled. At the same time, these previous programs left policy gaps. The CPI provided an additional critical component of the *YouthVisions* pilot: a comprehensive curriculum that had been missing from both *Envirothon* and *Earth Connection*. The CPI introduction to critical issues of community preservation, smart growth, and sustainable development in Massachusetts provided participating teachers and youth group advisors with a well-defined framework for introducing their young people to community issues. The CPI also provided a framework for selecting workshops and for identifying experienced EOEA, community agency, and UMASS staff to offer these workshops.

It quickly became clear, however, that merely reusing the CPI curriculum "as is" would be an unsuccessful way to recycle CPI ideas and frameworks. We found that the *YouthVisions* curriculum was most successful when adaptations of CPI curriculum were made to achieve maximum opportunities for interactive learning. As one example, in the "Planning the Good City" workshop, UMASS Amherst professor Elisabeth Hamin asked the youth to assume the role of city planners and determine where to place residential, commercial and industrial development, transportation structures and open space in order to balance these various interests to create a community for people to live, work and play. Three "good cities" resulted, each with their own distinctive character, and each, understandably, capturing the experience of the youthful city planners. One group, with members from urban communities, drew a core inner circle filled with housing around a common green and they surrounded this circle with municipal buildings and commercial and retail establishments. Industrial uses were located on the outer edge of the community. Another group laid the city out in a grid, making it easy to navigate. The third group, with members from more rural areas, drew a river and built the city along the river, emphasizing parks and open space and placing cultural amenities close to the river. As the groups shared their visions, they learned about each other's communities as well as their own values. In many ways, the workshop captured the essence of *YouthVisions*—encouraging youth as visionaries and leaders by promoting the value of community, and introducing the skills needed to be effective citizens.

Students indicated through their feedback that they found most useful the interactive curricula such as the "Planning the Good City" workshop and the GIS lab where each student had a computer to test the applications; they found other parts of the CPI curriculum less compelling. Regardless of the topic, youth participated more fully and reported that they learned better when the activities were highly interactive. Many experts were very generous with their time and saw the value of involving young people. Although lecture presentations can work with a youth group when the group is already highly engaged in the topic, we found that the initial introduction of sustainable development topics to youth audiences benefited from interactive, hands-on methods and examples.

Many decisions contributed to the success of the *YouthVisions* conference, but perhaps one of the most important—and central to our discussion here—was the decision to emphasize the offering of resources rather than imposing prescriptions or prepackaged curricula. Often the assumption in developing a curriculum is that the key to its successful use will depend on spelling out exactly what should be done with each lesson and then ensuring that all users exactly follow each of the steps outlined in the curriculum. Thus, university/agency outreach efforts to high schools often invest much time in developing a uniform curriculum of this sort and training teachers in exactly how such materials should be used to achieve their intended effect. A different approach was adopted for *YouthVisions*. Here the aim was to offer resources and guidance rather than a recipe or exact formula. This choice was deliberate. Rather than attempt to create a one-size-fits-all program or curriculum, *YouthVisions* planners opted to expose participants to ideas and resource people that teachers could then use to expand their own teaching and learning. This approach recognized that each educator operates under his or her own constraints of curriculum, time, calendar, and funding, and so will not be able to implement a program exactly as dictated. It was also recognized that each community has different issues that will be of highest priority, and each educator has his/her own particular teaching style and relationship with youth. The *YouthVisions* approach provided important resources while leaving the creative initiative for education in the hands of the most experienced professionals—the teachers and youth leaders who brought groups to *YouthVisions*.

YOUTHVISIONS' NEXT STEPS

The *YouthVisions* pilot illustrated one way that state agencies and the state university could come together to support community and school-based initiatives that involve youth in community preservation. The question is how to continue such work. Three strategies for follow-up are suggested below; we then turn to the more general question of how groups can draw upon, reuse, and recycle ideas, programs, and best practices.

First, in keeping alive the various *YouthVisions* initiatives, the pilot continues in the form of an advisory committee, composed of the adult advisors who participated in *YouthVisions* and have agreed to advise EOEA and UMASS as we develop future offerings. Their input will be important in the ongoing work of linking young people with community-preservation learning opportunities in Massachusetts communities. Second, EOEA is designing a classroom exercise that allows students to create a community using "game pieces" of housing, industrial and commercial development, and parks. The exercise can be expanded, at the teacher's discretion, to include GIS and additional state mapping resources. It is intended to help students think about balancing a variety of interests in a community to achieve the best impact on quality of life and the least impact on the environment. Third, UMASS Extension is developing a major proposal for private funding for a project that will introduce Community Preservation/ sustainable-development knowledge, skills, and values into the formal and informal Massachusetts high school curriculum. The proposed project would combine professional development with curriculum development for schools and communities, providing educators with the opportunities and support to research, experiment with, and share innovative approaches to teaching environmental and civic literacy. We remain particularly interested in community-connected projects that encourage youth in their efforts to become leaders in addressing community issues.

IMPLICATIONS FOR THE REUSE AND RECYCLING OF IDEAS: THE CHALLENGES AHEAD

Throughout the community preservation initiatives described above, there are those who continue to wonder whether it might be better to locate such efforts under well-grounded and widely-used concepts such as sustainable development or smart growth. Community preservation continues to be regarded by some as an instance of reinventing the wheel. But through this work, we have come to realize that the familiar admonition to use that which already exists (and don't we all agree at some level!) may not be helpful for individual communities. A basic assumption underlying all such calls is that the act of reinvention (that is, the failure of communities to simply reuse ideas that are already out there) is a problem—that it reflects knowledge forgotten and time wasted on rediscovery, rather than perhaps representing a necessary step in community involvement. The former view also assumes that the effort groups devote to coming up with the ideas themselves stands in the way of those same groups moving forward to the new, more pressing tasks, attention to which would rapidly bring about more effective education for sustainability. But are community efforts to generate their own ideas in fact best conceived of as redundant effort? Indeed, might there be unrecognized benefits to developing programs anew? Is a part of bottom-up as opposed to top-down approaches that the former are focused on communities finding their own way? Such efforts tend to be viewed as communities making the same mistakes over and over again, when sometimes such efforts may represent a mix of rediscovering and then tailoring the apt or good solution to fit local needs.

The reinvention of approaches happens so often that either this is entirely accounted for by the faulty ways humans have of remembering what has gone on before or perhaps this raises the possibility that other, more powerful, dynamics are at work that make reinvention a crucial part of the process by which we become committed to ideas and make them our own. That is to say, a potential problem with all admonitions to avoid re-creations is that such cautions may fly in the face of the psychological, motivational, and mobilization processes needed to make the ideas work in actual practice. Indeed, advice to avoid re-creation may well misunderstand the dynamics of how communities, teachers, and others learn from each other and solve local problems.

Take the case of the preexisting or canned curricula that was discussed previously. By giving teachers everything already thought out in the form of some entirely prepackaged curriculum, there is the potential that teachers may not be mobilized to use the information. Teachers may have little sense of ownership or discovery when everything has already been generated and someone else is responsible for originating all of the crucial ideas. In effect, the wind may be taken out of our sails when we are told that someone else has already developed all of the ideas and our role is simply to follow the rules exactly in teaching what we have been given or applying the approved ideas. Prepackaged curricula too often present answers without first giving teachers or others a chance to formulate questions in such a way that the answers become truly their own.

In our view then, a basic problem in education for sustainability that remains in need of solution is that of how information sharing and customization should take place. Clearly we need to share information with each other in some way and are not fully doing so. Consider the fact, for example, that the U.S. Environmental Protection Agency (EPA) has announced that it will no longer fund the creation of new environmental educational curricula because so much already has been produced that continues to go untapped. In EPA's view, we are not benefiting from each others' experiences; we are not recycling and reusing ideas.

How then do we share and use each others' ideas? How might we customize information and make it useful for our particular situations? Perhaps sharing *is* going on, but we haven't looked in the right places to understand the kind of idea sharing and adapting that may be occurring. Consider advice giving as one possible overlooked example. All of us engage in considerable advice giving and advice seeking, and from close scrutiny of such efforts, we might learn something about the effective recycling and reuse of ideas among teachers and across communities. Advice giving and advice seeking could represent some of the ways that we draw on existing ideas while at the same time customizing those ideas so that they better fit our needs in the area of education for sustainability. In his book *The Art of Advice* (1994), Salacus provides a variety of instructive and provocative case examples of advice giving in its many forms.

List making reflects yet another common but in many ways less effective form of knowledge dissemination. Consider all the lists that have been created in recent years that tell communities which steps to take and which to avoid in going about the business of smart growth or sustainable development. When communities are presented with lists of steps that should be followed, they are being told how to learn from the experience that other communities have had. The difficulty with lists—in contrast to the give and take of effective and tailored advice giving—is that such lists are often too generic and fail to take context into account. Lists don't easily capture the questions people are asking; they aren't flow charts. Knowledge is assumed to be static and to remain useful across time and across circumstances. Questions of customization are likely to be the key issue here: how do we customize smart-growth ideas, ideas from other states, ideas that in their raw form are unworkable in Massachusetts because of particulars of the Massachusetts political structure?

These issues of information sharing return us once more to the citizen leaders who remain the central focus for much of the education for sustainability efforts reported in this chapter. Comments can often be heard in which the knowledge shortfalls of citizen leaders are compared with the presumably vaster knowledge of experts. Professionals worry about whether the citizen leaders can be brought up to the level of the planning experts, and there can be a tendency to design education for sustainability toward the end of making citizen leaders as much like planners as possible by prepackaging lots of information that can be communicated in a short time. But such efforts may miss the mark on how citizen leaders want to be involved in community preservation and therefore what they need to know to recycle ideas and develop new ones. Citizen leaders may learn from experts and from each other in very different ways than we suspect. Those developing education programs for sustainability need to be able to deal with this notion as well as with the fact that new community leaders will continue to become involved at new points in time, and these new leaders won't necessarily bring relevant expertise or have the expertise of other citizen leaders who have been involved in community planning for some time.

Questions also emerge with regard to youth and their role in community preservation: Is their involvement important to us as adults because youth participation provides opportunities for us to train them into particular points of view; or, on the other hand, do we value youth involvement because we hope that through the fresh perspectives they bring they will teach us new ways of looking at community problems? Is the involvement of youth valued because to some degree they are starting over from the very beginning and are engaged in reinventing the wheel? These questions are far from idle. The nature of community follow-up from conferences such as *YouthVisions* hinges on answers to such questions. Are we merely indulging youth when we remark that they bring something new to our understanding of community preservation or do we indeed expect that they can offer significant contributions to community conversations about sustainability? How will we frame future efforts?

With materials recycling, we have learned that there must be a market out there if recycling is to be successful; is the same true for ideas, and do we need to place more emphasis on creating a market for these ideas? As we continue to struggle with the issue of reusing and recycling ideas in new ways, how do we prepare for the emergence of new problems in sustainable development? How do we create trainings that prepare us to deal with problems we can't even yet imagine? And how do we deal with trainings that may not themselves have continuity? Like most trainings, the CPI may not go on indefinitely; indeed the political realities in Massachusetts are changing once again. Alterations in support for trainings should come as no surprise, but how then do we recycle and reuse CPI ideas, suggestions, and considerations? In education for sustainability: What should we take from each others' experience? How do we learn from each other? How do we adapt and reuse ideas and where, ultimately, does innovation fit in?

REFERENCES

Eady, V. (in press). Brownfields redevelopment: Reconnecting economy, ecology and equity. In E. Hamin, L. Silka, & P. Geigis (Eds.), *Citizens as planners*. Amherst: University of Massachusetts Press.

Geigis, P., Hamin, E., & Silka, L. (2005). Community preservation: Collaborations for smarter growth. In W. Wiewel & G-J. Knapp (Eds.), *Partnerships for smart growth: University-community collaborations for better public places*. New York: M. E. Sharpe.

Geigis, P., & Silka, L. (2003). *The Community Preservation Institute: Opportunities for reflecting on education for sustainability*. Presented at the CITA Conference "Education for Sustainability," October 2003. Full text available at http://www.uml.edu/com/CITA/conference%202003.html#program.

Hamin, E., Silka, L., & Geigis, P. (Eds.). (in press). *Citizens as planners*. Amherst: University of Massachusetts Press.

Ryan, R., & Bergeson, A. (in press). Natural land: Preserving and funding open space. In E. Hamin, L. Silka, & P. Geigis (Eds.), *Citizens as planners.* Amherst: University of Massachusetts Press.

Salacus, J. W. (1994). *The art of advice.* New York: Times Books.

Silka, L., & Eady, V. (in press). Diversity: Multiple cultures forming one community. In E. Hamin, L. Silka, & P. Geigis (Eds.), *Citizens as planners.* Amherst: University of Massachusetts Press.

Wickersham, J., & Wiggin, J. (in press). Creative zoning: Putting the teeth in your planning. In E. Hamin, L. Silka, & P. Geigis (Eds.), *Citizens as planners.* Amherst: University of Massachusetts Press.

CHAPTER 9

Merging Academics and Operations in a Statewide University Consortium

Patricia Jerman, Christy Friend, Corinna McLeod, Summer Smith Taylor, and Bruce Coull

South Carolina's three research universities—Clemson, the Medical University of South Carolina (MUSC) in Charleston, and the University of South Carolina (USC)—are now in the sixth year of a productive partnership: the Sustainable Universities Initiative (SUI). In 1998, the presidents of the three schools signed a pledge to cooperate in leading the way toward a more sustainable future through teaching, research, community service, and facilities management. The initial phase of the effort was funded by a generous grant from the V. Kann Rasmussen Foundation. In 2000, the foundation assisted the universities in obtaining $300,000 in one-time funds from the General Assembly to expand the program to other state-supported institutions of higher education. To date, 13 four-year and technical schools have joined. The largest of the three founding schools, USC, has approximately 30,400 full-time equivalent students at its Columbia campus and four-year and two-year regional campuses around the state. Clemson, the state's land grant university, has approximately 17,000 students, while the Medical University in Charleston has approximately 2,500.

SUI's principal mission can be summarized as a two-pronged effort: to help students understand the effect they have on the world around them and to assist our universities in reducing their institutional environmental footprint. We realize that we can make progress toward both goals by encouraging students and faculty to use the campus as a laboratory, exploring ideas and principles using the infrastructure that surrounds them daily. Students learn practical, real-world skills, and the campus benefits from their efforts. This chapter will describe several variations on the "campus-as-laboratory" theme.

A. CAMPUS AS LABORATORY—ENVIRONMENTAL ASSESSMENT

Much of the faculty at our member schools have carried out interesting and effective "campus-as-laboratory" projects with small groups of students. Students in a USC sustainable-design engineering class audited campus buildings and made recommendations to increase energy efficiency. A civil and environmental engineering class required students to monitor and document construction of USC's new "green dorm" being built across the street from their classroom.

As the state's land-grant institution, Clemson provides even more diverse opportunities to use the campus as a laboratory. A graduate student in biology documented the relationship between nonnative (potentially "invasive") land-scaping plants and the biodiversity of reptiles, amphibians, and small mammals on both a section of Clemson's experimental forest and the state's botanical garden, housed on campus. Another Clemson student developed a draft tree-management plan for campus as part of his urban-forestry classwork. Students in the sustainable-agriculture program grew organic vegetables and flowers as well as free-range chickens and sold their products in a biweekly farmers market at the student union. Students studying streamside management tested classroom theories by restoring an eroded stream on campus. College students in a variety of disciplines, including sociology, horticulture, and landscape architecture, worked with elementary-aged students, many deemed to be "at risk," to teach them a variety of life skills using gardening as the "text." Older students helped younger students to construct beds, plant and tend vegetables and herbs, harvest their crop, and prepare meals using the fruits of their labor. Along the way, the younger students learned where their food comes from, as well as principles of ecology, responsibility, and a bit about the culinary arts. The college-aged mentors refined their own thoughts about sustainability as they struggled to teach children from varied backgrounds.

Many projects involved assessing campus environmental management. One of our earliest efforts united faculty, administrative staff, a graduate student, and many undergraduates at USC in an effort to understand waste management on campus. A graduate student in the Masters in Earth and Environmental Resource Management program worked with the manager of the university's recycling program to assess both the quantity of waste in each of the university's dumpsters and the amount of recyclable materials improperly consigned to the dumpsters. Students in a basic environmental science class conducted assessments of dumpsters on a schedule determined by the graduate student, with at least two teams assigned to each dumpster for quality control. The undergraduates became recycling advocates as they realized how much reclaimable material was being landfilled. They also learned statistical methodology and the importance of replicability. The university learned that many of the dumpsters were less than half full when emptied, leading to a revamping of the disposal schedule and a potential savings of $10,000 per year. Another graduate student organized undergraduate labs around documenting litter with disposable cameras and audited classroom buildings for leaking faucets and toilets. Other graduate students worked with faculty in "University 101" courses to develop projects for freshmen required to complete service hours. Students worked according to their own schedule to assess lights left on in classroom buildings after normal hours and to determine attitudes toward bicycle use on campus.

While these projects have been valuable to both the universities and the students involved, they have not been effective in helping the schools to monitor their overall environmental performance. Several student-led efforts intended to do that are underway.

Students at both Clemson and USC prepared campus environmental assessments in the early 1990s, but the assessments were not repeated due to changes in personnel and funding. Sparked by SUI, both schools established (or in the case of Clemson, revitalized) environmental committees consisting of faculty, staff, and students. At both schools, committee members expressed an interest in assessing campus environmental performance. At USC, a graduate-student team prepared a "snapshot" report of environmental activities in various university operations units for the year 2000. They developed their model questionnaire from a combination of past campus audits, the National Wildlife Federation's Campus Ecology program materials, and information relevant to development of an Environmental Management System (EMS). The report was expected to provide a baseline from which progress could be measured on an annual basis. Assessments, including the initial questions, are posted on the USC Environmental Advisory Committee (EAC) Web site at www.sc.edu/EAC/Dept.Assess.htm.

Unfortunately, it has proven to be easier said than done. Several issues interfered with our ability to maintain a consistent monitoring program. The EAC was informally staffed by a graduate student and the overall SUI manager. No one was able to provide the assessment activity the leadership and attention it deserved.

Another issue was changing personnel, both within SUI and within individual departments. Although the questionnaire was intended to be administered on an annual or biennial basis, successive cohorts of graduate students identified weaknesses or improvements in the instrument or simply interpreted questions differently than their predecessors. While we wanted to use the most effective assessment instrument possible, and we did not want to stifle graduate students' creative impulses, we lost some consistency with each alteration in the questionnaire.

More troublesome was personnel change within departments. New managers might view a department more critically than their predecessors. Conversely, they might be unfamiliar with the EAC and the SUI program and might have less trust in the process than their predecessors. In one case, a new manager declined to answer a significant number of questions for which his predecessor had supplied data. Fortunately, our relationship with the new manager was a good one, and he was very forthright in sharing his concerns. It seems that he had no confidence in the answers given the previous year since there was no data collection system in place to provide the information. While he declined to guess at answers, he established a tracking system so that in subsequent years he would have a better idea of chemical usage. Our reporting was inconsistent, but the metagoal of the EAC was met, in that the new system will lead to better environmental management on campus.

Another frustration has been the difficulty of identifying quantitative measures for each facilities management department. We tried very hard to avoid creating new reporting requirements, in part because the EAC had no authority to do so, and in part to avoid losing the good will of department officials. We recognized that in trying to maintain the delicate balance between getting the information we needed and inconveniencing administrators, we perhaps favored conserving the time of administrators to the detriment of long-term monitoring efforts. It was an unfortunate consequence of attempting to carry out a task for which there was no internal or external mandate. Interestingly, very few departments seemed to have ongoing reporting programs, and, indeed, few seemed to recognize the value that documenting improvements has in garnering support for future efforts. This fact is not surprising in a time of reduced budgets, staff cutbacks, and the demands of an intensely managed urban campus. It is, however, a significant challenge to graduate students who have had little or no experience in designing assessment tools.

B. CAMPUS AS LABORATORY—ENLISTING LIBERAL ARTS IN AN ENVIRONMENTAL MISSION

Although many valuable projects have been successfully completed, and many courses incorporating principles of sustainability have been taught, finding creative ways to bring our message to large numbers of students remains a significant challenge. By assisting English department faculty to adopt the campus-as-laboratory principle and incorporate environmental considerations into courses required by a large number of students, we reached many students who do not enroll in more traditional environmental courses.

University of South Carolina English 101

At the USC in Columbia, approximately ninety percent of the 3,500 incoming freshmen are required to take English 101. Using a minigrant from the SUI faculty, graduate student instructors developed sections designated as "environmental," which included a 10-hour community-learning component related to the environment. By the end of the trial semester in 2001, 220 first-year students had performed approximately 2,200 hours of community service for thirty campus and community agencies. The number of students enrolled in the special environmental sections more than doubled during the second year, and dropped slightly in the third year (see Table 1).

A list of agencies served includes Carolina Native Grass Society, Columbia Historical Preservation Society, Congaree Swamp National Park, Habitat for Humanity, Harbison State Forest, Harvest Hope Food Bank, Oliver Gospel Mission, Riverbanks Zoo & Botanical Gardens, Salvation Army, Sierra Club, and SUI On-Campus projects.

Each 101 section focused on a different topic related to environmental sustainability, around which reading and writing assignments were organized. Topics ranged from "Environmental Citizenship" to "Writing and the Global Environment." In her course titled "Composition and Environmental Sustainability" (Fall 2001), instructor Denise Shaw used the text *The Environmental Predicament: Four Issues for Critical Analysis,* by Carol Verburg, along with a more traditional composition text. Verburg's text is divided into four main issues: Our Responsibility in Sustainability Efforts, The Problem with Garbage, Global Warming, and The Environmental Predicament. Shaw divided her course into four units to follow the text. Through readings, library research, and their community service activities, students discovered and understood (but did not always agree with) arguments relevant to the four issues.

The course required intensive planning. The instructors met over the summer to plan their courses, review composition and environmental textbooks, discuss issues and ideas about sustainability, and decide how the goals of SUI could be incorporated into the classroom. During summer freshman enrollment, an informational flyer was distributed to academic advisors and department heads asking them to inform registering first-year students about the themed 101 sections.

Once registration was completed, the instructors developed an informational packet and letter that was sent to students enrolled in the themed sections explaining how the section would be organized. The prospective students were given an opportunity to withdraw from the courses should they object to the theme or the

Table 1. USC Environmentally Themed English Summary

Impact	Year 1	Year 2	Year 3
Number of sections	9	18	17
Number of instructors	6	9	8[a]
Students	220	560	409
Community service hours	2,200	5,600	4,090

[a]Ten instructors were trained and prepared syllabi; however, because of enrollment pressures in other undergraduate courses, one instructor was assigned upper-level literature courses and another assigned to teach business writing, so that they didn't have an opportunity to teach their 101 and 102 theme syllabi during year 3.

community service/service-learning component. Every section experienced some turnover in enrollment, though there were only three cases that were determined to have occurred directly as a result of the stated requirements (Friend & McLeod, 2002).

A questionnaire was developed to gauge student reactions to the pilot program and to gain a better understanding of the students' response to the course and its theme. The majority of the students reacted positively to the course and indicated that the course increased their environmental awareness. Statistical analysis of the survey responses, completed with the assistance of the USC office of Institutional Planning and Research, indicated, among other patterns, that students felt more knowledgeable about community environmental agencies, that they more regularly kept up with current events, and that they felt more confident about making public arguments than they did before taking the environmental theme course.

We are confident that most of the students were "touched" in some way by the course. One section, focusing on urban environments, sent students into the community to document conflicts arising over potentially incompatible uses—the homeless shelter located across the street from the county library, for example. Students struggling to understand these issues grew in significant ways over the course of the semester.

Student comments indicated that the portion of the course that focused on environmental issues was appreciated. Sample comments included, "I enjoyed the discussion on environmental issues the best of all," "What I enjoyed most about this theme course was being able to learn more about real-world issues," and "I also learned about South Carolina. I am not from here, and it was interesting to see how South Carolina differs from the state I'm from" (First Year English Writing Programs Web site, 2003).

One interesting piece of anecdotal evidence attested to the degree to which these courses connected with students. The Heifer Project is a nonprofit organization that has worked for sixty years to improve the environment and end world hunger by promoting environmentally sound agroecology—using social, cultural, economic, political, and ecological methods that work together to achieve sustainable agricultural production. Donor contributions are used to supply needy families around the world with animals that are appropriate to the community, provide food and a source of income for the recipients, and reproduce so that the gift can be passed along to others, making the entire community stronger and more sustainable. Members of one class presented their teaching assistant/professor with a "gift of bees" (made as a donation to the Heifer Project) at the end of the course. "It struck us all as an enormously successful outcome for Jon's class: not only did the students learn about sustainability in South Carolina, but they then reached outside of the classroom—even outside of the service-learning classroom—into the arena of an international organization that was seeking to provide environmentally sound solutions to the world's problems" (McLeod, 2004). The program began its fourth year during the Fall semester of 2004.

Problems identified by instructors and students included the difficulties in identifying and contacting appropriate service agencies and placing students in a timely fashion. Efforts to enlist the campus Office of Community Service Programs to help were only partly successful; some student resistance to what they perceived as an additional workload and cost (additional texts, etc.) of the environmental sections versus a standard 101 section; instructors had to spend more time on course development and supervision than anticipated; stipends weren't commensurate with the extra work load (Friend & McLeod, 2002).

Expansion of the program in 2002 attempted to address problems reported during the program's first year. Additional teaching assistants were added, stipends were increased, and one graduate assistant received additional stipend monies to coordinate contacts with service agencies. Nine graduate student instructors taught eighteen sections of English 101 and 102. Approximately 560 first-year students performed approximately 5,600 hours of community service for agencies in the community and on campus. The 2002 expansion included development of several environmentally themed sections of English 102, a literature course. A significant number of students from the themed sections of English 101 opted to continue in an environmentally-themed 102 section, many asking for the same faculty member.

One example of an environmental literature course was Corinna McLeod's "Composition and Environmental Literature," which used the anthology *Literature and Nature: Four Centuries of Nature Writing* (Keegan/McKusick, Prentice Hall, 2001). Assignments included reading early exploration literature focused on landscape and the new environments the authors were "discovering," and reading "The Legend of Sleepy Hollow" from the perspective of the environment—how the main character's attitude toward the environment contributed to the suspense and tone of the story. The students read Thoreau's Walking and then went for a walk. A key exercise was placing students in different environments (indoors, outdoors in a busy pedestrian walk versus a more secluded garden spot) and having them write, then examine how the setting affected their thoughts and feelings. Once students saw that environment has an impact on writing, they were better able to see how environment is significant in literature. Students in another English 102 section read about landscapes and worked with the campus landscape architect to relate creation of a landscape to the development of an essay.

The program continued in 2003–4, training 10 instructors who taught 17 course sections, enrolling a total of 409 students. In Fall 2004, the program entered its fourth year, with a somewhat reduced roster of classes. This fact was due in part to key doctoral candidates graduating, coupled with funding issues. One issue peculiar to USC is the fact that the vast majority of the English 101 courses used a textbook published by the English department, meaning that any departure from that text costs the department lost revenue. Since the university has recently adopted a value-centered management approach, no department can afford to bypass a possible revenue stream. At the same time, faculty and students alike are reluctant to endorse a specialized course section that requires buying at least twice as many textbooks as the standard version of the course. In addition, the faculty member who had supervised the graduate assistant instructors and coordinated the program found it increasingly unwieldy to find time for the program on top of her regular duties in the department. When she was asked to assume an administrative position in the First-Year English Program, she was forced to scale back the size of the environmental theme section project.

Clemson University Business and Technical Writing Classes

Clemson's Department of English piloted the Client-Based Program in Business and Technical Writing classes in 2002–3. Eleven sections of English 304 (Business Writing) and English 314 (Technical Writing) participated in the pilot program. Like English 101 at USC, Business Writing and Technical Writing reach many students in a variety of disciplines. The courses are required for majors ranging from agriculture and the sciences to engineering and business. Other students take them in order to fulfill the university's writing requirement. The courses are intended to prepare students for the types of writing tasks they will encounter in the workplace. Six faculty, five campus and two community clients, as well as 260 students were involved in the pilot program.

Potential clients were identified in several ways. Most were known to be interested in or working in environmental sustainability and were simply approached about whether they might need any written products. Some had already established connections to the writing program as guest speakers in writing classes (through a different initiative that parallels the Client-Based Program). After the first semester, many clients continued in the program and told others about the program. Potential clients began to contact the program with ideas. Now the program director no longer has to recruit clients; clients come to the program. The director simply matches the client with a class. First year clients were Clemson Farmers' Market—publicized the existence of the market for food products grown by students and faculty as part of classes or research on campus; Clemson Dining Services—worked with one dining hall to publicize recycling and other "greening" efforts; Clemson Housing—developed materials to highlight environmental programs and projects and educate students living in residence halls; Clemson Calhoun Field Lab—publicized sustainable agriculture research facility and its products; Clemson University Environmental Committee (CUEC)—developed logo and promotional display; Clemson Elementary School—local public school, students developed materials to assist families in caring for community gardens developed by other Clemson classes; and Code Elementary School—local public (Title I) school wrote grant proposals and fundraising booklet to assist in transforming an abandoned football field into a community park. Pilot semester deliverables were 66 poster/signs; 43 flyers and brochures; 22 instruction manuals; 18 white papers and reports; 14 poster presentations; 6 radio, TV, and print ads; 5 Web sites; 2 PowerPoint presentations; and 16 letters, forms, logos and other materials.

A workshop in November 2002 launched the program by bringing together the writing faculty and the clients. The workshop allowed them to learn about each other's needs and about sustainability and to plan for integration of the projects into classes. Classes were held during the Spring semester of 2003.

Work products included reports analyzing possible approaches to "green building" for the Clemson Housing Department, ads promoting conservation and recycling for campus print and electronic media, and promotional brochures for the new campus agriculture and farmers market initiatives. Students also worked with community organizations, assisting in a community consensus-building effort in the nearby town of Seneca and preparing instructions for parents and other volunteers involved in constructing and maintaining the storybook gardens at the new Clemson Elementary School.

In addition to these tangible products, the projects also led to significant changes in the students' own environmental awareness. Instructors reported that students: changed to more sustainable habits by reducing their use of clothes dryers and other "energy hogs"; printed drafts of their documents on recycled paper; made efforts to recycle glass, plastic, and other materials; became more aware of the volume of waste on campus and the costs of disposal; began to under-stand the complexity of environmental policies and practices; and saw themselves as agents of change in the university and community (Taylor & Haque, 2003).

The students clearly engaged in learning about both the environmental issues and the writing skills needed to complete their projects. They also gained practical, real-world experience that will serve them well in their chosen pro-fessions. They learned to cope with the joys and frustrations of team efforts, with jobs that change course at midstream, and with pressures of deadlines and limited resources. The written products that the students produced for their clients will advance the clients' goals to improve environmental sustainability and awareness on the Clemson campus and in the surrounding community. One faculty client said that he "would have had to pay at least $30,000" to obtain the equivalent services from a professional vendor and added that he wasn't sure the product would have been as carefully targeted to the Clemson audience (Skewes, 2003).

The instructors felt that their students were more motivated to learn writing skills because they wanted to complete effective deliverables. They noted that their students were "excited about the projects," "worked hard to meet every deadline," "took on more responsibility for their learning," "wrote much better than students in previous semesters," and "moved way ahead of where I envisioned them to be on such large projects." In short, one teacher said, "The class atmosphere was exciting and a joy to come into every Tuesday and Thursday" (Taylor & Haque, 2003).

The first year of the Client-Based Program produced deliverables for the clients as well as a substantial body of teaching and programmatic materials that can be used in other departments and universities to develop similar programs. In addition to the large binder of teaching materials developed for the workshop, the program now benefits from a client-recruiting packet that includes a booklet about how the program works as well as samples of deliverables produced by students.

Response to the program from teachers, clients, and students has been overwhelmingly positive. In 2003–4, the program included 17 sections, with four new faculty and four returning faculty. Clients have learned from past experiences that the classes are particularly effective in projects that involve the students in communicating to their peers on campus. The clients realized that the students could come up with ideas that appeal to their peers and that faculty/staff would never think of. There were nine clients in 2003–4. Both elementary schools and the Clemson Farmers Market continued and the following were added: CU Library—assessed and addressed problems related to recycling and waste management; CU Environmental Health and Safety Office—developed a manual for individual departmental responsibilities related to regulatory compliance; CU Utility Services—wrote an informational booklet about the utility systems and ways to conserve resources; CU Environmental Committee—began an extensive environmental audit of campus operations; CU Geology Department—educated about and publicized the geology major; AMECO division of Fluor Corporation—(community client) wrote work process procedures to be used for training and monitoring employees.

Clemson continued the program in 2004–5 with $3,500 in donations from the clients to help fund the program. Because it was a pilot effort, the program included only three faculty members teaching four sections. Clients for Fall 2004 were Michelin Corporation, Clemson's Environmental Health and Safety Office, and the Clemson Architecture Library Print Facility.

C. CAMPUS AS A "LIVE-IN" LABORATORY—
USC LIVING/LEARNING CENTER FOR SUSTAINABLE FUTURES

The third example of the integration of academics and operations offers a very different approach. USC's newest residence hall opened in Fall 2004. It is a 500-bed apartment-style complex, incorporating many lessons in cutting-edge design and technology to reduce the structure's impact on the environment. It received the U.S. Green Building Council's Leadership in Energy Environmental Design (LEED) silver rating. It is one of only a few LEED-certified residence halls in the country and the largest in the southeast, if not the world. Students who live in the building cannot help but learn about sustainability as they go through their daily activities.

The building came about as the result of conversations begun in the university's Environmental Advisory Committee and continued between the Director of Housing and the Dean of the School of the Environment. The director simply decided to proceed with a green building, aided by the department's environmental manager (perhaps the first such housing environmental manager in the country).

One of the most remarkable features of the building is that the decision to "go green" was made after the university's board of trustees approved the budget and timetable. Thus, the building was *built in the standard time frame and within the budget allowed for standard construction,* making it clear that "green building" doesn't have to impose burdens on the building owner. The university did receive a small amount of assistance from SUI, as well as a grant of approximately $100,000 from the U.S. Department of Energy, matched by $50,000 from the state energy office, for the experimental fuel cell, but these amounts are inconsequential when viewed within the context of a $32-million construction budget.

The building uses 45 percent less energy and 30 percent less water than similar residence halls on campus built within the last few years. Features include the use of a fuel cell, passive solar and day lighting, light shelves, solar heating for domestic hot water, high efficiency utility equipment, and systems integration and commissioning. Student apartments are individually metered to allow for incentive rebates and close monitoring of energy use by residents. The building is constructed on a slope, allowing for a turf "green roof" over a portion of the facility. The stormwater management system also teaches as it works, since it includes constructed wetlands, xeriscaping, permeable concrete, and a series of terraces that filter water while they provide an amphitheater for student activities.

Students were involved in the development of LEED documentation for the project, and an environmental engineering professor designed a sustainable construction course using the complex. Students and faculty continue to be actively involved in assessing and managing environmental impacts from building operation. For example, students will be allowed to select and maintain plantings on the perimeter of the turf roof, a biology professor and his students are experimenting with a variety of genetically enhanced plants for phytoremediation of stormwater, and several interdisciplinary master's students in Earth and Environmental Resource Management are planning theses based on assessment of the multifaceted stormwater management system.

The Living Learning Center for Sustainable Futures is fully integrated with the residential buildings. The center incorporates classroom and tutoring spaces and creates opportunities for research and learning by making the building's advanced technology as transparent as possible. In addition, the center has a faculty director who organizes learning opportunities and ensures that students are included to the maximum extent possible in events taking place in the center.

Thus, the building not only educates its 500 occupants, but provides a real-world laboratory for students from a number of disciplines.

CONCLUSIONS

As Bruce Herzberg wrote in "Community Service and Critical Teaching," "[s]tudents will not critically question a world that seems natural, inevitable, given; instead, they will strategize about their position within it. Developing a social imagination (through service learning) makes it possible not only to question and analyze the world, but also to imagine transforming it" (Herzberg, 1994). Our mission is to send students into the world prepared to question, to analyze, and to not only "imagine transforming it," but to effect that transformation.

We find that students who become actively engaged in transforming the campus and surrounding community learn not only classroom lessons, but also life skills. The advantages range from resumé-building experiences for students, to products of genuine value to campus administrators. There also are benefits particular to the types of service-learning or campus-as-laboratory experiences we have chosen to highlight.

On a small campus, a single course or activity can sometimes make a significant difference. At sprawling research campuses, on the other hand, even a large number of courses focusing on environmental sustainability may not enroll enough of the student body to make a difference. We have found that reaching out to liberal arts faculty has been an excellent way to carry our message to large numbers of students. We've also found that surrounding students with our message, so that they see it on a daily basis and come to expect a more effective approach to environmental management, is also a way to reach large groups of students. We hope students who have been "immersed" in green buildings demand the same efficiency in buildings they build or buy in the future, and that students who have actually worked on projects related to sustainability will understand its relevance to their careers, regardless of discipline.

Service learning using the campus as a laboratory to test theories of environmental sustainability has not been without its problems. Like any non-traditional activity, the projects described here require more time and effort on the part of faculty and staff involved. As long as grant funds are available to provide stipends, additional materials, and the like, faculty and staff seem willing to participate. When external funding is not available, faculty enthusiasm wanes. Many, if not all, campus laboratory projects require the cooperation and assistance of staff or administrators. These individuals have many demands on their time, a problem exacerbated by dwindling state support for higher education. There is always a tradeoff involved when asking for cooperation; time and energy given now, which may come at the expense of later projects; staff time devoted to working with students may displace time spent on other "conserving" activities, or, in extreme cases, a staff member's experience with students may result in a refusal to cooperate in the future. On balance, however, we find that the advantages far outweigh the disadvantages.

REFERENCES

Friend, C., & McLeod, C. (2002). *Sustainable universities initiative final grant report* at http://www.sc.edu/sustainableu/2002funded.htm.

Herzberg, B. (1994). Community service and critical teaching. In *CCC* 45.3 October, 307-319.

McLeod, C. (2004). Personal communication to P. Jerman.

Taylor, S., & Haque, M. (2003). *Sustainable universities initiative final grant report* at http://www.sc.edu/sustainableu/2003funded.htm.

Skewes, P. (2003). Personal communication to P. Jerman.

University of South Carolina Department of English. Environmentally-themed English 101 Web site.

CHAPTER 10

Teaching Sustainability and Professional Ethics: Production and Values In and Outside the Work Place

William Mass

In this chapter, I report on a single case study as participant observer of a relatively distinctive undergraduate course that I have taught for eight semesters. The course is organized around aspects of sustainable development and primarily oriented to teach technical students, mostly computer science (CS) majors, although the course is open to all students at the University of Massachusetts Lowell (UML). The course structure and content have been shaped by both the initial considerations that motivated and facilitated the course offering and the experience of student/teacher interactions over the last four years. In addition to both spontaneous and structured feedback on assigned material, the course emphasizes class participation in the seminar-teaching style and the value of participation by communities and affected groups in the process of setting goals and implementing programs to achieve sustainable development. Students in the first courses began requesting specific topics for inclusion, and this process was formally included as an opportunity for student/teacher negotiations over course topics to be covered in the last six classes. Introducing unanticipated final topics during the semester was a challenge for instruction both in terms of the intellectual background of the teacher and the time demand of researching topics and developing lesson plans during the busiest part of the academic season. However, the pedagogical payoff was the experience of empowering students to significantly define at least a small part of their own educational experience, and it also provided a laboratory (without controls) for an initial assessment of several influences on the negotiations. Specifically, the influencing factors include prior coursework; the interests students brought to the course, and the dramatic events that occurred during this period, particularly September 11 and the Iraq war and its aftermath. The topicality of major national and international issues defined student interest more than limited perceptions of the immediacy of any local application of the lessons learned from studying the challenges facing the attainment of sustainable development.

This chapter reports on the process and conditions shaping the original development of the course and the background of students enrolled in eight sections (one per semester) from Fall 2001 to Fall 2004. The second section will briefly review the significance of teaching sustainable development within a course also designed to meet the ethics requirement of the CS department. The third section will review the instructor's learning and changes in thematic focus and pedagogy prompted by student response to required readings, resources, and writing assignments. The fourth and final section will describe the dynamics of student/teacher negotiation over course content and the results in terms of topics selected for the final six class meetings and some final observations from the instructor's point of view.

THE DEVELOPMENT OF "SUSTAINABLE DEVELOPMENT: PRODUCTION, WORK, AND VALUES"

Regional Economic and Social Development (RESD) was formed in 1996 as a multidisciplinary department offering a master's degree program. Faculty also taught undergraduate courses as part of their workload, most often out of interest in maintaining engagement with and teaching and service support for the discipline-based departments in the social sciences and humanities. At the same time, departmental-signature-interdisciplinary undergraduate courses were developed as a resource aligned with the general education mission and to introduce undergraduates to the themes and career-development possibilities provided by the department's graduate program as a way to attract applicants. Although there are now six such courses, only two are offered each semester. Both of the courses evolved through collaborative efforts of RESD faculty members of different disciplinary backgrounds. One is "An Introduction to Regions: The Merrimack Valley," which begins with a focus on the disparate paths of development of the two Massachusetts cities of Lowell and Lawrence. This course investigates a variety of social, economic, and environmental themes primarily through contrasting the experiences of other cities and their surroundings as the primary unit of analysis. The course was designed and scheduled by classroom location (see below) to attract primarily social-science and humanities students. The other regularly offered course is "Sustainable Development: Production, Work and Values" (hereafter "SD" or "Sustainable Development") which I have taught once a semester for the last four years.

The UML campus is geographically fragmented, although not to the degree of a C. P. Snow-like two-culture cleavage; science and engineering departments and courses are located on North Campus, while the social sciences and humanities are on South Campus. This arrangement makes it difficult to attract students from the technical disciplines to attend courses in the social disciplines and vice versa.

This interdisciplinary course grew out of an interest in providing a complementary undergraduate course that would focus more intensively on the workplace, the firm, and industry as the primary units of analysis. The goal was to develop a course to service students in technical disciplines that would provide a broad and integrative approach to a variety of social, economic, and environmental concerns. The first effort at developing SD was a collaborative effort with my colleague Sarah Kuhn. Sarah is a planner by training, with expertise in issues related to the development of software-work organization, work process, and professional development. The course linked a study of firm and industry development through three industry case studies of textile, auto, and computer-software industries with considerations of design concepts as an approach to ethical conflicts common to professional experience and environmental practices in particular.

SD was scheduled for Fall 1998, but it failed to attract sufficient enrollment to be held. During the academic year, the course secured approval to meet an undergraduate general-education requirement for social sciences as well as satisfy a CS department requirement that majors take an ethics-related course. For CS majors, the course was thus a "twofer"—it satisfied both a general education and an ethics requirement. This dual designation was critical for attracting the core student enrollments as summarized below. Six courses that fulfill the ethics requirement, have been approved by the CS department; each one also satisfies a general education requirement.

The SD course is structured as a seminar, and enrollment is capped at 30 students. The new course in Spring 2001 attracted 12 students, but enrollment increased over the four years that it was offered so that it has remained in the mid-20s. The proportion of CS majors has ranged from 61 to 75 percent, while the majority of the other students major in social sciences or business. There are always a few students majoring in the sciences and usually one or more in the fine arts or humanities. Since most students are CS majors, the most frequent focus of examples used in class are chosen to emphasize software engineering and electronic appliance industries. However, since the use of computers, the Internet, and software is ubiquitous in modern life, particularly for college students, these topics and examples have been generally more appealing to students. In fact, the special knowledge the CS students bring to class has been valuable in stimulating discussions, as has the range of concerns introduced by students with other expertise and interests to the CS students.

THE ROLE OF PROFESSIONAL EDUCATION
AND ETHICS REQUIREMENTS

In general, the emergence of engineering ethics and computing ethics as academic fields of study has developed more or less concurrently over the last two decades. The intellectual history of the relation of these developments is beyond the scope of this chapter (see Herkert, 2003 for an introduction to the issues). The increasing recognition of the importance of education about professional ethics is reflected in the changing criteria for accreditation in both fields. Here, too, there has been increasing overlap and formal organizational relations. Recently, the accreditation board for computer science was integrated with the Accreditation Board for Engineering and Technology (ABET). The CS department at UML is accredited, and the development of its ethics course requirement for majors was a part of the process. There was no explicit priority on sustainability as a focus for ethical considerations, only an acceptance of this choice as one among others.

Engineering ethicists have distinguished between micro- and macrolevels of analysis and ethical considerations. "Micro-level" analysis of "individual technologies or practitioners" identifies microethical questions focused on the relationships between individual engineers and their clients, colleagues, and employers. "Macrolevel" analysis of "technology as a whole" addresses the collective social responsibility of the profession and public policy.

Joseph Herkert writes that

> . . . engineering ethicists seem more interested in and better prepared to deal with micro-ethical issues, while computing ethicists are much more willing and able to take on macro-ethical concerns. It seems to us that this distinction results at least partly from the strong tradition of professional practice and professionalism in engineering and the important role it has played in the development of engineering ethics. Given that the roots of computing are more abstract and academic than those of engineering, computer ethics has developed in an atmosphere that does not parallel the professional traditions of engineering. On the other hand, unlike engineering ethicists, from the very beginning computer ethicists have more naturally turned to the broader social implications of information and computing technology. (2003, p. 36)

If this course attracted a larger number of engineering students, it would be possible to evaluate the extent to which this difference would be reflected in the response of CS and engineering majors to the SD course.

The distinction between macro- and microethical levels of analysis is helpful in distinguishing the approach in the two major sections of the SD course. The course primarily focuses on macroethical themes in introducing the concept of sustainable development in the first half of the course, while shifting to emphasize microlevel ethical considerations after the midterm. The importance of order and relationship of ethical considerations is neither accidental nor incidental. In addition, the SD course adopts the point of view of Whitbeck, who views ethical problems as practical issues, where identifying an effective response is analogous to approaching a design challenge. Design problems are highly constrained, as are ethical problems. Rarely, if ever, is there a unique correct solution, and outcome evaluation is dependent upon whether the design is more or less effective in "coping," as opposed to whether it reflects a unique optimal solution. Often it is possible (and desirable) to partially satisfy many of the demands simultaneously, and initial assumptions that conflicts are irresolvable may be misguided.

Whitbeck further identifies dimensions of design problems significant for ethical problems: 1) There may not be one correct solution, but some solutions may be clearly wrong; 2) Alternative solutions may differ as to their relative advantages or merits; 3) Solutions must achieve the desired performance or end result, conform to specifications or explicit criteria; be reasonably secure against negative consequences, i.e., "do no harm" (Hippocratic oath), be consistent with existing background constraints. Furthermore, the problem of treating ethical dilemmas from the perspective of a judge or an outside critic is more to insulate oneself from criticism rather than stimulate creativity in looking for solutions; even excellent solutions can be improved upon (1996).

The design analogy is important throughout the course, and Whitbeck's analysis is assigned reading. Particularly for students engaged in technical/ professional training, the use of a design approach is significant in both defining context (performance standards and constraints) and as practical application of the more abstract goals of sustainability. There remains a tension between approaching design challenges in terms of rationality and the role of authority—that is, who determines, and how, the weighting of priority dimensions of the performance standards to be met? The course incorporates both a search for better designs and the role of conflicting values and interests as well as the exercise of social, political, and economic power in standard setting.

As described further below, a design exercise in the first half of the course requires each student to develop a "sustainability indicator." They must address some combination of environmental, economic, and community dimensions of SD and assess the indicator's relative strengths and weaknesses in terms of precision, data accessibility, and ease of comprehension. In the second half of the course, there are two in-class exercises in particular that present a succession of scenarios where students discuss in small groups and report on their approach to responding to ethical challenges and business goals. The in-class exercises are adapted from online available cases. One of the exercises focuses on the pressure to recommend a specific product-development strategy in response to management directives. The initial conditions present uncertainty and unevenness in the early indications from the research team's findings and past experience. The influencing factors include relations among the research team, immediate and higher-level supervisors and what is known about competitors' strategies. The exercise also echoes earlier course discussion of the relative clarity of scientific evidence to take action relative to a standard of indication of possible harm to human health and the environment known as the "precautionary principle." (Adapted from "LAROM Case Study: Data and Decisions" at http://ethics.tamu.edu/pritchar/larom.htm).

The second exercise presents the process of developing a plan for expansion of new production facilities into a new, low-density community where one of the employees serving on the town's environmental quality planning committee resides. (Adapted from "PARKVILLE : Moral conflicts and conflicts of interest" at http://ethics.tamu.edu/pritchar/parkvill.htm). This case investigates alternatives to responding to a situation rife with conflicts of interest and varying pressures and expectations from supervisors. It also presents an opportunity to consider aspects of design alternatives for "Smart Growth" in terms of commuting, preservation of the natural environment, and mitigation of the environmental impacts of economic development. In both cases, limited information is presented in the first scenario, and students discuss what responses are preferred, what information may clarify alternatives, and what determines their choice of action. In subsequent scenarios, new information is added, and they consider both how robust their initial choice is under changed circumstances and the considerations outside the limited scenario-based information that influence the choices made by various participants.

In this regard, the educational impact of an ethics course and concern for sustainability within the context of professional training in particular, is in part a reflection of what is context for what. Fletcher and Dewberry have developed a graphic image (see Figure 1) to illustrate contrasting approaches. On one end, concerns for sustainability are introduced as exemplary cases within the context of

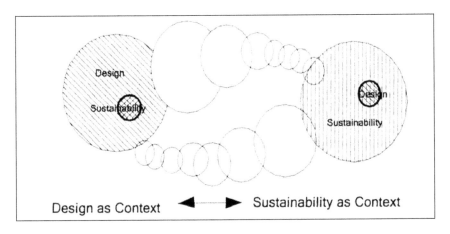

Figure 1. Sustainability and context.
Source: Fletcher & Dewberry, Fig. 1, p. 40. Adapted and reproduced with permission, Emerald Group Publishing Limited.

professional design training (whatever the particular design-focused discipline—including engineering and computer science as applied in product development contexts) and, on the other end, a broader education about sustainability provides the general framework within which all design challenges must be addressed. These considerations parallel a debate about the relative effectiveness of meeting educational goals for ethical themes in general, or sustainability in particular, and whether it is more effective to develop stand-alone ethics courses or incorporate ethical considerations within the more technically-oriented required courses. Joseph Herkert states: "The ideal solution (where practical in terms of staffing requirements and room in the curriculum) is to use a combination of methods— a required course in engineering ethics and an engineering curriculum that recognizes the importance of ethics throughout" (Herkert, 2002, p. 11). In other words, the ideal is not a choice along the Fletcher and Dewberry spectrum, but practicing educational models at both ends. However, the important caveats within the Herkert ideal recognize the regulating constraints of staffing and curriculum overload so that the UML experience of separate course themes is likely the rule rather than the exception.

CONTENT, PEDAGOGY, AND STUDENT-TEACHER MUTUAL LEARNING

Teaching an introductory survey course about sustainable development to technically oriented students, mostly CS majors, without prior orientation to any previous studies of environmental issues of any type, is a challenge and has provided unexpected teaching satisfaction. (Self-report—described further below.) To be frank, I did not expect the near-complete lack of environmental awareness of most students or the eye-opening responses of so many to the course. The overall experience has increased my enthusiasm for teaching the course and, to a significant degree, has altered one stream of my research agenda to include aspects of renewable energy.

A heuristic model, which is useful in a snapshot for communicating the challenge of an integrative approach to multidisciplinary learning in a design context, is provided from the work of Fletcher and Dewberry (see Figure 2):[1] The six design principles identified in their work are efficiency, appropriateness, sufficiency, equity, systems, and scale.

Although the course fails to offer exercises in the sense of a design-studio course where teams share information and disciplinary-based expertise, it aspires to accomplish similar aims through assignments requiring student-directed learning, information sharing from a variety of perspectives, and simulation of

[1] The Design for the Environment Multimedia Implementation Project—demi—links design and sustainability information in a Web-based resource and was set up in response to a number of UK Government reports which highlighted the dearth of knowledge and activity about sustainability in higher education design courses across the country" (Fletcher & Dewberry, 2002, p. 45).

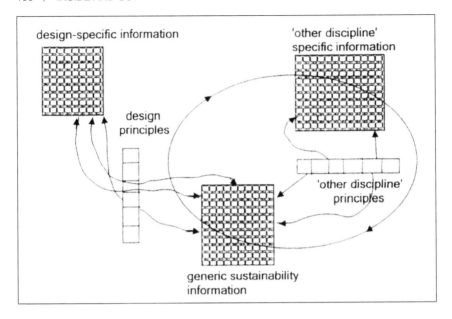

Figure 2. Knowledge transfer in the design framework.
Source: Fletcher & Dewberry, Fig. 2, p. 40. Adapted and reproduced with permission, Emerald Group Publishing Limited.

design-inspired exercises. While Fletcher and Dewberry's insights were not known prior to the author's research into pedagogy related to sustainability undertaken for this chapter, the six principles are a useful guide and succinctly capture much of the directly developed theory and metacontent of the course examples. What is left out of their list is an emphasis on the importance of innovation to achieve sustainability goals. An explicit focus on innovation is presented through the reading of two classic articles by Michael Porter and Claas van der Linde, and William McDonough and Michael Baumgarten. The latter authors in particular draw an important distinction between eco-efficiency and eco-effectiveness, where the latter term refers to ecologically based innovations rather than the former term's indication of a standard for improvements that merely diminish harmful environmental impacts. The distinction is drawn from McDonough's expertise as a leading innovative architect concerned with integrating ecological principles in the design of products, processes, and structures (McDonough & Braungart, 1998; Porter & van der Linde, 1995).[2]

---

[2] Also an inspirational video—"The Next Industrial Revolution"—featuring McDonough and Braungart, available through Bullfrog Films: http://www.bullfrogfilms.com/catalog/next.html.

What follows is an overview of the goals of the course readings, seven short writing assignments, the take-home midterm, and the final essay examination. Early readings are designed to introduce terms and concepts related to ecology, economics, and sociology while concurrently requiring students to explore these concepts through Internet searching and application of concepts developed in the readings and class discussion. With one exception, students select the content and are evaluated according to their ability to creatively apply class concepts, thus the assignments are referred to as Learning Exercises (LEs). The purpose of each LE is mutual learning through shared results and findings the day the LE is due.

The first LE directs students to visit several notable sites that define sustainable development, requires that they find additional sites of value in understanding sustainable development, choose one of their Web sites, explain their choice, and finally evaluate the Web site in terms of criteria developed by Paula Hammett (1999).[3] The discussion serves the dual purposes of focusing on both sustainable development concepts and applications, as well as identifying strengths and limitations of Web resources. A follow-up second LE directs students to Maureen Hart's Sustainable Measures Web site (http://www.sustainablemeasures.com/) and requires that they develop an indicator of sustainability and discuss the significance of their measure for environmental, economic, and social/community aspects of sustainability as well as the strengths and limits of their indicator. As explained to students and as in systematic investigations in all disciplines, the notion of sustainability requires the development of theoretical constructs and measures that attempt to evaluate whether there is progress or regress in relation to identifiable goals. The LEs have been refined and altered over the last four years. The major change is that there now exist many more relevant Web sites as resources because students continue to add to my inventory of valuable sites. The third and fourth LEs have changed the most since the course was first taught in response to students' complaints and suggestions. The process of securing their responses has been primarily through the seventh and final LE, so explaining this last LE is important to understanding the changes in the third and fourth LEs.

The seventh LE provides systematic feedback by a list of questions that is introduced with the statement: "This exercise does not ask for an overall evaluation of the course or my instruction, but rather asks you to provide evaluations of specific aspects of the course." This assignment provides written feedback, a basis for class discussion at the end of the term that has proved more valuable than the spontaneous and informal statements that otherwise supplement my own limited observations and opinions.

---

[3] For a handy guide incorporating Hammett's schema with useful illustrations see the Sonoma State University Library guide at http://libweb.sonoma.edu/assistance/eval.html

As a result of the formal student feedback, the most significant changes in the first half of the course were the increase in the focus on sustainable alternatives to existing practice relative to critiques of current poor environmental practices, increased use of videos, and the selection of examples that pertained more directly to CS students. Meeting these three goals sometimes was achieved within the same new course material. I was initially skeptical about the value of videos and the media- and monitor-prone student orientation, but the heightened animation of class discussion, the increased availability of high-quality videos, and continued student feedback has won me over. I have balanced what I refer to as disaster tales of near (or actual) criminal environmental behavior and inspirational examples of the application of green technologies and principles. I used one video the first semester (on pollution prevention) and now have students view four.[4] The videos provide narrative and imagery in context and deepen acceptance and understanding of the validity of the readings, if only because they are more vivid and are as close a substitute for field trips as possible. The student-prompted subject matter changes in the course-introduced material on computer and related electronic appliances. A pollution-prevention video focused on the semiconductor industry, and LE three focused on the Silicon Valley Toxics Campaign Web site, especially the Annual Computer Report Card (for example, http://www.svtc.org/cleancc/pubs/2003report.htm) on corporate environmental policies, as well as other readings on e-waste.

The fourth LE requires review of a survey on trends in occupational health, and additional readings focus on occupational exposures for workers in the electronics sector. The student feedback has expressed dissatisfaction with these readings more often than any other section of the course. Finding a well-written and relatively succinct general reading on occupational health and safety appropriate to an introductory survey course has been quite difficult, and several selections have been used. The electronics-sector occupational examples have been well received. The non-CS majors appear to value this extended focus on the electronics sector, I believe, primarily because of the increased importance of electronics appliances in all aspects of their lives, at work and at home. After the concepts have become more familiar, there are no videos after the midterm, and instead, the student feedback prompted the development of more case-study material, which was used as the basis of in-class exercises requiring small-group, question-guided discussions, and feedback reports to the class as a whole. The availability of Web sites with engineering and CS ethics case studies has been a valuable resource for adapting case studies for in-class exercises as described earlier in this chapter.

---

[4] "Trade Secrets: A Moyer's Report" http://www.pbs.org/tradesecrets/ "The semiconductor and electronics industry" Preserving the Legacy series produced by: Intelecom Intelligent Communications, and distributed by Magic Lantern Communications; "The NEXT Industrial Revolution" see footnote 2; and "A Dangerous Business" http://www.pbs.org/wgbh/pages/frontline/shows/workplace/

One final observation about the first half of the course concerns advancing awareness among students of university environmentally related activities. I am able to take advantage of many opportunities to introduce students to the leading work of departments as well as research and outreach centers at the university within the context of the discussion of assigned readings. For example, the Department of Work Environment at UML has both faculty directors from the nation's first state-funded Toxics Use Reduction Institute and leaders in defining alternative environmentally appropriate materials policies. The Lowell Center for Sustainable Production has provided leadership for promoting and educating around the precautionary policy and its application in state initiatives, as well as product stewardship principles extending throughout a product's lifecycle from design to recycling or disposal. Furthermore, I can refer to the Center for Sustainable Energy's development of photovoltaic systems and their application in developing economies. Experiments contributing to the development of electric cars and rooftop windmills take place at the Center for Electric Cars and Energy Conversion. (More information about the activities of UML centers is available at http://www.uml.edu/research/centers.htm) The significance of the ability to identify ongoing activities related to the course subject matter is reflected in one student's comments:

> There were many aspects of this class that I found very valuable. One of the most important was the emphasis on groups and programs in the Lowell area that are leading the way in sustainable development. I felt it was very educational to have a local perspective on these issues.

The fifth and sixth LEs focus each student on the microethical challenges confronting individuals, whatever professional career path they pursue. These LEs are better presented and explained in the context of the second half of the course, when the focus turns to the role of professional codes of ethics and ethical considerations in professional development more generally.

DECISION MAKING AND PROFESSIONAL MICROETHICAL CHALLENGES

In 1993, the IEEE Computer Society (IEEE-CS) and ACM established a Joint Steering Committee for Establishment of Software Engineering as a Profession. With nearly 100,000 members, the IEEE Computer Society is the world's leading organization of computer professionals. The ACM is an international scientific and educational organization dedicated to advancing the arts, sciences, and applications of information technology. With a worldwide membership of 78,000, ACM functions as a locus for computing professionals and students working in the various fields of Information Technology. The committee established a Task Force on Software Engineering Ethics and Professional Practices that eventually produced Version 5.2 of the "Software Engineering Code of Ethics and Professional Practice" in 1998. It was jointly approved and accepted by the IEEE-CS and ACM in December 1998. The code has the status of an IEEE standard.

Without elaborating all of the distinguishing features of the new IEEE-CS/ACM Code of Ethics, suffice it to note the prominent inclusion of a new primacy clause and the explicit statement that the public interest is central. The preamble notes: ". . . concern for the health, safety and welfare of the public is primary. . . ." In contrast to previous versions, the current code strives to more thoroughly address three levels of obligations (humanity, professional obligations in general, and the software engineering profession in particular); helps clarify the distinction between potentially conflicting choices; provides moral principles as a guide for decision making; and charts a strategy for moral decision making. The code gives examples and details of how these aspirations change the way individuals behave as software-engineering professionals (see Gotterbarn, Miller, & Rogerson, 1999, and the full code at http://www.acm.org/serving/se/code.htm). "Without the aspirations, the details can become legalistic and tedious; without the details, the aspirations can become high sounding but empty; together, the aspirations and the details form a cohesive code" (Lobo, 2001, p. 2).

A fifth LE requires students to find a different professional code of ethics of their choosing with instructions to explain: "How (in contrast to the software engineering code of ethics) are the two codes similar and different? What is your opinion about these codes, and about codes of ethics in general?" The usual practice is to find a code of ethics of a profession that students aspire to or one with which they have personal, often family, exposure.

The fifth LE was introduced as a preliminary to the sixth, which is the most demanding of a student's time and was generally experienced as the single most important course experience, often reported to me as one of the most interesting and valuable of their undergraduate experience. Students are required to identify and arrange an interview with someone with at least 10 years of experience in a profession that they most want to learn more about. They are provided directions on conducting and writing a report of the interview and are instructed to minimally: inquire as to the interviewee's education about and familiarity with his/her profession's code of ethics; show the individual a copy of their profession's code of ethics if they are unfamiliar and ask them to evaluate its purpose and value; and ask about the most common and most challenging ethical dilemmas they have encountered in their careers.

Despite the advances in defining ethical standards and professional interests for inducing and influencing ethical behavior, their purpose and function are examined for relevancy and serving selfish interests. The interests of professional societies and the functions of ethical codes are investigated and discussed as they concern protection from regulation and public relations. These aspects may or may not conflict with the stated broader aims of the code of ethics.

In the intervening three weeks, between the fifth and sixth LEs, the course readings have varied over the eight semesters, but typically they identify a range of ethical considerations in the workplace setting. In response to student request for examples of direct application of ethical considerations in the professional setting and in light of common experiences reflected in the reported interviews, I developed the in-class exercises described above. The readings emphasize 1) decision making by technologists with incomplete data and significant uncertainty, yet the outcome is significant for job performance evaluation; and 2) moral conflicts and conflicts of interest within a context of environmental impacts. The direct purpose of these in-class exercises is to provide a more compelling practical context requiring individual reactions; they are "warm ups" to the sixth and culminating LE.

I encourage the CS majors to interview a software engineer professional, excluding their CS professors. Typically, they do not have trouble contacting a professional with the requisite experience, and CS faculty have been helpful in providing contacts for students when necessary, often with UML CS alumni. Students are given three weeks to complete the assignment compared to the usual one week in addition to time required to present the readings and the in-class exercises. They are forewarned that the greatest difficulty in arranging an interview is scheduling with a busy professional on relatively short notice, even one amenable to making his or her time available. A small percentage of CS majors and almost all non-CS majors choose to interview non-CS professionals from a range of professions including lawyers, healthcare professionals, retail managers, counselors, and realtors. Interviews also have been conducted with art dealers, police, firepersons, and coaches.

The class energy for and discussion of this exercise are invariably the liveliest of the semester. The aim of the exercise is to complement the preceding lessons that focus primarily on macroethical questions with an environmental emphasis. Personal contact with someone in a profession that a student is interested in and hearing stories and lessons with ethical dimensions of practical importance are reported in the seventh and final LE, described above, as a highlight of the course experience.

Although it was not a conscious intention, I believe the experience is, in a sense, an academic climax and intellectual integration of the self-directed learning aspects of the class. I believe it sustains if not enhances class energy, focus, and commitment at a point in the semester when exhaustion and preoccupation with reaching the finish line begin to predominate. The range of issues raised in student interviews is too broad to cover here completely, but almost universally students are surprised by what they learn from the interviews, including and especially when a working student interviews an older colleague they have known for a considerable period of time. Even when the general issues are familiar, the particularity of context and outcome enhances the value and importance of asking the types of questions raised in class readings and discussion, if not the specific examples.

I reviewed 15 interview reports from the Spring 2003 course from retained e-submissions, which I encourage but do not require. The types of microethical challenges discussed included product reliability versus early release of products for competitive advantage; confidentiality; intellectual property rights; management pressures to "cook the books" or "fix the data"; representation of product performance characteristics to prospective buyer or customer; differences in experience as a worker and a supervisor responsible for enforcing ethical behavior; unethical if not illegal bidding, budgeting, and billing practices; worker responsibility without adequate competence or support; company policy to limit documentation so as to limit liability; and software designed for invasion of privacy.

While many of these examples have been consistent over the period this course has been taught, there have been some recent changes. In particular, during the recent severe downsizing in high technology firms, which has been more severe in Massachusetts than in most other states, one student and his interviewee eloquently described an increasingly common dilemma:

> Whether it's relocation or all-out termination, changes will come whether the workers like it or not. As a lab manager in charge of hundreds of pieces of equipment and the lab in which they are housed, it is necessary to have knowledge of the equipment being relocated. This often means that the manager knows an employee's fate before the employee himself does, but does not yet have authorization to pass on this information. The situation becomes even more difficult when the manager must extract information about that worker's equipment without letting on to the worker why he needs that information. These kinds of circumstances can breed hostility and resentment because it is often apparent that the manager knows more than he is willing to say. It would be against company policy to inform the employee of his fate within the company, but it is morally taxing to withhold the truth. It becomes such a problem, that a manager may find himself going against the wishes of his supervisors and informing an employee of his fate. While discussing this very problem, my own supervisor told me in an interview, "Sometimes you have to pick certain people to take into your confidence, whether it's what upper management would like you to do or not."

In addition, I discovered the following unsolicited comments that, even discounting for the possible perceived value of a compliment to the teacher, reflected my overall sense of student appreciation and surprise at the value of the assignment: "This has to be the most exciting homework I had in a while; being used to resolving problems and writing essays, having to do this interview was rather refreshing and amusing at the same time"; "Reading the theories about ethics is beneficial, but it's not possible to fully understand their influence until you talk to a real person in an industry"; "It is startling that only twelve years ago there was this much sexist behavior"; "After my experience in interviewing a professional in the software engineering field, I have learned that there are frequent ethical decisions to be made, some more important than others, and that it is important as a professional to do your best to make good choices."

Finally, one evaluation of LE6 captured the surprise and value of the interview experience very directly and summarized my central explicit goals in requiring the interview:

> The most striking thing I discovered was the frequency with which ethical dilemmas occur in professional life. It is not once a year or once a month, as I would have assumed prior to the interview, but these dilemmas occur on a near daily basis. It is something that must be constantly pondered and dealt with. As a result of this perspective on ethics I now have, I feel I am better prepared to pursue a profession.

NEGOTIATED COURSE TOPICS: STUDENT INTEREST AND GLOBAL EVENTS

The last phase of the course is defined through negotiations with the class over the topics to be selected. I allow great latitude for topics under consideration given the introductory survey breadth of the course and my priority on sustaining enthusiasm for the continuing development and challenge of applying a sustainable-development conceptual framework. The topics chosen have surprised me, and I have valued what I have learned by the students' priorities as well as the occasional content contributed by the students directly. The process generally has been a matter of alerting students to the prospect and their responsibility to develop topics along with my willingness to accept the student vote. Although I reserved the right to veto, I have not exercised my authority since the topics chosen so far have been appropriate. I have shaped the way the topics chosen by the class were explored by maintaining responsibility for selecting readings and directing or facilitating class discussion. Very often, students have identified readings they wish to share with the class and discuss more generally.

The first semester I taught SD, I expected to respond to student interest in the final "to-be-determined" readings to end the course, but I did not have a process in mind. I expected to select the final course topics, but student interest was strong, so I engaged the students in defining their topics of interest. The list of topics selected in this and subsequent semesters is a record of how current events dominated the process. Very few topics selected were primarily focused at the microethical level or stimulated by issues primarily identified in the university or surrounding community.

In early 2001, the U.S. financial bubble burst and the economy slid into a recession. The Spring 2001 topics selected by students included: Are Current U.S. Income and Wealth Trends Sustainable?; Is the U.S. Trade Deficit Sustainable?; Biotechnology: The Basics and Engineering Humans; Intellectual

Property, Commerce, and the Internet. Topic selection in this first semester exceeded my expectations for breadth and student interest, so I formalized the process in subsequent semesters by announcing early in the course that the topics required in the final six class meetings would be jointly negotiated with the class. The required readings for the selected topics were noticeably longer than was typical for other assigned readings, but the level of class participation and individual responses on the final learning exercise indicated that the level of reading prior to class meeting was not systematically different than earlier in the course. I did continue to list possible topics on the syllabus without listing any associated required readings to illustrate the possibilities. I listed the topics selected by students the previous semester on the syllabus of the succeeding semester and expected more continuity in topic selection. However, in general, macro developments dominated student selection, and the subsequent wars in Afghanistan and Iraq dominated student interests.

The first dominant event was, of course, the terrorist attacks of September 11. It was a topic of interest from early in the Fall 2001 semester, and there were occasions to discuss news events early in the semester. Students were aware that related subjects could be a focus of the final course topics. In addition, the interest and selected readings on economic issues were refocused on the changes in federal tax policy and a greater interest in aspects of globalization. At the same time, student interest in software-related topics focused on the role of Microsoft, and I selected readings concerned with intellectual property, market dominance, the character of innovation, and consumer impact. In Spring 2002, interest in economic issues continued, but it was focused on Enron and similar corporate scandals. The semester saw another round of escalating violence in the Palestinian-Israeli conflict in the wake of the "War on Terror." The students' topic choices prompted my selection of readings relating the two. The class chose for the first time to study the topic of biotechnology as defined by a previous class.

As the political and military build-up to the Iraq war dominated the news during the Fall 2002 semester, student interest shifted from September 11 and Afghanistan and prompted new readings on the geopolitics of Iraq, oil, and the Middle East. Interest in biotechnology was focused on human cloning. Student awareness of Bush Administration environmental policies was more acute than in previous terms for reasons I cannot now reconstruct. Two students in particular with backgrounds in chemistry (one a chemical engineering student and the other a CS major) were struck by the importance of materials policy during the classes focusing on clean technology and the precautionary principle. They were very articulate in persuading the class to select the developing field of "Green Chemistry," a topic that proved the most challenging for me to find teachable materials for nonchemists (both the other students and me).

The dominating event in the Spring 2003 term was the U.S.-Iraq war and, in highly animated discussions, students defined and selected topics solely related to the war including Islam, Terrorism and the West; Ethnic Divisions in Iraq; The Geneva Conventions and Weapons of Mass Destruction; and Post-War Iraq. The last topic focused on Iraqi oil, the challenges of reconstruction, and the political "fallout" of the war.

During Fall 2003, students maintained interest and concern about post-war Iraq and focused on "Stabilization, Exit Strategy, and Nation Building." Also, continuing debate about long-term U.S. interests and commitments reinforced a repeated topic from the prior semester with updated readings on "The Bush Doctrine and American Empire—Facts and Contested Policy." A new topic was introduced, with significant leadership from one student who provided an article about the activities of Lawrence Lessig, and a topic was defined as "Free Software Movement and the Creative Commons." Lessig's work was particularly apt for CS students studying sustainability, and the link was made quite immediately based on the metaphor of the "Commons." Lessig is a Professor of Law at Stanford Law School and founder of the school's Center for Internet and Society. He also chairs the Creative Commons project (see http://creativecommons.org/). Creative Commons is a nonprofit organization that offers a flexible range of protections and freedoms for authors and artists. The first reading assignments in the SD course build on the metaphor of the commons to explain the challenge of maintaining healthy ecological systems in the face of counterproductive individual incentives (Hardin, 1977; Commoner, 1971, 2001). Lessig's pioneering activities have identified a parallel and increasingly significant problem of private intellectual property rights that impoverish common cultural possibilities, including the development of software applications (Lessig, 2002, 2003).

This chapter's final revision took place during Fall 2004. The students' selected topics included focus on the events in Iraq, the U.S. occupation, and efforts at stabilization; but there was apparent exhaustion with topics related to the campaigns, especially after the presidential election. To my surprise, students are very interested in and have chosen topics related to alternative fuels and vehicles. I believe the interest is spurred by the significant recent rise in the cost of gasoline and the students' underlying long-term interest in a broader choice of vehicles. The topic reflects a type of collective interest in future individual modes of transportation that can be environmentally friendly and what it will require to reduce their relative cost and attain commercial viability.

Several general dynamics are apparent from a review of the course's topic definitions and students' topic selections. First, student choices were not dominated by my suggestions, which, after the first two semesters, were the choices of students in the prior semester. Second, students were interested in a diversified if small portfolio of topics that were reflective of the environmental and economic breadth of the course except when events of global significance dominated the news. Third, such news-dominating events, specifically related to 9/11, foreign policy, and military action in Central Asia and the Middle East, created teaching opportunities the likes of which I have rarely experienced in terms of intense classwide interest at the undergraduate level. The reality of the role of and impact on U.S. energy and economic policy that bears directly on issues of environmental, economic, and community sustainability could not be more acute. I believe the relationship between of energy security, foreign policy, and environmental policy was the elephant in the room that had to be discussed, given student interest, to reinforce if not legitimize the relevance of this introductory survey course on sustainable development. As foreign and military policy dominate national policy considerations, the already inadequate domestic priority on environmental quality and economic equity concerns is downgraded further, as are the prospects for effective global coordination necessary to meet environmental challenges. The macroethical questions regarding U.S. policy selected by students provides an opportunity to address such concerns with the benefit of empowered students, hopefully motivated to consider these issues more deeply and with a broader sustainable-development perspective.

CONCLUSION

Appropriate to this chapter's emphasis on students' participation in structuring their own educational experience, even in a field of study almost always previously unexplored in a classroom setting, I will close by drawing on two students' reflections. One wrote, "(T)he fact that the material for the last part of the course was chosen by the students themselves was wonderful. I've never before been in a class structured this way. It really helped to bring the course into my field of vision, especially since all my votes were winners." Beyond the extra satisfaction of being on the winning side in a majority vote, and as stated by many students in many different ways, the engagement of responsibility for defining possible options and setting the direction of their own learning was a value of empowerment in itself. Furthermore, I believe, as this student suggested, that it deepened the sense of utility of the preceding learning experiences in the course. Another student wrote, "Furthermore, I liked the fact that we were able to choose topics of our own interest. This made the course very unique and helped me being (sic) more knowledgeable about day-to-day social discussions." This statement captures what I believe was the dominant impact of the most significant, newsworthy developments that focused the attention of students' interests when defining options for further study. The exceptions were the topics chosen that were related to software and intellectual property concerns. The majority CS students were aware of their topicality as well as the professional and general significance of these issues to a degree unlikely to be duplicated by a class of students from a different field of study. The drawback of the microlevel focus on professional development is that while it prepares students as participants in a work or professional setting, aware of their community responsibilities, it does not enhance or promote an immediate focus on how to more effectively participate in microlevel, community-based environmental activities. The course undoubtedly increases student awareness of the latter possibilities, but it would take significant changes and reorientation of the course, or more likely follow-up courses, to more directly advance microlevel, community-based environmental educational and action goals.

ACKNOWLEDGMENT

The author is greatly indebted to Sarah Kuhn for the original course-development collaboration, her pioneering staffing of this course the first time it was offered, and her general introduction into the design approach to professional education. I also am appreciative of specific assistance from Dongsheng Li and Robert MacAuslan. I also want to thank editor Robert Forrant for his helpful questions and suggestions that improved this chapter. Finally, I would like to thank the nearly 200 students who have taken a course in Sustainable Development with me over the last four years and what I have learned with and from them. As usual, I claim all responsibility for the errors of omission and commission remaining in this chapter.

REFERENCES

Commoner, B. (1971). *The closing circle: Nature, man, and technology.* New York: Knopf.

Commoner, B. (2001). *The impacts of humankind's industrial activities on our health and ecosystems.* Presented at the International Summit on Science and the Precautionary Principle, Lowell, MA, September 20-22.

Fletcher, K., & Dewberry, E. (2002). Demi: A case study in design for sustainability. *International Journal of Sustainability in Higher Education, 3*(1), 38-47.

Gotterbarn, D., Miller, K., & Rogerson, S. (1999, October). Software engineering code of ethics is approved. *Communication of the ACM, 42*(10).

Hardin, G. (1977). The Tragedy of the Commons. *Science, 162*(1968), 1243-1248. Also Crowe, B. (1996). The tragedy of the common revisited. Reprinted in G. Hardin and J. Baden (Eds.), *Managing the Commons,* San Francisco: W. H. Freeman.

Herkert, J. R. (2002, Fall). Continuing and emerging issues in engineering ethics education. *The Bridge, 32*(3).

Herkert, J. R. (2003, Spring). Back to the future: Engineering, computing, and ethics. *Phi Kappa Phi Forum, 83*(2), 34-40.

Lessig, L. (2002, August 15). Free culture. Keynote from OSCON 2002, *The O'Reilly Network,* retrieved online at http://www.oreillynet.com/lpt/a/2641.

Lessig, L. (2003, March 13). Wireless spectrum: Defining the 'commons' in cyberspace. *CIO Insight.*

Lobo, A. (2001, August). Whose Concern Is It Anyway? An appreciation of the ACM & IEEE Computer Society's Software Engineering Code of Ethics and Professional Practice. The ACM Newsletter, Mumbai.

McDonough, W., & Braungart, M. (1998, October). The NEXT industrial revolution. *Atlantic Monthly, 282*(4), 82-92.

Porter, M., & van der Linde, C. (1995, July/August). Green and competitive. *Harvard Business Review.*

Whitbeck, C. (1996, May/June). Ethics as design: Doing justice to moral problems. *Hastings Center Report, 96*(3).

Contributors

ALAN BLOOMGARDEN is Director of Faculty Grants and Government Relations at Smith College and a doctoral student in higher education at the University of Massachusetts, Amherst, studying community partnerships, faculty role integration, and community-based learning and research in the liberal arts setting. He was a 2004 American Association of Higher Education K. Patricia Cross Future Leaders Award recipient for civic responsibility in higher education.

MARY BOMBARDIER is the Director of Community Partnerships for Social Change at Hampshire College, the community-based program for students and faculty engaged in collaborative research projects, social action, and community education with local grassroots organizations. Her work focuses on creating community/academic partnerships in Holyoke, Massachusetts. She was a primary organizer of the 2002 Planners Network National Conference held in Holyoke and is a founding member of the Holyoke Planning Network.

MYRNA M. BREITBART is a Professor of Geography and Urban Studies and faculty coordinator of community-based learning at Hampshire College. Her teaching and research interests focus on participatory planning and the use of urban public space. She is an active participant on the Five College community-based learning committee and is a founding member of the Holyoke Planning Network and the Holyoke ARTeS Alliance. She also works on a Community Outreach Partnership Center Grant that connects area colleges with Holyoke community organizations.

BRUCE COULL holds the title of Carolina Distinguished Professor and was appointed Dean of USC's newly formed School of the Environment in 1996. USC's School of the Environment approaches environmental issues through multidisciplinary research, education and community outreach. He heads the South Carolina Sustainable Universities Initiative and is the leader of USC's environmental efforts in the Ukraine related to the Chernobyl nuclear accident of 1986. His research is in the area of benthic marine ecology.

JAMES EFLIN is a geographer and faculty member in Natural Resources and Environmental Management at Ball State University. A Colorado native, he serves as Energy Education Scholar for Ball State's Center for Energy Research/Education/Service (CERES). His research emphasizes issues of sustainability, industrial ecology, and renewable energy systems.

DANIEL EGAN is Associate Professor and chair of the Sociology Department at the University of Massachusetts Lowell. He has conducted research on worker cooperatives, local socialism, globalization, and the role of corporations in public policy. He is writing a book on corporate welfare subsidies.

JUDY K. FLOHR is a lecturer in the Isenberg School of Management's Department of Hospitality and Tourism Management at the University of Massachusetts Amherst. Her research interests include employee training and development, hospitality education and food safety education. Prior to teaching, she held management positions in healthcare food service.

ROBERT FORRANT is a Professor in the Department of Regional Economic and Social Development at the University of Massachusetts Lowell. He is the co-editor of two volumes on sustainable regional development and the author of numerous articles on industrial development and decline in the Connecticut River Valley and New England. He serves as a regional economy analyst for the journal *Massachusetts Benchmarks* and is on the editorial boards of the journals *New Solutions* and *Labor History.* In 1998 he received the University of Massachusetts President's Award for Public Service.

CHRISTY FRIEND is Associate Professor of English at the University of South Carolina, where she teaches courses in rhetoric and composition pedagogy and serves as Associate Director of the First-Year English Program. Since 2001, she has directed the Program's "Writing About the Environment" project. Her work has appeared in *Rhetoric Review, jac: a Journal of Composition Theory,* and *College English,* and she is a co-author of several writing textbooks, including *The Scott, Foresman Handbook for Writers.* A textbook, *Beyond Words: Reading and Writing in the Media Age,* is forthcoming from Longman Press.

PRISCILLA GEIGIS is former Director of Community Preservation (CP) in the Massachusetts Executive Office of Environmental Affairs and is now Director of State Parks and Recreation for the Commonwealth. Her accomplishments as Director of CP include managing the state's buildout analysis project; overseeing 20 Summits and sis SuperSummits to present buildout information; leading the creation of the interagency Community Development Planning program; initiating and managing the Community Preservation Institute; and managing the *UrbanRiver Visions* program in which seven urban communities created revitalization visions. Under Geigis's leadership, Community Preservation won three national awards, including a National Award for Smart Growth Achievement from the U.S. Environmental Protection Agency in 2002.

KENNETH GEISER is an internationally recognized specialist on pollution prevention, clean production, and industrial chemicals policy. He is a Professor of Work Environment at the University of Massachusetts Lowell and is Co-Director there of the Lowell Center for Sustainable Production. He co-authored the Massachusetts Toxics Use Reduction Act and for 12 years served as the director of the Toxics Use Reduction Institute. He has been a policy advisor to the U.S. Environmental Protection Agency and the United Nations Environment Program.

He is the author of many articles on pollution prevention, toxic chemical policy, and sustainable development and a book, *Materials Matter: Toward a Sustainable Materials Policy,* MIT Press.

VANESSA GRAY is Assistant Professor of political science at the University of Massachusetts Lowell. She writes on transnational environmental organizations and Colombia and teaches comparative politics, environmental politics, and Latin American politics. Her current research is on the environmental dimensions of civil conflict in Colombia.

ELISABETH M. HAMIN is an Assistant Professor in the Landscape Architecture and Regional Planning Department at the University of Massachusetts Amherst. Her book, *Mojave Lands: Interpretive Planning and the National Preserve,* (2003) examines resident and lobbyist perspectives on the designation of the new national park unit and makes an argument for how qualitative research can be better included in planning processes. She co-edited *Preserving and Enhancing Communities: A Guide for Citizens, Planners and Policymakers*, with Linda Silka and Priscilla Geigis (University of Massachusetts Press, forthcoming). She has published articles in numerous planning journals including the *Journal of the American Planning Association* and the *Journal of Planning Education and Research*.

PATRICIA JERMAN has degrees in biology from Bucknell University and public administration from the University of South Carolina. She has managed the Sustainable Universities Initiative since its inception in 1997. Prior to coming to the University, she was Executive Director of the South Carolina Wildlife Federation, a consultant for a Fortune 500 engineering and environmental firm, and environmental advisor to former Governor Dick Riley.

WHITLEY KAUFMAN is an Assistant Professor in the Philosophy Department at the University of Massachusetts Lowell. He has a Ph. D. from Georgetown University and J.D. from the Harvard Law School. His teaching and research interests include Ethics (Theoretical and Applied), Philosophy of Law, Environmental Philosophy, and Philosophy of Religion.

ROBERT KOESTER is a Professor of Architecture at Ball State University and a Registered Architect and LEEDTM Accredited Professional. He directs the Center for Energy Research/Education/ Service, which supports 50 affiliated faculty engaged in energy-related research, education and service. Publications include a chapter in a major text on work environments, a book on building-systems integration, a computer software manual, monographs on energy and environmental systems education, and an interactive CD-Rom developed for Johnson Controls International.

LINDA L. LOWRY is a professor in the University of Massachusetts Amherst Isenberg School of Management's Department of Tourism and Hospitality Management. She has published her research in several management journals and consults on projects related to tourism policy, tourism and development, and cultural tourism. Her current research interests include the social and cultural impacts of tourism and sustainable tourism development.

WILLIAM MASS is an Associate Professor in the Regional Economic and Social Development Department and a Director of the Center for Industrial Competitiveness at the University of Massachusetts Lowell. Trained in economics and public health, he conducts interdisciplinary research on transitions in economic leadership among firms and industries, and studies public policies that influence the impacts of economic development on regions, human health, and the environment. He has served as a member of the Board of Trustees of the Business History Conference and as an officer and board member of MassExcellence, which administers the Massachusetts Performance Excellence award program.

CORINNA McLEOD is Assistant Professor of English at Grand Valley State University, where she teaches courses in World Mythology and World Literatures in English. Her research centers on postcolonial theory, ecocriticism, and questions of national identity in literature. She is also interested in the relationship between sustainability, service learning, and pedagogy.

CHAD MONTRIE is an Assistant Professor of History at the University of Massachusetts Lowell, where he teaches U.S. environmental, labor, and social history. His book, To Save the Land and People: A History of Opposition to Surface Coal Mining in Appalachia (2003) was published by the University of North Carolina Press. He is currently working on a project titled "Making a Living: Work and Environment in the United States'."

KIARA NAGEL graduated from Hampshire College with a concentration in urban studies and community development. While Project Coordinator for Community Partnerships for Social Change from 2000–2004 at Hampshire College, she promoted collaborative projects and equitable partnerships between Holyoke, Massachusetts community organizations, and the college. Currently she is working on a Master's Degree in City Planning from the Massachusetts Institute of Technology.

LINDA SILKA develops programs that create community and university partnerships at the University of Massachusetts Lowell. Recent partnerships include the Southeast Asian Environmental Justice Partnership, started with funding from the National Institute of Environmental Health Sciences; and the Community Outreach Partnership Center, begun with funding from U.S. Department of Housing and Urban Development's Office of University Partnerships. She teaches graduate courses in community mapping, grant writing, program evaluation, and research ethics with underserved communities and consults widely on capacity-building strategies and program evaluation. In 1999 she received the University of Massachusetts Distinguished Professional Service Award.

PRESTON H. SMITH II directs the community-based learning program at Mount Holyoke College, where he is an associate professor of politics and African American Studies. He co-directs the Puerto Rican Studies Faculty/Community Seminar and is a project coordinator for economic reinvestment in South Holyoke,

MA as part of a HUD Community Outreach Partnership Center grant. Interests include black class politics, black and Latino coalitions, and community economic development. He is a co-National coordinator of the Free Higher Education campaign of the Debs-Douglass-Jones Institute, educational and cultural arm of the Labor Party.

WILL SNYDER is an Extension Educator with the Natural Resources and Environmental Conservation Division of the University of Massachusetts Extension Service. He has been a leader in developing innovative environmental-education programs intended to strengthen the ability of youth to play leadership roles in protecting and enhancing the environment.

SUMMER SMITH TAYLOR is Assistant Professor and Director of the Advanced Writing Program in the English Department at Clemson University. The Advanced Writing Program includes undergraduate business and technical writing classes and features a project-based and client-based approach. Taylor teaches technical writing, technical editing, research methodologies, and the teaching of technical writing. Her research focuses on assessment of student writing, engineering communication, and administration of writing programs.

JOHN VANN is Associate Professor of Marketing at the Miller College of Business, Ball State University. He is the Ball State University Green Initiatives Coordinator and member of the University's Council on the Environment.

STEPHEN VIEDERMAN retired from the presidency of the Jessie Smith Noyes Foundation in 2000. There he focused on economic and environmental justice, sustainable communities sustainable agriculture, and reproductive rights. He led the foundation in an effort to reduce the dissonance between its asset management and grant making through mission-related investing, an effort that he continues with foundations, university endowments, and public pension funds. He lectures and writes on institutional fiduciary responsibility and problems of philanthropy and consults with communities of color in the Southwest on culturally and environmentally sensitive economic development.

Index

Advice giving/seeking, 131
Agenda 21, 30–31, 36
Amherst College, 105
  See also Community/university
    partnerships in a metropolitan
    setting
Art of Advice, The (Salacus), 131
Association of Computing Machinery
    (ACM), 159–160
Association of University Leaders for
    a Sustainable Future (ULSF),
    32, 59
AT&T Foundation's Industrial Ecology
    Faculty Fellowship, 56
Authoritative model, 76
Avanza Resource Development Team,
    114

Ball State University, 42
  See also Integrating academia/
    operations/community
Baumgarten, Michael, 156
Black Environmental Justice Coalition,
    37
Bloomgarden, Alan, 114
Bok, Derek, 22
Bombardier, Mary, 110
Boundaryless principle, 22
Breitbart, Myrna, 110

Campus-as-laboratory theme, 135

See also Merging academics/operations
    in a statewide university
    consortium
Carson, Rachel, 22
Center for Clean Products and Clean
    Technologies, 30
  See also Education for a transition to
    sustainability
Center for Family, Work, and Community
    (CFWC), 6
Chargoff, Erwin, 22
Chipko people, 73
Citizens as Planners (Hamin, Silka &
    Geigis), 123
Citizens Planning and Training
    Collaborative, 122
Cleaner production, training environ-
    mental leaders for, 36–39
Clean Production Action, 30, 37–38
Clemson University, 135, 142–144
  See also Merging academics/operations
    in a statewide university
    consortium
Coleman, James, 23
Collaborative activities/new approaches
    to teaching, need for, 9
  See also Community/university
    partnerships in a metropolitan
    setting; Integrating academia/
    operations/community; Merging
    academics/operations in a
    statewide university consortium
Committee on Industrial Theory and
    Assessment (CITA), 68

Community-based learning (CBL), 90–91, 105–106
See also Community/university partnerships in a metropolitan setting
Community-based organizations (CBOs), 106
See also Community/university partnerships in a metropolitan setting
Community-based research (CBR), 87, 90–91
See also Curriculum, embedding concepts of sustainable development in the
Community Outreach Partnership Center (COPC), HUD's, 111–114
Community Partnerships for Social Change (CPSC), Hampshire College's, 110
Community preservation
advice giving/seeking, 131
Community Preservation Institute, 121–123
Environmental Protection Agency, 130
implications for reuse and recycling of ideas, 129–132
list making, 131
policy arm and education arm working together, 123–124
problems with admonitions to avoid re-creations, 130
smart growth, as an alternative to, 120–121
training ingredients, reusing/recycling, 125–129
YouthVisions program, 124–129, 132
Community Preservation Institute (CPI), 121–123
Community service learning, 89–90, 105–106
See also Community/university partnerships in a metropolitan setting
Community/university partnerships in a metropolitan setting
challenges to building, 116–117

[Community/university partnerships in a metropolitan setting]
Community Outreach Partnership Center, HUD's, 111–114
initial efforts to forge, 109–111
literature on, 107–108
"New Visions for Historic Cities: Bridging Divides, Building Futures," 110–111
Planners Network, 109–110
projects, recent
archive project, 115
grant-writing workshop in Holyoke, 114
Puerto Rican studies seminar, 115
summary/conclusions, 117
See also Integrating academia/operations/community; Merging academics/operations in a statewide university consortium
"Composition and Environmental Literature" (McLeod), 141
Conferences, declarations from university/educator, 31
Corporations and discussions on the externalities they generate, 27
Council on the Environment (COTE), Ball State University's, 51–52, 57–59
Culture change needed for learning/ acting for sustainability to occur, 25–27
Curiosity, licensing in people a sense of, 27
Curitiba (Brazil), 73
Curriculum, embedding concepts of sustainable development in the
best practices, finding, 88–89
examples
honors thesis, undergraduate, 94–95
industry research project, a graduate-level, 96–97
junior-level class project, 95–96
overview, 92–94
experiential education and learning
community-based learning/research, 90–91

[Curriculum, embedding concepts of sustainable development in the] community service learning, 89–90
defining terms, 89
students as thinkers/leaders, 91–92
summary/conclusions, 97–99
See also Education *listings;* Ethics, teaching sustainability and professional; Teaching sustainability: the shrinking professor

Decision making and microethical challenges, 159–163
Declarations from university/educator conferences, 31
Deliberative model, 76
Denmark, 36
Domination/mastery over the environment as a theme in modern life, 21
Doubt, licensing in people a sense of, 27
Durand, Robert, 120–121
Durkheim, Emile, 66

E (environment/economy/equity) approach, three, 80–81
Eagle Eye Institute, 124
Earth Connection, 125–127
Ecological Literacy (Orr), 55
Ecological sustainability, 69
Ecology of Hope (Bernard & Young), 84
Economics, ethics/the real world as intrusions in field of, 23–24
Economy/environment/equity (three e) approach, 80–81
Education for a transition to sustainability advancing, 39–40
cleaner production, training environmental leaders for, 36–39
conventional higher education compared to, 33
declarations from university/educator conferences, 31

[Education for a transition to sustainability]
Education for Sustainable Development, 31–32
integrated into daily needs of professionals/activists, 32–33
international training for clean production, 38–39
toxics use reduction, training professionals for, 34–35
See also Curriculum, embedding concepts of sustainable development in the; Ethics, teaching sustainability and professional; Teaching sustainability: the shrinking professor
Education for Sustainability/Sustainable Development
curriculum transformation, 53–55
principles of, 31–32
United Nations designating the Decade of Education for Sustainable Development, 32
See also Humanities/social sciences, role of the; Integrating academia/operations/community; Merging academics/operations in a statewide university consortium
Education for Sustainability Western Network, 60
Eflin, James, 9
Egan, Daniel, 10, 66–68
Ehrenfeld, David, 24
Ehrlich Award, 90
Einstein, Albert, 23–24
Encountering Global Environmental Politics: Teaching, Learning, and Empowering Knowledge (Maniates), 69
Energy Department, U.S. (DOE), 145
Engineering ethicists, 152–155
Enstructuration approach, 81
Environmental Predicament: Four Issues for Critical Analysis (Verberg), 139
Environmental Protection Agency (EPA), 130

[Envisioning a sustainable future]
Envirothon, 125–127
Envisioning a sustainable future
    difficulty that universities have in
        fostering sustainability, 22–25
    higher education and sustainability,
        20–21
    overview, 17–18
    proposals, some modest, 27–28
    sustainability, 19–20
    system change needed for
        learning/acting for sustainability to
        occur, 25–27
    vision, 18–19
Epistemology of sustainability, 80–81
Equity, sustainability concerning issues
    of, 27, 80
Essex Agricultural High School, 124
Ethics, teaching sustainability and
    professional
    content/pedagogy/student-teacher
        mutual learning, 155–159
    decision making and microethical
        challenges, 159–163
    negotiated course topics, 163–166
    overview, 149–150
    production/work/values, 150–151
    role of professional education and
        ethics requirements, 152–155
    summary/conclusions, 166–167
Europe, 36

Field Station and Environmental
    Education Center (FSEEC), 45
Finkel, Donald, 83
Five College Consortium, 105, 106
    See also Community/university
        partnerships in a metropolitan
        setting
Flohr, Judy, 10
Fluor Corporation, 144
Foundation Center, 114
Friedan, Betty, 22

Geigis, Priscilla, 11

Geiser, Kenneth, 11, 12
Gerber, John, 81–82
Gibson, James, 21
Giles, Dwight, 90
Global Alliance for Incinerator
    Alternatives (GAIA), 30, 38–39
Global Higher Education for
    Sustainability Partnership, 32
Gourman Report: A Rating of
    Undergraduate Degree Programs
    in American and International
    Universities, 87
Gray, Vanessa, 68–73
Green Committee Report, 43–45, 47
Greening of the Campus Conferences,
    five international, 46–50
    See also Integrating academia/
        operations/community
Greider, Will, 23, 26

Halifax Declaration (1992), 31
Hamin, Elisabeth, 10, 127
Hampshire College, 105, 106
    See also Community/university
        partnerships in a metropolitan
        setting
Harrington, Michael, 22
Hart, Maureen, 157
Hawken, Paul, 24
Hayek, Fredrich von, 20
Heifer Project, The, 140
Herkert, Joseph, 152, 155
Higher Education Network for
    Sustainability and the Environment
    (HENSE), 60
History and role of the humanities/social
    sciences, 63–66
Holyoke Community College (HCC)/
    Holyoke Planning Network (HPN),
    108
    See also Community/university
        partnerships in a metropolitan
        setting
Hospitality and Tourism Management
    (HTM), 87–88

See also Curriculum, embedding concepts of sustainable development in the
Housing and Urban Development, U.S. Department of (HUD), 3, 111–114
HUD. *See* Housing and Urban Development, U.S. Department of
Humanities/social sciences, role of the
historian's perspective: Chad Montrie, 63–66
philosopher's perspective: Whitley Kaufman, 73–77
political scientist's perspective: Vanessa Gray, 68–73
sociologist's perspective: Daniel Egan, 66–68
summary/conclusions, 77
Hutchins, Robert, 25

IEEE Computer Society (IEEE-CS), 159–160
Indigenous knowledge, little acceptance of, 24
Industry and Environment Office in United Nations, 36
Institute for Plastics Innovation, 5–6
Institute of Electrical and Electronics Engineers-Computer Society (IEEE-CS), 159–160
Integrating academia/operations/ community
applications to institutions other than Ball State University, 59–60
Council on the Environment, 51–52
curriculum innovations, 53–55
extending the Green for Green outreach, 52–53
faculty, summer development workshops for, 45–46
Field Station and Environmental Education Center, 45
frustrations and successes, 57–59
Green-2, 51
Green Committee Report, 43–45
Greening of the Campus Conferences, five international, 46–50

[Integrating academia/operations/ community]
origins of greening movement at Ball State University, 42–45
other campus-based programmatic efforts, 56–57
overview, 41–42
research, campus-based sustainability, 55–56
summary/conclusions, 59–60
Talloires Declaration, 50–51
See also Merging academics/operations in a statewide university consortium
Interaction beyond campus usually rejected by universities, 7–8
International Association of Universities, 32
International Journal of Sustainability in Higher Education, 32
Investments in community development, 28
Iowa State University, 85
Iraq-U.S. War and teaching ethics, 164–165

Justice, sustainability concerning issues of, 27

Kaufman, Whitley, 73–77
Kenet, Lord, 24
Kindelberger, Charles, 23
Koester, Robert, 9

Learning, community-based, 90–91, 105–106
See also Community/university partnerships in a metropolitan setting
Legislation
Community Preservation Act in Massachusetts, 120, 121
Levin, Richard, 21
Liberal pluralism and university's reluctance to teach values, 75

Literature and Nature: Four Centuries of Nature Writing (Keegan & McKusick), 141
Living/Learning Center for Sustainable Futures, USC's, 144–145
Lowell Center for Sustainable Production, 5, 29–30
See also Education for a transition to sustainability
Lowell Historical Preservation Commission, 7
Lowell National Historical Park, 6, 7
Lowell Textile School, 2
Lowry, Linda, 10

Macro-level analysis and engineering ethicists, 152
Management focused on technology or values, 23
Marx, Karl, 64, 66–68
Mass, William, 10
Massachusetts, 119
See also Community preservation
Massachusetts State Normal School at Lowell, 2
Massachusetts Toxics Use Reduction Institute, 29–30, 34–35
See also Education for a transition to sustainability
Material flow analyses (MFA), 56
McDonough, William, 82, 156
Medical University of South Carolina (MUSC), 135
See also Merging academics/operations in a statewide university consortium
Merging academics/operations in a statewide university consortium
environmental assessment, 136–138
liberal arts enlisted in an environmental mission
Clemson University business and technical writing classes, 142–144
University of South Carolina English 101, 138–142

USC Living/Learning Center for Sustainable Futures, 144–145
overview, 135
summary/conclusions, 146
See also Integrating academia/operations/community
Merrimac River, 73
Micro-level analysis and engineering ethicists, 152
Mills, C. Wright, 67
Monsanto, 82
Montrie, Chad, 3, 63–66, 69
Moral education, need for humanities to lead way in emphasizing, 76
Mount Holyoke, 105
See also Community/university partnerships in a metropolitan setting
Mundell, Robert, 23

Nagel, Kiara, 110
National Commission on Service Learning, 90
National Conference on Science, Policy and the Environment (2003), 60
National Council for Science and the Environment, 60
National Planners Network, 109–111
National Service-Learning Clearinghouse, 90
National Wildlife Federation's Campus Ecology program, 59–60
Netherlands, 36
"New Visions for Historic Cities: Bridging Divides, Building Futures" (2002), 110–111
Nueva Esperanza, 106, 110

Occidental Petroleum, 72
Orr, David, 79

Participatory processes for envisioning a different society, 27
Peer learning/collaboration for students, 83

Philosophy and role of the humanities/
social sciences, 73–77
Planners Network, 109–111
Pluralist model, 76
Political science and role of the
humanities/social sciences, 68–73
Politics omitted from sustainability
disciplines, 24
Porter, Michael, 156
Positivism and university's reluctance to
teach values, 75
Precautionary principle, 24
Preservation, community. *See*
Community preservation
Production, training environmental
leaders for cleaner, 36–39

Quabbin Regional High School, 124

Ralston, John, 23
Ramsey, Bill, 89
Rawls, John, 75–76
Reardon, Ken, 106, 109
Recession (U.S.) in 2001 and teaching
ethics, 163–164
Recycling/reusing past insights/ideas, 119
See also Community preservation
Regional Economic and Social
Development (RESD), UML's,
150
Research, scientific
community-based research, 87, 90–91.
See also Curriculum, embedding
concepts of sustainable develop-
ment in the
integrating academia/operations/
community, 55–56
as investigator generated and
responsive to industry, 24–25
Revkin, Andrew, 24
Rio de Janeiro Conference (1992),
30–31, 36
River Ambassadors Program, 124
Russell, Sara L., 105

Science and uncertainty, 24
Second Nature, 60
Sen, Amartya, 23
September 11th terrorist attacks in U.S.
and teaching ethics, 164
Service learning, community, 89–90,
105–106
See also Community/university
partnerships in a metropolitan
setting
Service-Learning Is, 90
Shaw, Denise, 139
Sigmon, Bob, 89–90
Silka, Linda, 11
Smart growth, community preservation as
an alternative to, 120–121
Smith College, 105
See also Community/university
partnerships in a metropolitan
setting
Snyder, Will, 11
Social sciences. *See* Humanities/social
sciences, role of the
Sociology and role of the humanities/
social sciences, 66–68
Software engineering and ethical issues,
159–163
Sophocles, 21
Southern Regional Education Board
(SREB), 89–90
Sovern, Michael, 22
Sustainable Universities Initiative (SUI),
135
See also Merging academics/operations
in a statewide university
consortium
Sweden, 36
System change needed for learning/acting
for sustainability to occur, 25–27

Talloires Declaration (1990), 31, 46,
50–51
Teaching sustainability: the shrinking
professor

[Teaching sustainability: the shrinking professor]
actions taking place at the site/community/regional scale, 80
alternative learning models and developing shared learning, 83
communities of learners/activists needed, 79
e approach, three, 80–81
enstructuration approach, 81
peer learning/collaboration, 83
policies/designs to implement key principles, 82
rapport/empowerment among students, developing, 84–85
students following their own interests/learning from each other, 82–83
summary/conclusions, 85–86
world view, pedagogic goal is to encourage a, 79
See also Ethics, teaching sustainability and professional
Thompson, Rob, 79
Tourism management, 87–88
See also Curriculum, embedding concepts of sustainable development in the
Toxics Use Reduction Institute (TURI), 5
Toxic Use Reduction Planners Association (TURPA), 35
Tsongas, Paul, 7
Tsongas Industrial History Center, 7

UML. See University of Massachusetts Lowell
United Nations
Conference on Environment and Development (1992), 30–31, 36
Environment Programme (UNEP), 36
Industry and Environment Office, 36
University Charter for Sustainable Development (1994), 31

University of Massachusetts Amherst, 87–88, 105
See also Community/university partnerships in a metropolitan setting; Curriculum, embedding concepts of sustainable development in the
University of Massachusetts Lowell (UML)
Center for Family, Work, and Community, 6
city/region and the university, 2–3
Committee on Industrial Theory and Assessment, 4
Community Outreach Partnership Program, 3
embedded in the region, becoming, 3–4
energy conservation/biodegradable materials/cleaner and safer production/environment, focus on, 5–7
obstacles inhibiting success, three institutional/organizational, 8
reflective discourse, 7–9
universities and sustainable development, 4–5
See also Education for a transition to sustainability; Ethics, teaching sustainability and professional
University of Massachusetts (state research university), 123
See also Community preservation
University of South Carolina (USC), 135, 138–142, 144–145
See also Merging academics/operations in a statewide university consortium
University of Tennessee, 30
See also Education for a transition to sustainability
USC. See University of South Carolina
U'wá people, 72

Values, trends contributing to reluctance in the university to teach, 75–76

Van der Linde, Claas, 156
Vann, John, 9
Vega, Carlos, 106
Viederman, Stephen, 11–12
Vision of a sustainable society, 18–19
    See also Envisioning a sustainable
        future
Weber, Max, 66
Welch, James E., Jr., 22
Western Massachusetts Funders Resource
    Center, 114
Whitbeck, Caroline, 152–153

Wiesel, Elie, 21
World Business Council for Sustainable
    Development, 74
World Commission on Environment and
    Development, 73, 74
World Trade Organization (WTO), 82
World view, pedagogic goal is to
    encourage a, 79

YouthVisions program, 124–129, 132

A SELECTION OF TITLES FROM THE

WORK, HEALTH AND ENVIRONMENT SERIES

Series Editors, *Charles Levenstein, Robert Forrant and John Wooding*

AT THE POINT OF PRODUCTION
The Social Analysis of Occupational
and Environmental Health
Edited by Charles Levenstein

BEYOND CHILD'S PLAY
Sustainable Product Design in the
Global Doll-Making Industry
Sally Edwards

ENVIRONMENTAL UNIONS
Labor and the Superfund
Craig Slatin

METAL FATIGUE
American Bosch and the Demise
of Metalworking in the Connecticut River Valley
Robert Forrant

SHOES, GLUES AND HOMEWORK
Dangerous Work in the Global Footwear Industry
Pia Markkanen

WITHIN REACH?
Managing Chemical Risks in Small Enterprises
David Walters

INSIDE AND OUT
Universities and Education for Sustainable Development
Edited by Robert Forrant and Linda Silka

WORKING DISASTERS
The Politics of Recognition and Response
Edited by Eric Tucker

LABOR-ENVIRONMENTAL COALITIONS
Lessons from a Louisiana Petrochemical Region
Thomas Estabrook

CORPORATE SOCIAL RESPONSIBILITY
FAILURES IN THE OIL INDUSTRY
Edited by Charles Woolfson and Matthias Beck